Gurney, Ireland, Quilter and Warlock

Gurney, Ireland, Quilter and Warlock

Michael Pilkington

ENGLISH SOLO SONG
GUIDES TO THE REPERTOIRE

Indiana University Press

Bloomington and Indianapolis

Manufactured in Great Britain

Library of Congress Cataloging-in-Publication Data

Pilkington, Michael.
    Gurney, Ireland, Quilter, and Warlock / Michael Pilkington.
       p.   cm.—(English solo song)
    Bibliography: p.
    Includes indexes.
    ISBN 0-253-34694-0
    1. Songs–England–History and criticism. 2. Gurney, Ivor,
1890–1937. Songs. 3. Ireland, John, 1879–1962. Songs.
4. Quilter, Roger, 1877–1953. Songs. 5. Warlock, Peter,
1894–1930. Songs.   I. Title.   II. Series: Pilkington, Michael.
English solo song.
ML2831.P54   1989
782.42168′092′242–dc20   89–11024

Contents

Peter Warlock

Foreword

Programme planning must be one of the most demanding jobs in a singer's career and one which consumes a great deal of time. It is rewarding when just the right balance is achieved but frustrating when that magic seems unattainable. This comprehensive guide will therefore be good news to performers, teachers and students. It covers all the songs, whether in print or not, of four of the most important composers of English Song. In providing concise information and helpful comments born of vast experience as a teacher of this genre, Michael Pilkington has done us a great service.

Noelle Barker OBE
Head of Vocal Studies
Guildhall School of Music and Drama

Erratum

p. 5, line 2: *for* 1880 *read* 1890

Preface

This book is one of a series, *English Solo Song: guides to the repertoire*, planned to cover the whole repertoire of English solo song. Songs which cannot be accompanied by piano alone are not included. The series is designed not merely as a practical guide for singers and teachers of singing, but also to be of use to those who wish to study any particular area of English song composition, in relation to the music or the poetry.

A full description of each song is given, as detailed in the Introduction. This may help to answer the question I have often been asked: 'Are there any English songs?' As these guides will show, there is an enormous repertoire available, which is unfortunately only too little known by those who should be most concerned – English singers themselves. It is hoped that the information provided here about variants in the poems, and the sources from which they were taken, will encourage singers to investigate the words as well as the music of the songs they sing. The composers started with the words, after all, and it will be helpful to good performance for the singer to take the same starting-point. Where the words of a song differ from the original poem the singer needs to decide whether this has happened by accident or design. Whether or not the original words are used in performance, it must surely be of value to know what the poet actually wrote. If more than one edition of a song is available any differences are recorded here. The original sources have not been researched, but if published evidence shows an edition to have modified the original this is made clear. So far as possible misprints have been noted, but it is inevitable that some will have been overlooked, and equally inevitable that there will be some errors in this book itself. Any information on this will be gratefully received.

I should like to thank my colleagues in the world of singing teaching for their encouragement. In particular Jack Coldiron and Bruce Lunkley of Texas, and many members of AOTOS (the Association Of Teachers Of Singing), led me to believe that this series would be of practical use to them in their work. The staff and students at the Guildhall School of Music have made many useful comments, not only in relation to draft versions of these guides, but during the whole course of the twenty-five years I have been teaching the Interpretation of English Song at the School. I am also grateful to Leslie East for allowing me to study his collection of Quilter MSS. Finally, I should like to thank my daughter Helen for her assistance with the laborious task of checking the indexes.

Old Coulsdon, 1988   M.P.

Introduction

The entries in this volume are set out as follows:

Title Printed in **bold** in the order detailed for each composer. In the case of cycles or sets of songs (printed in capitals), much information appears only under the name of the set, and is not repeated for individual songs.

First line First line of the poem, if different from the title.

Poet Source and date of first publication of the lyric, if known. A date in square brackets after the publication date indicates the date of actual composition, if known.

Composition Date of composition of the music, if known.

Publication Name of original publisher, date of original publication, and whether issued in more then one key. If the song is included in a volume this is given as a Collection number in square brackets, for example [Coll 3], immediately after the key (high, medium, or low, etc) printed in that volume (for Collections, see individual composers).

Tonality Normally the original key, but see individual composers.

Range Lowest and highest notes of voice part; optional notes are given in round brackets (); pitches shown in square brackets [] indicate the range of the main body of the song. This is followed by a listing of any other published keys. If the original key is known other keys are given in italics. Key to pitch symbols: C = c below bass clef; c°, c' (middle c), c″, c‴; for example, f' is the f above middle c.

Meter C is given as 4/4, cut C as 2/2. If more than one time signature is used it implies frequent alternation.

Tempo The tempo indication, as shown at the start of each song, followed by metronome mark, if given.

Duration Given in minutes and seconds. This is clearly a subjective matter, but the times given will produce satisfactory tempi.

Difficulty Voice (V) and piano (P) are graded separately as easy (e), moderately easy (me), moderate (m), moderately difficult (md), and difficult (d). Again a matter for personal judgment, but a glance at a few known songs will indicate the standards used.

For Most suitable voice or voices. If the original key is known other possible voices are given in italics. See individual composers. Square brackets imply that some such singers might find the text of the song unsuitable.

Subject A paraphrase of the text, usually in a form suited to programme notes.

Voice Description of vocal line, with reference to shape, size of leaps, extremes, rhythms, and any special problems. Syllabic word setting is assumed.

Piano Description of accompaniment, with reference to texture, layout, harmony, rhythm, and any specific problems.

Comment Any further information which might be of value, including any misprints noticed, and explanations of unusual words. Variant versions of the words are given in italics, explanations in roman.

An example of one of Ireland's songs should make the system clear:

9 Love is a sickness full of woes (Samuel Daniel, *Hymen's Triumph*, 1615, Act I, Scene v.) Comp. July 1921. Pub. W.R., 1921. *High* [Coll 3], *Medium*, Low.

        Gb major, e'b-g″, [g'b-g″b]; *F major*, Eb major. 3/4,2/4, Allegretto con moto, crotchet = 72-76. 1'45″. V/m, P/m.

For: *Sop, Ten*; *Mezzo, Bar*; Cont, C-Ten, Bass.

Subject: Love is a torment, whether or not we have it.

Voice: Steps, many skips; 6th drop, 8ve leap; lies high; ends on soft held g″b; rhythms quite straightforward.

Piano: Chordal, fairly thick; very chromatic; some decoration.

Comment: The chromatic dissonances appear slightly forced, but this can be an effective song if well performed. Ireland's MS in BL (Add. MS 52898) is in Eb major.

Explanation

The title is also the first line. The lyric will be found in Act I, Scene v of Samuel Daniel's *Hymen's Triumph*, which was first performed in 1615. Ireland composed the song in July 1921, and it was published by Winthrop Rogers the same year, in high, medium and low keys. The low key is the original, and the high key is the version printed in *A Heritage of English Song*, vol 2.

Gb major is the key given in *The Complete Works*; in this key the lowest note is e'b, the highest note is g″; there are few notes lower than g'b or higher than g″b The other keys printed were F major and Eb major, the latter being the original. The time signature varies between 3/4 and 2/4. The tempo instruction is Allegretto con moto. The metronome mark is crotchet = 72-76. The song should last about 1 minute 45 seconds. The voice part is of a moderate standard, as is the piano.

Transposed versions of the song would suit soprano, tenor, mezzo-soprano or baritone; the original key would suit contralto, counter-tenor or bass.

Abbreviations

For details see Select Bibliography

Ault	*Elizabethan Lyrics*, edited by Norman Ault.
Bailey	J.O. Bailey, *The Poetry of Thomas Hardy*.
B & H	Boosey & Hawkes
BL	British Library.
Cambridge Guide	Michael Stapleton, *The Cambridge Guide to English Literature*.
Cat.	John Ireland, *A Catalogue of Published Works*, by Ernest Chapman.
Coghill	Chaucer, *The Canterbury Tales*, edited by Neville Coghill.
Copley	Ian Copley, *The Music of Peter Warlock*.
Davies	*Medieval English Lyrics*, edited by R.T. Davies.
Davis	*The Works of Thomas Campion*, edited by W.R. Davis.
EEL	*Early English Lyrics*, edited by E.K. Chambers and F. Sidgwick.
EV	*English Verse 1300-1500*, edited by John Burrow.
Georgian	*Georgian Poetry*, edited by Edward Marsh.
Latham	*Ralegh: The Poems*, edited by Agnes Latham.
NOB	*New Oxford Book of English Verse*, edited by Helen Gardner.
OB	*Oxford Book of English Verse*, edited by Arthur Quiller-Couch.
OB 16	*Oxford Book of 16th Century Verse*, edited by E.K. Chambers.
OBC	*Oxford Book of Carols*, edited by Percy Dearmer, R. Vaughan Williams and Martin Shaw.
OED	*Oxford English Dictionary*.
OUP	Oxford University Press.
S & B	Stainer and Bell.
Stevens	John Stevens, *Music and Poetry*.
Tomlinson	F. Tomlinson, *A Peter Warlock Handbook*, vol. 1.
Tydeman	*Four Tudor Comedies*, edited by W. Tydeman.

Vivian	*Campion's Works*, edited by Percival Vivian.
W.R.	Winthrop Rogers.
War Letters	*Ivor Gurney: War Letters*, edited by R.K.R. Thornton.
WSNL	Warlock Society Newsletter.

Note on publishers

Many of the publishers mentioned in this volume have changed ownership since the songs were first published. The list below shows which present firms have acquired their catalogues:

Augener: now published by Stainer & Bell
Boosey: now published by Boosey & Hawkes
Elkin: now published by Novello
Galliard: now published by Stainer & Bell
Hawkes: now published by Boosey & Hawkes
Joseph Williams: now published by Stainer & Bell
Winthrop Rogers: now published by Boosey & Hawkes

IVOR GURNEY
1880-1937

Gurney's songs are set out in the order given in the five volumes published by Oxford University Press. These are followed by the volumes printed by Stainer & Bell and Boosey & Hawkes, ending with single songs, mostly now out of print. Collections are referred to as follows:

Heritage 1 = *A Heritage of English Song*, vol 1, B & H, 1977.
50 Modern = *Fifty Modern English Songs*, B & H, ?1927.

IVOR GURNEY

1 A FIRST VOLUME OF TEN SONGS. Pub. OUP, 1938.

(1) **The singer**. In the dim light of the golden lamp. (Edward Shanks, *The Queen of China and other poems* 1919.) Comp. High Wycombe, November 1919.

	B minor, d′b-f″#, [e′-e″]. 2/2, Quasi andante. 2′15″. V/m, P/m.
For:	Mezzo, high Bar.
Subject:	The pleasure of listening to music.
Voice:	Mostly by step; diminished 4th and two 7ths; sustained f″# at end; speech rhythms, but stretched out in places; some modulation.
Piano:	Quaver broken chords against minim chords; generally fairly thin texture; many accidentals; big stretch desirable, or a careful rearrangement of notes between the hands.
Comment:	The phrasing marked needs considerable breath control, but extra breaths can be taken with a careful use of rubato. An effectively atmospheric song.

(2) **The Latmian shepherd**. The moon's a drowsy fool tonight. (Edward Shanks, 'Song for an unwritten play', *Songs*, 1915.) Comp. Gloucester, 1920.

	Eb major, c′-e″, [e′b-d″]. 2/4, Adagio quasi andante con moto, quaver = 72. 3′45″. V/m, P/md.
For:	Mezzo, C-Ten, Bar.
Subject:	Night on Latmos hill, where the Moon looks down on Endymion; she loved him, and to prevent his death caused him to sleep there for ever.
Voice:	Steps, small skips, broken chords; many short melismas; some modulation; essentially speech rhythm.
Piano:	Fairly thick texture, changing chords with continuous semiquaver movement; chromatic; some awkward stretches.
Comment:	A well-shaped vocal line, but the accompaniment can easily sound too thick and congested. Where Gurney has misremembered the poem it is better to use the original words, given in small print.

(3) **Black Stichel**. As I was lying on Black Stichel. (Wilfrid Gibson, *Neighbours*, 1920.) Comp. 1920.

7

F major, d'*b*-e", [d'-d"]. 4/4, Allegro. 2'. V/m, P/md.

For: Mezzo, C-Ten, Bar.
Subject: South wind for happiness, West wind for love, the North for wrath, and the East for pity.
Voice: Steps and simple skips; semi-strophic with strong rhythm and sustained ends of stanzas; third stanza a dramatic climax, with held e"; fairly chromatic.
Piano: Rhythmic, with running quavers; third stanza very chromatic with broken chords, not easy at the tempo indicated.
Comment: A fine romantic song with a good climax and a moving finish.

(4) Down by the Salley Gardens my love and I did meet. (W.B. Yeats, *Crossways*, 1889). Comp. September-October 1920.

Ab major, d'*b*-f ", [e'*b*-e"*b*]. 3/4, Poco andante. 2'15". V/me, P/me.

For: [Mezzo], Bar.
Subject: My love advised me to take love and life easy, but, to my sorrow, I did not agree.
Voice: Steps, simple skips; some wide-ranging phrases; not a single accidental.
Piano: Simple chordal, with decorated interlude and coda.
Comment: A beautiful folksong-like melody; a good exercise in breath control and phrasing, particularly if the rather demanding phrase-marks are followed. Page 13, bar 2: there should be a comma after 'foolish'. Correct Gurney's verbal error. Yeats's original title, 'An old song resung', refers to the fact that he based the poem on one stanza from an old broadside ballad, 'The rambling boys of pleasure'.

(5) All night under the moon plovers are flying. (Wilfrid Gibson, *Friends*, 1916.) Comp. Winter 1918.

G# minor, d'#-f "#, [g'#-e"]. 3/4, Poco adagio. 3'. V/m, P/m.

For: Mezzo, high Bar.
Subject: Birds fly, crying of love; we, being in love, are flying.
Voice: Mostly by step, some broken chords; smoothly flowing speech rhythms; some enharmonic and chromatic writing.
Piano: Chordal; continuous quavers; chromatic.
Comment: The tempo must not be too slow, in view of the long phrasing. Gurney's verbal alterations are better for singing. Page 17, bar 9: in *Georgian 1916-17* the poem reads *in silvery light*, with no *the*, but *the* is given in the *Collected Poems* of 1926. The poem ends with a question mark in *Georgian*, though not in *Collected Poems*. Gibson published another version of this poem as 'The empty cottage'. A very atmospheric song.

(6) Nine of the clock oh! Wake my lazy head. (John Doyle [pseudonym for Robert Graves], *Country Sentiment*, 1920.) Comp. July 1920.

G major, d'-e", [g'-d"]. 2/4, Andante con moto. 45". V/me, P/me.

For: Mezzo, C-Ten, Bar.

Subject: Get up, it's late!

Voice: Steps, simple skips; straight-forward modulation; bouncy rhythms; short melisma at end.

Piano: Crotchet chords, with some LH quaver arpeggios; slightly awkward coda.

Comment: A delightfully cheerful little song, which would make a good encore or finisher. Page 20, bar 1: use Graves's original word. This is the first of two poems under the joint title 'Nine o'clock'. The second was also set by Gurney, see 3 (10). The collection of poems *Country Sentiment* was published under Graves's name in 1920.

(7) You are my sky; beneath your circling kindness. (J.C. Squire, *Poems, Second Series*, 1922 [1919].) Comp. Autumn 1920.

Db major, c'-f ", [e'b-e"b]. 4/8, Poco andante. 2'. V/m, P/md.

For: Mezzo, Bar.

Subject: My mood depends on yours, whether happy or sad.

Voice: Steps and skips; somewhat chromatic; very wide-ranging: f " to c' to e"b within two bars; Sustained f " at end; speech rhythms.

Piano: Thick texture, with many broken chords and 8ve doublings; several 9ths for RH; chromatic; enharmonic notation makes for some difficulty in reading.

Comment: A rather complex setting of a comparatively simple poem. Gurney has altered the balance of the poem on the second system of page 23; to use Squire's complete line give two notes to *I* and one to each of the remaining syllables.

(8) Ha'nacker mill. Sally is gone that was so kindly. (Hilaire Belloc, *Sonnets and Verse*, 1923.) Comp. 1920.

F major, c'-f ", [f'-e"b]. 2/4, Andante. 2'15. V/me, P/m.

For: Mezzo, Bar.

Subject: The end of the old familiar English countryside.

Voice: Steps and 3rds, a few simple skips; some accidentals; rhythmically clear, with a few triplets and Scotch snaps.

Piano: Fairly continuous semiquaver patterns, not too thick; some modulation; some LH 10ths could be helped by RH.

Comment: Taken at a slowish tempo this can be a very moving song. Page 25, bar 1: Belloc's words cannot be made to fit here; bar 10; *fallen* is the word in the original poem, not *falling*, as given here in small print.

(9) When death to either shall come. (Robert Bridges, *New Poems*, 1899.) Comp. London-Minsterworth, July 1920.

Db major, d'b-e"b [e'b-d"b]. 4/8, Andante con moto, quaver = 100. 1'15". V/me, P/me.

For: Mezzo, C-Ten, Bar.

Subject: After my death be happy with the child, and read the songs I wrote for you.

Voice: Mostly by step, a few simple skips; no accidentals; speech-related rhythms.

Piano: Continuous semiquavers over quaver bass; no accidentals.

Comment: The quaver = 100 seems on the fast side; it must remain 4/8 rather than 2/4, and never sound hurried. It is not a sad song, on the contrary, it exudes contentment with what life has given, and is one of Gurney's most satisfying songs. Use the small print words throughout.

(10) Cathleen ni Houlihan. The old brown thorn-trees break in two. (W.B. Yeats, *In the Seven Woods*, 1904.) Comp. Minsterworth, June 1919.

A minor, c'b-f " , [e'-d"]. 4/4, Allegro con moto. 2'45". V/md, P/m.

For: [Mezzo], Bar.

Subject: We are afraid, and may well die; but we have in our hearts the spirit of Cathleen ni Houlihan [that is, of Ireland].

Voice: Mostly by step, with occasional big skips; much chromaticism; a long chromatic climb to a ff held e" for the climax; several melismas; strong driving rhythm at the start of each of the three stanzas, each ending with a free, almost prayerful, passage.

Piano: Crotchet bass with off-beat chords leading to thick slower chordal passages, in each verse; becomes fairly chromatic.

Comment: A magnificent dramatic song, needing wide contrasts of mood and dynamic. Excellent for the singer who thinks English song only suitable for the drawing-room! Yeats's title is 'Red Hanrahan's song about Ireland'. Page 29, bar 5: Cummen Strand is on the southern side of the estuary, to the north-west of Sligo; bar 10: the left hand is unlucky. Page 30, bar 11: Cathleen is the old woman who symbolises Ireland in Yeats's play *Cathleen ni Houlihan*. The end of the play describes her: *'Peter* – Did you see an old woman going down the path? *Patrick* – I did not, but I saw a young girl and she had the walk of a queen.' Yeats's beloved Maud Gonne played the part of Cathleen. See 2 (7). Page 31, bar 3: Knocknarea – the Mountain of the Kings, overlooking Sligo; bar 9: Queen Maeve's supposed burial cairn is on top of

Knocknarea. Page 32, bar 14: Clooth-na-Bar is Lough Ia,
Sligo. Page 33, bar 13: Rood = crucifix.

2 TWENTY SONGS, Volume II. Pub. OUP, 1938.

(1) **The Scribe**. What lovely things Thy hand hath made. (Walter de la
   Mare, *Motley and Other Poems*, 1918.) Comp. 1919.

	B minor, b°*b*-e″, [e′-d″]. 2/4, Poco allegretto. 3′. V/m, P/m.
For:	Mezzo, C-Ten, Bar.
Subject:	God's creations are too many and wonderful to be described.
Voice:	Steps, broken chords; some chromatics; speech rhythms with extended phrases, end quasi recit; e″ and b°*b* are sustained when reached.
Piano:	Starts simple; builds into throbbing repeated triplet chords; chromatic – harder to read than to play.
Comment:	An ambitious and successful song, with real scope for imaginative performers. Page 4, bar 2: reeds are used to make pens.

(2) **The boat is chafing** at our long delay. (John Davidson, *Plays*, 1889.)
   Comp. Minsterworth, July 1920.

	D*b* major, d′*b*-e″, [g′*b*-e″*b*]. 2/4, Andante con moto, quaver = 100. 1′45″. V/me, P/me.
For:	Mezzo, C-Ten, Bar.
Subject:	We must set sail for an unknown land; Thetis protect us.
Voice:	Steps and simple skips; slightly chromatic with some enharmonic notation; mostly flowing quavers.
Piano:	Flowing semiquavers with quaver chords; not too thick; some modulation.
Comment:	A pleasantly straightforward song. Thetis was a sea goddess, the mother of Achilles.

(3) **Bread and cherries**. 'Cherries, ripe cherries', the old woman cried.
   (Walter de la Mare, *Peacock Pie*, 1913.) Comp. 1921.

	E minor, e′-f″#, [g′-e″]. 2/4, Allegro. 30″. V/me, P/m.
For:	Sop, Ten; Mezzo, high Bar.
Subject:	Little boys come to the cherry-seller.
Voice:	Steps, skips of all sizes; crotchets and quavers changing to triplets, a semiquaver melisma at end, after sustained e″.
Piano:	Starts with simple chords and LH quaver broken chords, then spread triplet arpeggios in both hands; ends with a flourish.
Comment:	Bright and cheerful, good encore or finisher. Be careful not to start too fast!

(4) **An epitaph**. Here lies a most beautiful lady. (Walter de la Mare, *The Listeners and Other Poems*, 1912.) Comp. Leigh, July 1920.

        D major, d'-e", [d'-d"]. 2/2, Andante. V/md, P/m.

For: Mezzo, C-Ten, Bar.
Subject: 'Beauty passes, however rare it be.'
Voice: Steps, broken chords; some modulation; speech rhythms with many crotchet triplets; long phrases, the last unaccompanied.
Piano: Chordal, sustained, and broken in quavers; some modulation.
Comment: Magically beautiful, but great demands are made on the singer's ability to handle long phrases, and both performers must go well behind the written notes for the shaping of this wonderful song. Many words here differ from the original poem, but it would seem in this case that it is not due to Gurney's failure of memory, but rather to his poet-composer's ear, for the alterations are all improvements from the singer's point of view, though not if the poem were to be spoken.

(5) **Blaweary**. As I came by Blaweary I heard a young wife sing. (Wilfrid Gibson, *Neighbours*, 1920.) Comp. 1921.

        F major, d'-d". 6/8, Andante. 1'30". V/e, P/me.

For: Mezzo, C-Ten, Bar.
Subject: I heard a young wife singing a lullaby.
Voice: Steps and simple skips; slightly uncertain tonality, though only one accidental; simple rhythms.
Piano: Quaver broken chords; mostly three-part writing, and not very conveniently placed for the hands.
Comment: The 'weary' from the title seems to have taken control of this rather strange little song! Gurney has omitted the second stanza, in which the two new lines run: 'Daddy's in the lambing-storm / Tending to the sheep.'

(6) **A sword**. As crowns to a king, as pennies to a pound. (Robin Flower, *Epigrams from an anthologia Hibernica*, 9th-17th century.) Comp. 1922.

        D minor, d'-e". 4/4, Allegro. 30". V/m, P/md.

For: Bar.
Subject: My sword is greater than all others.
Voice: Broken chords; strong rhythms; ends with sustained d"s and e"s, in surprising rhythms.
Piano: Thick chordal writing in quavers and triplets.
Comment: A shout of defiance; if the performers can manage it well, a fine finisher. Bar 3; *to a king* makes the better rhythm, but *to kings* makes better sense!

(7) **The folly of being comforted**. One that is ever kind said yesterday. (W.B. Yeats, *In the Seven Woods*, 1904.) Comp. Bangour-Seaton Delaval, October-December 1917.

        C# minor, c'#-g''#(f''#), [e'-d''#]. 2/4, Andante. 4'30''. V/md, P/m.

For: Ten; high Bar.

Subject: A friend has suggested, kindly, that it will be possible for me to give up my hopeless love, now that the woman I have loved in vain is growing old; but he is quite wrong.

Voice: Steps and simple skips; some modulation; based on speech rhythms, with many short repeated phrases, and some very extended ones; two phrases lie high, e'' and f''#s, and the ending is a seven-bar phrase on f' and e'.

Piano: Very chromatic; some counterpoint; broken phrases; heavy chordal climaxes.

Comment: A fine song, intensely emotional, written while Gurney was in the trenches. Both poem and music pose problems of interpretation, but they are well worth tackling. Page 18, bar 9, to page 19, bar 10: in *The Collected Poems* (Macmillan, 1982) these lines read ' "Though now it seems impossible, and so / All that you need is patience." Heart cries, "No, / I have not a crumb of comfort, not a grain." ' There is also a colon after *again* at the end of the next line, which makes the sense clearer. However, Gurney has set the poem exactly as published in 1904. Page 17, bars 5-6: possibly Lady Gregory. The subject of the poem is Maud Gonne, whom Yeats first met in 1889.

(8) **Hawk and Buckle**. Where is the landlord of old Hawk and Buckle. (John Doyle [pseudonym for Robert Graves], *Country Sentiment*, 1920.) Comp. 1920.

        G minor, d'-e''b, [d'-d'']. 3/4, Allegro. 1'15''. V/me, P/me.

For: [Mezzo], C-Ten, Bar.

Subject: Where is the landlord? – drinking; the ostler? – dozing; the daughter? – trimming her hat.

Voice: Steps and 3rds; a little modulation towards the end; almost entirely in crotchets.

Piano: Rhythmic chordal with a few decorations.

Comment: A straightforward and energetic song, if a little monotonous in total effect. The words in small print cannot easily be made to fit. Gurney has set stanzas 1, 3, 2, in that order, and omitted the remaining three.

(9) **Last hours**. A grey day and quiet. (John Freeman, *Memories of Childhood and Other Poems*, 1919.) Comp. 1918.

E minor, b°*b*-e″, [e′*b*-e″*b*]. 6/8, Largo. 4′15″. V/m, P/m.

For: Mezzo, C-Ten, Bar.
Subject: A winter landscape.
Voice: Steps, simple skips; somewhat chromatic; very sustained; long slow melisma at end; never rises above mf; quite simple rhythm.
Piano: 3/4 and 6/8 combined most of the time, with overlapping pairs of contrapuntal parts in the two rhythms; highly chromatic.
Comment: A very slow and sustained piece which can, if performed with conviction, be a wonderful evocation of a grey winter's day. The tempo must be slow in spite of the risk of monotony; in only two songs did Gurney use Largo for his tempo mark. The original words should be used in bars 6 and 7, since Gurney's faulty memory loses the rhyme; but in bars 8 and 9 *hangs* may be thought better for singing than Freeman's *falls*.

(10) **Epitaph in old mode**. The leaves fall gently on the grass. (J.C. Squire, *Poems, Second Series*, 1922 [1919].) Comp. 1920.

D*b* major, d′*b*-f″*b*, [f′-d″*b*]. 4/8, Andante. 2′30″. V/m, P/m.

For: Mezzo, C-Ten, Bar.
Subject: The willow sighs above her grave; pity her, for she never told her love.
Voice: Starts with steps and simple skips, then many small chromatic steps, with enharmonic notation; flowing speech rhythm.
Piano: Mostly diatonic chordal basis, connected by flowing semiquavers; two passages of surprising chromatic harmony.
Comment: A beautiful song, whose elegiac mood must not be allowed to become sentimental. Page 29, bars 3-4: *upon* is the word given in *Poems, Second Series*. Page 30, bars 5-9: the poem reads simply, 'She loved so tenderly, so tenderly, / And never told them whom.'

3 A THIRD VOLUME OF TEN SONGS. Pub. OUP, 1952.

(1) **Shepherd's song**. Though I am young and cannot tell. (Ben Jonson, *The Sad Shepherd*, 1640, Act I, Scene v.) Comp. 1919.

D*b* major, c′-f″*b*, [e′*b*-d″]. 3/8, Andante. 2′20″. V/m, P/m.

For: Mezzo, C-Ten, Bar. Subject:Love and death are similar, for both can kill.
Voice: Steps, small skips, broken chords; some chromatics, with enharmonic notation; speech rhythms with many triplets.
Piano: Fairly continuous semiquaver broken chords, sometimes in bare 8ves, sometimes thickly laid out; a few big stretches.
Comment: Rather unconvincing as a whole, though there is an effective romantic climax.

(2) **The happy tree**. There was a bright and happy tree. (Gerald Gould.)
　　Comp. 1920.

	E major, c'#-f"#, [f'#-e"]. 2/4, Andante. 2'15". V/me, P/me.
For:	Mezzo, high Bar.
Subject:	A happy tree was a home for birds; but jealous men cut it down and made it into a cross.
Voice:	Steps and 3rds; some fairly simple modulation; straightforward rhythms.
Piano:	RH semiquavers, LH quavers, becoming a little more chordal as it progresses.
Comment:	Pleasant, but the turn to tragedy at the end is too abrupt to be managed easily in performance.

(3) **The cherry trees bend over**. (Edward Thomas, *Poems*, 1917 [Hare
　　Hall? 7-8 May 1916].) Comp. 1920.

	E major, e'-e", [g'-e"]. 2/4,3/4, Poco andante. 1'. V/m, P/m.
For:	Mezzo, Bar.
Subject:	The cherry trees shed their petals as if for a wedding, though there is none.
Voice:	Steps and simple skips; some modulation; three bars of alternate e" and d"; mostly twos against the triplets of the piano.
Piano:	RH broken chords against sustained bass line, becoming wide-ranging broken chords in both hands; some chromatics; some two against three.
Comment:	An attractive song in spite of the problems. Page 10, bar 6: Thomas wrote *when*, not *though*.

(4) **I shall ever be maiden**. (Bliss Carman, *Sappho: One Hundred Lyrics*,
　　1921.) Comp. 1919.

	G major, d'b-g", [e'b-e"]. 2/4,3/4, Andante con moto. 2'15". V/m, P/m.
For:	Sop, high Mezzo.
Subject:	Only you shall love me, and bless the coming years with gladness.
Voice:	Many phrases rise by step, to fall in broken chords; quite a wide dynamic range required; sustained g" forte near end, followed by some bars of recit, pp; some modulation; basically speech rhythms.
Piano:	LH semiquaver arpeggios, RH crotchet chords, blending after a while, and then reversed; fairly chromatic.
Comment:	An enjoyable song for all concerned. One of 'Two Sappho Songs'; the pair to this is 'Love shakes my soul', 4 (3); they go well together musically, but the range of the second is rather lower, which could be a problem.

(5) **Ploughman singing**. Here morning in the ploughman's songs is met. (John Clare, *Poems Chiefly from Manuscript*, edited by Edmund Blunden, 1920.) Comp. 1920.

<blockquote>B major, d'-g″, [f' #-f ″#]. 4/4, Poco andante. 2′45″. V/m, P/d.</blockquote>

For: Sop, Ten.
Subject: I arose early and went out, and heard the ploughman's song – how simple is happiness.
Voice: Steps and broken chords; long flowing lines mostly in quavers; fairly frequent modulations.
Piano: Semiquaver sextuplet figuration in RH throughout, over simple LH chords, which cover wider and wider spaces; much modulation.
Comment: An excellent song, but needing a pianist with a good technique; it is by no means easy to play. However, the RH could be simplified, without too much damage, by omitting some of the lower notes on the beats; and the song really should be sung.

(6) **I praise the tender flower**. (Robert Bridges, *Shorter Poems*, Book III, 1880.) Comp. 1912-13?, revised February 1917.

<blockquote>F major, c' #-e″, [f'-d″]. 2/4, Poco andante. 3′. V/m, P/me.</blockquote>

For: [Mezzo], C-Ten, Bar.
Subject: A flower and a girl made me happy; I can tell neither, so I have made this song instead.
Voice: Steps, simple skips, broken chords; some modulation; speech rhythms with some triplets; Gurney's phrase marks seem over-generous – many pairs of phrases would be better combined, though this would require good breath control.
Piano: Chordal, with many passages of parallel semiquavers; some modulation.
Comment: A charming and tender song. Page 20, bar 11: RH first beat a' needs a flat.

(7) **Snow**. In the gloom of whiteness. (Edward Thomas, *Last Poems*, 1918 [Steep, 7 January 1915].) Comp. 1921.

<blockquote>F minor, e'b-g″, [e'b-f ″]. 3/4, Adagio. 2′. V/m, P/m.</blockquote>

For: Sop, Ten.
Subject: In the snow a child is weeping.
Voice: Mostly 3rds, a few steps and skips; simple rhythms, mostly minims and crotchets; some modulation; some long phrases, high-lying at end, and some short ones which might well be better combined in pairs.
Piano: Broken chords in quavers, with parallel movement between the hands; many accidentals.
Comment: A fine atmospheric song, which lingers in the mind. Page 25,

bar 2: first bass note should be A♭ not G. The child was Thomas's younger daughter Myfanwy, then aged 4½.

(8) Thou didst delight my eyes. (Robert Bridges, *Shorter Poems*, Book III, 1880.) Comp. 1921.
D♭ major, d′♭-e″♭, [e′♭-d″♭]. 4/4, Poco andante. 3′. V/md, P/m.

For:	Mezzo, C-Ten, Bar.
Subject:	I am but one of the many who love you, but I shall not forget your kindness.
Voice:	Steps and simple skips, mostly in crotchets; much modulation involving enharmonic notation.
Piano:	A long series of offbeat chords at the start of each stanza, moving into quaver arpeggios with thick texture; much modulation.
Comment:	A rich, warm and beautiful song, with an unforgettable melody; the offbeat accompaniment can cause difficulties for the musically insecure singer. The modulations are magical, some rubato is needed to make the most of them.

(9) The ship. There was no song nor shout of joy. (J.C. Squire, *Poems, First Series*, 1918 [1913].) Comp. 1920.
D♭ major, d′♭-e″, [e′♭-d″♭]. 2/4, Moderato. 1′45″. V/me, P/e.

For:	Mezzo, C-Ten, Bar.
Subject:	There was no excitement when the ship came home with neither slaves nor gold, but the tired seamen were content and proud.
Voice:	Steps and broken chords; some modulation; simple, fairly regular rhythms.
Piano:	LH quavers, RH semiquavers, all harmonically filled in; some modulation; not always comfortable for the hands.
Comment:	Pleasant though unexciting, like the ship it describes.

(10) Goodnight to the meadow. (Robert Graves, *Country Sentiment*, 1920.) Comp. 1920.
E♭ major, c′-e″♭, [e′♭-d″]. 2/4, Poco allegretto. 1′. V/m, P/me.

For:	Mezzo, C-Ten, Bar.
Subject:	It is evening; 'Does he love me'? The moon appears.
Voice:	Many small skips; very varied rhythms, with some patter; ends legato in contrast.
Piano:	Chordal, with moving quavers; a rather awkward coda.
Comment:	Lightweight, but enjoyable. One of 'Two Songs from *Country Sentiment*'. See 1 (6).

4 A FOURTH VOLUME OF TEN SONGS. Pub. OUP, 1959.

(1) **Even such is time**, which takes in trust. (Sir Walter
Raleigh,   'Epitaph',   *The   Prerogative   of   Parliaments*,
1628.) Comp. Arras, June? 1917.

	E minor/major, b°-e″, [d′-d″]. 2/2, Andante con moto. V/m, P/m.
For:	Mezzo, C-Ten, Bar.
Subject:	Death is inevitable, but I hope for resurrection.
Voice:	Mostly by step; many 4ths and 5ths and one 8ve leap; Some modulation: simple rhythms, but several melismas; long climbing phrase to final sustained e″.
Piano:	Thick chordal writing, possibly with full orchestra in mind; many big stretches; a twelve-bar postlude in E major.
Comment:	A powerful song, quite unlike Gurney's usual style. Gurney told Herbert Howells it could be orchestrated. The verbal discrepancies are curious: the old *Oxford Book of English Verse*, which Gurney must have had, is the source of the words given in small print. However, both *OB 16* and *NOB* agree in giving the first two pages exactly as Gurney wrote them, following Latham, and agree in giving page 3 as 'And from which earth and grave and dust, The Lord shall raise me up, I trust'. Ault gives *and* for *our* in bar 7 and *which* for *who* page 2 bar 1, but otherwise agrees with Latham. It would seem the best solution would be to sing what Gurney wrote for the first two pages, and the words given above for the third; even if it is thought better to keep to Gurney throughout, on page 3 bar 4, *his* is surely a miscopying of *this*. Page 3 bars 18, 19: it seems possible the b′s in the RH should not be tied, since this appears to be a final statement of the leitmotif of the whole song.

(2) **Brown is my love**, and graceful. (Anon in Yonge's *Musica
Transalpina*, Book 2, 1597.) Comp. Kensington, Autumn 1920.

	Db major, d′b-g″b, [e′b-e″b]. 3/8, [Andante]. 1′30″. V/m, P/m.
For:	Ten; high Bar.
Subject:	My love is beautiful, but scornful.
Voice:	Many broken chords; steps and skips; fairly complex rhythms; some modulation.
Piano:	Fairly continuous semiquavers, with much 8ve doubling between the hands, texture rather thick; many accidentals.
Comment:	A pleasant start, but becomes harmonically rather congested on the second page. The small print words should be used.

(3) **Love shakes my soul** like a mountain wind. (Bliss Carman, *Sappho: One Hundred Lyrics*, 1921.) Comp. 1920.

B minor, b°-f"#, [e'-e"]. 4/4, Allegro moderato. 2'15". V/md, P/md.

For: Mezzo.

Subject: I am overwhelmed by love.

Voice: Steps; rapid climbing phrases to sustained f"s; chromatic; long phrases, many triplets; wide dynamic range.

Piano: Four bars of scalic semiquavers with crotchet chords, not easy; much arpeggio work; 8ves in quaver triplets; very chromatic; some big stretches; wide dynamic range.

Comment: An exciting romantic song, perhaps not entirely successful, but well worth tackling. One of 'Two Sappho Songs'; see 'I shall ever be maiden', 3 (4). Note: the small print words should be used. Daphne became a laurel-tree to escape the love of the sun-god, Apollo; Syrinx, afraid of the love of Pan, was turned into a bed of reeds, from which Pan then made his pipes.

(4) **Most holy night** that still does keep. (Hilaire Belloc, *Verses and Sonnets*, 1896.) Comp. 1920.

Eb major, e'b-e", [e'b-d"b]. 4/8, Poco adagio. 3'15". V/m, P/m.

For: Mezzo, C-Ten, Bar.

Subject: May I have rest and peace this coming night.

Voice: Steps and 3rds until verse 3, which has 5th drops and leaps, a quick melisma and long climb to held e"; rhythms easy, though again verse 3 is more complex; only slightly chromatic.

Piano: Semiquaver RH over quaver LH, but the thick and rather dissonant writing needs careful control over balance of tone and use of sustaining pedal.

Comment: A beautiful vocal line handicapped, after the first verse, by a congested and harmonically confusing accompaniment; however it is well worth trying. Use small print words throughout. The note that Gurney omitted two verses is incorrect; only one verse is left out. It is included in Warlock's setting.

(5) **To violets**. Welcome, maids of honour! (Robert Herrick, *Hesperides*, 1648.) Comp. November 1920.

G major, c'-e", [e'-e"]. 2/4, [Poco allegretto]. 1'. V/me, P/me.

For: Mezzo, C-Ten, Bar.

Subject: Violets bring in the spring, but are soon forgotten when the roses arrive.

Voice: Lots of little skips; arpeggio from c'-e"; a surprise little modulation at end; basically simple rhythms.

Piano: Much in only three parts; fair variety of rhythm; slightly
              chromatic.

Comment: A charmer! The small print words on page 15 do not fit the
              shape of Gurney's melody as well as his alteration, which
              should be retained.

(6) On the downs. Up on the downs the red-eyed kestrel hovers. (John
  Masefield, *Lollingdon Downs and Other Poems*, 1917.) Comp.
  September 1919.

              G minor, c'-e″, [d'-d″]. 4/4, Allegro [molto moderato]. 1′45″.
              V/md, P/m.

For: Mezzo, C-Ten, Bar.

Subject: Men are burning gorse on the downs; once they burned men
              there, and today I can feel something in the air.

Voice: Many 5th drops, broken chords, steps; many triplet and
              semiquaver figures; needs strong and precise diction, and
              accuracy in the varied rhythms.

Piano: LH quaver melody with off-beat quaver chords in RH;
              middle section has semiquaver arpeggio figuration, which
              must be allowed to determine the tempo.

Comment: A dramatic and highly atmospheric song, full of mystery and
              indefinite threat. Unusually for Gurney the word-setting is
              rather awkward, making it hard to convey the full meaning
              of the poem to the listener. However, an imaginative singer
              will find great opportunities here. It is better to use the
              small print words, even though harder to sing. Masefield's
              long lines may have twenty-one or twenty-four syllables, but
              all have five stresses; the short lines have from four to six
              syllables, but always two stresses. The words omitted by
              Gurney at the bottom of page 16 are essential to this stress
              pattern, and can be included by changing the first note of
              page 17 from a minim to two quavers and a crotchet. Page
              17, bar 4: *these* is not only Masefield's original but the third
              stress word of the line; there should be no comma after the
              following *downs*. Try making the final two semiquavers of
              bar 4 into a quaver for *on*, and using the first two notes of
              bar 5 for *these downs*; the stresses should be on 'tribe', 'thus',
              'these' and 'burn'. Page 18, bar 4; *hawkes* = *hawks*, this is
              just a misprint. The other small print words provide a good
              example of Gurney's memory at work: page 16, bar 4, *kestrel
              hovers* for *kestrels hover*, is unimportant; *drift* in bar 11 has
              come from the next bar, and *burning*, page 17, bar 8, has
              come from bar 5 of the same page. Both these should be
              altered.

(7) **A piper** in the streets today. (Seumas O'Sullivan, *Verses, Sacred and Profane*, 1908.) Comp. 1920.

> G major, e'-f ", [g'-e"]. 2/4, Andante. 1'20". V/me, P/me.

For: Mezzo, Bar.

Subject: When the piper came we all danced in the streets.

Voice: Steps, 3rds, broken chords; some accidentals; simple rhythms with a few triplets.

Piano: Semiquaver broken chord patterns; a fair amount of modulation.

Comment: Not as cheerful as the words would lead one to expect. Use the small print words; but the missing line on page 20 cannot be included.

(8) **A cradle song**. The angels are stooping above your bed. (W.B. Yeats, *The Rose*, 1893.) Comp. 1920.

> Eb major, e'b-f "b, [f'-d"]. 6/8, Andante. 1'45". V/e, P/me.

For: Mezzo, C-Ten, Bar.

Subject: The angels are pleased with you – I shall miss you when you are grown.

Voice: Steps and 3rds; a sustained e"; simple rhythms, some hemiolas.

Piano: Simple three and four part crotchet and quaver movement, becoming a thicker texture with big stretches on second page.

Comment: A tender little song, with charming words. Gurney set Yeats's original version of the poem – the small print words come from the revised version of many years later, and can be ignored. Page 22, bar 12: the shining Seven = the planets.

(9) **The fiddler of Dooney**. When I play on my fiddle in Dooney. (W.B. Yeats, *The Wind among the Reeds*, 1899.) Comp. 1917, revised September 1918.

> Eb major, b°b-f ", [d'-d"]. 6/8, Allegro, dotted crotchet = 100. 1'45". V/m, P/m.

For: Bar.

Subject: My cousin and brother are priests, and I am just a fiddler, but when we reach heaven I and my music will go in first!

Voice: Steps and 3rds; some sustained e"bs; some chromatic passages; a fair variety of rhythms, with two long phrases.

Piano: Two chords a bar, and running quavers, often in 8ves in RH.

Comment: One of Gurney's few genuinely quick songs, it has life and a fair amount of variety. Use the small print words. At the end of the first verse there is a note in *Collected Poems*: ' "Mocharabuiee" pronounced as if spelt "Mockrabwee" '; this would mean using both c" and d" for the first syllable.

(10) **In Flanders**. I'm homesick for my hills again. (F.W. Harvey, *A Gloucester Lad at home and abroad*, 1916 [September 1915].) Comp. Crucifix Corner, Thiepval, finished 11 January 1917.

E*b* major, c'#-f ", [d'-d"*b*]. 2/4, Andante espressivo. 2'45". V/m, P/m.

For:　　　　Mezzo, Bar.
Subject:　　Homesick for the Cotswolds, while in the trenches.
Voice:　　　Steps and broken chords; much modulation; mostly simple rhythms; big climax on f ", five bars sustained b'*b* to finish.
Piano:　　　Chordal, gradually quickening and thickening, much 8ve work; many modulations.
Comment:　　Both words and music were written in the trenches during the First World War; this is an intensely emotional song that in the hands of sympathetic performers can be heart-rending.

5 **A FIFTH VOLUME OF TEN SONGS** edited by Michael Hurd. Pub. OUP, 1979. Songs with publication dates before 1979 were originally published separately.

(1) **By a bierside**. This is a sacred city, built of marvellous earth. (John Masefield, *The Tragedy of Pompey the Great*, 1910.) Comp. France, August 1916. Pub. OUP, 1979.

C major, a°-f ", [c'-e"]. 4/4, Adagio quasi andante, crotchet = 60. 3'45". V/md, P/m.

For:　　　　Mezzo, Bar.
Subject:　　A funeral oration on the grandeur of death.
Voice:　　　Many skips, arpeggios, repeated notes, long melisma; climax on four bars held e", fortissimo; starts 'as a recitative, with simplicity', but soon becomes an aria, with two big climaxes.
Piano:　　　Heavily chordal; several bars repeated, needing variety of colour, since Gurney had future orchestration in mind, though he never carried it out.
Comment:　　A big dramatic song, needing a big voice, and a pianist ready to play like an orchestra. 'The accompaniment is really orchestral, but the piano will get all that's wanted very well' (Gurney, August 1916). The words in small print are taken from the version entitled 'The Chief Centurians', in *The Complete Poems*, first published in 1924. However, the version given in *Poems of Today*, 1915, is called 'By a Bierside', and agrees with Gurney's version in all but the following points, where the small print is correct: Page 2, bar 5: *here*; bar 8: *this brain*; bar 9: *this*; page 4, bar 1:

drives. This must be the version Gurney knew, and should surely be used.

Page 4, bars 9-13: in a letter of 15 December 1916 Gurney gives a totally different version of this passage, lasting 8 bars, given in *War Letters*. Page 4, bar 13: the original had a crotchet rest and three crotchet e″s for the voice; on 25 October Gurney wrote to Marion Scott: 'The 4 Es must stand, even if the lady should need trumpets to back her up. She is supposed to make a row like a brass band there. This only is admissible besides the written notes and it is from an unwilling writer – (crotchet rest and e′ a′ b′, all crotchets).' Five days later Gurney wrote to Howells: 'I cannot agree with you about the repeated Es. Somehow they will have to sound like an immortal challenge after the recital of deaths damages and wrongs to man. If the Es are impossible then g′ a′ b′ or g′ a′ e″, all crotchets.' Page 5: 'The repetition of that figure in the orchestral version would insist bar after bar on a different thread of the counterpoint, or at a different octave, then at an octave higher and so forth, with trumpets especially at the loudest with accented notes. In my mind I saw a picture of some poet-priest pronouncing an oration over the dead and lovely body of some Greek hero' (Gurney to Marion Scott, 13 September, 1916). Further information can be found in *War Letters*.

(2) **Desire in spring**. I love the cradle songs the mothers sing. (Francis Ledwidge, *Songs of the Fields*, 1915.) Comp. December 1919. Pub. OUP, 1928. *High* and Low keys.

        E major, b°-e″, [e′-e″]; *G major*. 3/4, Andante. 2′30″. V/m, P/m.

For:	*Sop, Ten*; Mezzo, C-Ten, Bar.
Subject:	I love the sounds and sights of a spring evening.
Voice:	Steps and 3rds, occasional broken chords; many flattened leading notes; some modulation; rhythm fairly simple, many semiquaver pairs, and some stretched phrases.
Piano:	Semiquaver patterns in RH over slower LH chordal writing; many accidentals; a few big stretches.
Comment:	A charming atmospheric song, a beautifully shaped vocal line over a flowing accompaniment, with convincing modulations. Francis Ledwidge was a young Irishman killed in the First World War, who has been forgotten as a Great War poet because he wrote of home and peace, not of life in the trenches.

(3) **Severn meadows**. Only the wanderer knows England's graces. (Ivor Gurney, *Severn and Somme*, 1917 [18 January 1917].) Comp. Caulincourt, Flanders. March 1917. Pub. OUP, 1928.

    D major, b°-d″, [d′-d″]. 3/2, Lento. 1′45″. V/me, P/e.

For: Mezzo, C-Ten, Bar; Cont, Bass.
Subject: Only the wanderer knows the true meaning of home.
Voice: Steps and 3rds; simple rhythms; some fairly long phrases.
Piano: Crotchet 3rds and 6ths moving above a minim bass.
Comment: Gurney's only setting of his own words, written in the trenches. Two short pages of pure anguish, almost unbearable in its controlled emotion; a great song.

(4) **Song of Ciabhan**. To the isle of peace I turn my prow. (Ethna Carbery.) Comp. June 1911. Pub. OUP, 1979.

    D major, d′-e″b, [e′-d″]. 9/8, Lento. 1′40″. V/me, P/e.

For: Mezzo, C-Ten, Bar.
Subject: Beloved and lover shall go to the isle of peace.
Voice: Steps, 3rds, broken chords; a few accidentals; pause on the e″b; simple rhythms, fairly long phrases.
Piano: Simple harmony, mostly in four parts; crotchet quaver rhythms.
Comment: An early song, with some charm.

(5) **The apple orchard**. In the apple boughs the coolness murmurs. (Bliss Carman, *Sappho: One Hundred Lyrics*, 1921.) Comp. Summer 1919. Pub. OUP, 1979.

    Eb major, d′#-e″b, [f′-c″]. 6/8, Quasi andante, dotted crotchet = 60. 1′. V/m, P/me.

For: [Mezzo], C-Ten, Bar.
Subject: From noon till twilight I await you in this garden.
Voice: Steps and 3rds; 8ve drop; sustained e″b, ending with two bars of d″ rising to one of e″b, all pp; some long phrases.
Piano: Dotted crotchet bass with off-beat quaver appoggiaturas in RH; some arpeggios; many accidentals.
Comment: Some two against three in the piano may cause the singer slight problems in this gentle song. Page 14, bar 6: line 3 starts with *Where* not *flicker*. See 3 (4) and 4 (3).

(6) **The cloths of heaven**. Had I the heaven's embroidered cloths. (W.B. Yeats, *The Wind among the Reeds*, 1899.) Comp. 1919. Pub. OUP, 1979.

    Eb major, e′b-g″, [g′-e″b. 6/8, Andante. 2′15″. V/md, P/m.

For: Sop, Ten.
Subject: I would give you the cloths of heaven, but can only offer dreams.
Voice: Mostly by step, with small skips; but a bar of g″ dropping to

another bar of g′, and ending with a long climb up to two
bars of g″, both phrases pp.

Piano: Starts with rocking quaver chords, adds semiquaver broken
chords, and then several arpeggios in three parts.

Comment: Could be effective, but it seems a rather elaborate setting for
such a simple poem. Yeats's title: 'He wishes for the cloths of
heaven'. The song was mentioned in a letter to Marion Scott
dated September 1918.

(7) **The fields are full** of summer still. (Edward Shanks, *The Queen of
China and Other Poems*, 1919.) Comp. 1919. Pub. OUP, 1929.
E major, c′#-e″, [e′-e″]. 2/4, Andante. V/me, P/me.

For: Mezzo, C-Ten, Bar.
Subject: Autumn is beautiful, and old age can be so too.
Voice: Steps and simple skips; some melismas; a little enharmonic
modulation; simple rhythms; long sustained notes at end.
Piano: Simple broken chord patterns in three parts; a little more
elaborate in the middle; many accidentals.
Comment: A nice simple setting of this rather lovely poem.

(8) **The night of Trafalgar**. In the wild October night-time. (Thomas
Hardy, 'Boatman's Song', *The Dynasts*, Part First, 1904, Act V, Scene
vii.) Comp. 1913? Pub. OUP, 1979.
D minor, d′-f ″, [d′-d″]. 4/4 Allegro. 1′45″. V/m, P/m.

For: Bar.
Subject: It was a stormy night, and we rowed home to bed, not
knowing what was happening off Cadiz, Trafalgar won and
Nelson dead.
Voice: Steps, skips, broken chords; strong straightforward
rhythms.
Piano: Chordal, with much 8ve work.
Comment: A real sea song, needing a strong voice and clear diction.
Page 22, bar 5: Back-sea – 'In those days the hind-part of the
harbour adjoining this scene was so named, and at high
tides the waves dashed across the isthmus at a point called
"The Narrows" ' (note by Hardy). The scene is Budmouth
(Weymouth). Page 23, bar 10: the small print words, though
Hardy's, are best ignored, unless the rhythms are adjusted
to match. Page 24, bars 8, 9: *Sou'-west, Sou'-west, Sou'-west
= The dark, The dark, Sou'-west*, in Hardy.

(9) **The twa corbies**. As I was walking all alane. (Border ballad.) Comp.
Summer 1914, and dedicated to C.H.H. Parry. Pub. OUP, 1928. (First
published in *Music and Letters*, April 1920).
A minor, c′-f ″, [e′-e″b]. Largo – quicker – mysterioso. 3′30″.
V/m, P/md.

For: [Mezzo], Bar.

Subject: The crows know where a dead knight lies; when they have picked his bones the wind shall blow over them evermore.

Voice: Steps; many 5ths and 6ths; climax on held e″ ff; rhythms fairly simple, with many triplets; two changes of key-signature.

Piano: Slow heavy chords, then 'quicker' in triplet quaver broken chords, which become thicker in texture, reaching a semi-quaver passage with big LH stretches; quiet finish.

Comment: A dramatic and effective setting. Page 28, bar 8; an accelerando into the new tempo is advisable. The words are as given in *OB*. 'The Twa Corbies' = 'The Two Ravens'. Page 28, bar 1: fail dyke = turf-built wall. Page 29, bar 8: hause-bane = neck-bone. Page 30, bar 3, beat 2, voice: c″ should probably be c″#; bar 4: theek = thatch. 'But of course "The Twa Corbies" is a man's song, if there were any left to sing it.' (Gurney to Marion Scott, July 1916).

(10) **Walking song**. O Cranham ways are steep and green. (F.W. Harvey, *A Gloucester Lad at Home and Abroad*, 1916.) Comp. 1919. Pub. OUP, 1928.

            F major, c′-f ″, [f′-f ″]. 4/4, Allegro. 45″. V/e, P/me.

For: [Mezzo], Bar.

Subject: The country is better than the town; since I cannot be there I will sing about it, loudly!

Voice: Steps and simple skips; no accidentals; mostly crotchets with some quaver pairs; f ″s are held for three beats, twice.

Piano: Crotchet bass with quaver broken chords above; not always quite comfortable under the hand; no accidentals.

Comment: Although marked allegro this is a 'walking song' and must not be taken too fast. A pleasant moment of relaxation for all concerned.

6 **LUDLOW AND TEME**. A Song-Cycle to Poems of A.E. Housman. Pub. S & B, 1923. (The poems are from Housman's *A Shropshire Lad*, 1896.) For tenor, string quartet and piano; a version for tenor and piano was issued simultaneously. A revised edition of the tenor and piano version, with Introduction and Notes by Michael Pilkington, was issued in 1982. Although entitled a song-cycle, there is no continuous story, nor is there any musical cross-reference between the songs, which can well be sung separately. These notes refer to the 1982 edition, which itself contains a full commentary on the 1923 versions.

For: Ten.

(1) **When smoke stood up** from Ludlow.

A major, d'*b*-a", [e'-f "#]. 4/4, Allegro con moto. 3'. V/md, P/md.

Subject: A blackbird told me I would be better off dead; I killed it, but then my soul sang the same song.

Voice: Steps, many 4ths and 5ths; much modulation; sustained a" at climax; mostly simple rhythms, some triplets and paired quavers; short recitative section in the middle.

Piano: Much tremolando; two against three; some leaping chords; much 8ve work.

Comment: A dramatic opening to the cycle.

(2) **Far in a western brookland**.

D*b* major, d'*b*-g"*b*, [f'-e"]. 3/4, Adagio. 3'. V/m, P/m.

Subject: I sleep in London; but in the west country a wanderer may hear the sighing of my soul in the poplars.

Voice: Steps, 3rds, and 4ths; 6th leap and drop, 7th drop; chromatic; quite simple rhythms, though many tied notes and some triplets; long phrases; sustained g"*b* pp near end.

Piano: Quaver movement over slower bass line; rich chromatic harmony; many 8ves.

Comment: A haunting song, in spite of occasional awkwardness. There are some verbal problems, which are discussed in the Introduction to the 1982 edition. Use the small print words in performance.

(3) **'Tis time, I think**, by Wenlock Town.

F major, e'*b*-g"*b*, [f'-e"*b*]. 2/4, Andante con moto. 2'. V/m, P/m.

Subject: It must be spring in Wenlock, but those who stay away will miss it; let it last long, though I am not there.

Voice: 3rds, steps, broken chords; some 5ths and 6ths; held g"*b* near end, mf; rhythms simple, with many paired semiquavers; some modulation.

Piano: Simple lines of semiquavers with chordal background; some big stretches; not many accidentals.

Comment: Gently attractive.

(4) **Ludlow Fair**. The lads in their hundreds to Ludlow come in for the fair.

C minor, e'*b*-g", [f'-e"*b*]. 9/8,6/8, Allegro moderato. 2'. V/m, P/m.

Subject: I wish one could know, among the crowds, those who are to die young and carry their truth and beauty to the grave; then one could wish them farewell.

Voice: Steps, skips, repeated notes; 8ve leaps to quaver g"s; held g" ff for four beats at end; simple rhythms, nearly continuous quavers.

Piano: Short chords on each beat, often with quaver melodies, sometimes in 8ves, above; last stanza has leaping chords with many 8ves and accidentals.

Comment: Much like other settings by Butterworth, Moeran and Somervell, but a less memorable melody; however it builds to a fine climax.

(5) On the idle hill of summer.

F major, e′b-a″, [g′-f″]. 4/4, Allegro. 2′30″. V/md, P/md.

Subject: I heard soldiers marching to war; they will die, but I too am a man, and will join them.

Voice: Steps and repeated notes; 6th and 8ve drops and leaps; broken chords; ends with held a″b and held a″, ff; Rhythms generally straightforward, but some quick diction needed.

Piano: 8ves and 3rds over repeated pedal F; becomes elaborate with much 8ve work, big stretches and triplet figuration.

Comment: A dramatic song with a big climax. In spite of the allegro marking too fast a start will cause problems later.

(6) When I was one and twenty.

A minor, e′-g″, [g′-e″]. 2/4, Andante. 1′45″. V/me, P/me.

Subject: A wise man told me not to give my heart away; I didn't believe him, but he was right.

Voice: Steps, 3rds, broken chords; simple rhythms with many paired semiquavers.

Piano: Quaver chords in alternate hands, with occasional melodic semiquaver passages.

Comment: Simple and quite effective.

(7) The Lent lily. 'Tis spring, come out to ramble.

A major, e′-a″, [f′#-f″#]. 2/4, Allegro con moto. 2′45″. V/m, P/md.

Subject: Spring is here; it does not last long, gather your flowers now.

Voice: Steps, skips, broken chords; 8ve drop, 7th and 6th leaps and drops. rhythms varied but not complicated; modulation; climax has held a″ followed by held g″#.

Piano: Triplet quaver broken chords, widely spaced, in both hands; some semiquaver passages making four against three; much 8ve work and some big stretches; many accidentals.

Comment: A romantic song which, though actually ending quietly, makes a good finish to the whole work.

7 THE WESTERN PLAYLAND (And of Sorrow). A Song-Cycle to Poems of A.E. Housman. Pub. S & B, 1926. (The poems are from Housman's *A Shropshire Lad*, 1896.) For baritone, string quartet and piano; a version for baritone and piano was issued simultaneously. A revised edition of the baritone and piano version, with Introduction and Notes by Michael Pilkington, was issued in 1982. Although entitled a song-cycle, there is no continuous story, nor is there any musical cross-reference between the songs, which can well be sung separately. These notes refer to the 1982 edition, which itself contains a full commentary on the 1923 versions.

For: Bar.

(1) **Reveille**. Wake, the silver dusk returning. Comp. High Wycombe, 1921.

F major, d'-f ″, [f'-e″]. 4/4, Poco allegro. 4'. V/md, P/md.

Subject: Get up, the day has begun; do not waste it.
Voice: Steps, broken chords; many 4ths and 5ths; some melismas; many accidentals; much variety in rhythm and phrasing.
Piano: Thickly chordal; much 8ve work; many triplets; some big stretches.
Comment: A dramatic start to the cycle, with plenty of variety. Page 3, bar 5, beat 3, bass: quaver rest missing. Page 7, bar 8; *daylight* is one word, not two.

(2) **Loveliest of trees**, the cherry now. Comp. Gloucester, 1908, revised High Wycombe, 1920.

Db major, d'b-f ″, [e'b-d″]. 2/4, Poco andante. 3'. V/m, P/m.

Subject: The cherry is in blossom; I must look at it while I can.
Voice: Steps and skips, many 4ths and 5ths; modulation; fairly simple rhythms with paired semiquavers.
Piano: Flowing semiquaver melodic lines; fairly thin texture, though a few big stretches; modulation.
Comment: A calm and beautiful song. Page 10, bar 2: delete hyphen between *woodland* and *ride*; bar 4: piano RH, 3rd note should be a semiquaver.

(3) **Golden friends**. With rue my heart is laden. Comp. London, 1920, revised High Wycombe, 1920.

Ab major, e'b-e″b, [f'-d″b]. 4/4, Andante. 2'. V/me, P/e.

Subject: I mourn the friends of my youth, now dead.
Voice: Steps, some broken chords; short melismas; simple rhythms; some phrases unaccompanied.
Piano: Mostly simple 4-part harmony.
Comment: A modal flavour to this quiet and simple setting. Page 14, Bar 3, Voice: the underlay printed is from the full score, in the vocal score notes 3 and 4 should not be tied, *foot* should last two crotchets and *lads* two quavers; the textual notes are misleading. Sing the small print *boys*.

(4) Twice a week the winter thorough. Comp. London, 1920, revised High Wycombe, 1920.

> B minor, b°-f ″, [e′-e″]. 4/4, Allegro molto. 1′15″. V/m, P/d.

Subject: Football in winter, cricket in summer; it is a wonder how such things can prevent despair.

Voice: Steps, 3rds, repeated notes; 7th leap and 8ve drop; strongly rhythmic, mostly crotchets and paired quavers; one phrase all in quavers needs quick diction; held b° in 3rd verse.

Piano: Continuous quavers, in 8ves, with chords attached irregularly; sometimes leaping; many accidentals.

Comment: The only really fast song Gurney wrote; exciting, but the speed makes great demands on the pianist. Page 15, bar 4; thorough = through. Page 16, bar 10: the rather cryptic remark in the Critical Notes means the full score has an extra bar between bars 10 and 11 of this page, which is more or less a repeat of the accompaniment in bar 10.

(5) The aspens. Along the field as we came by. Comp. High Wycombe, 1921.

> F major, c′-e″, [f′-d″]. 3/4, Andante. 4′. V/m, P/m.

Subject: Last year the aspen told me my girl would die and that I would find another; it happened, and now I hear nothing, but perhaps the aspen speaks to her of my death this time.

Voice: Steps, 3rds, broken chords; 8ve and 5th drops; two melismas; few accidentals; simple but varied rhythms; some long phrases.

Piano: Many broken phrases; fairly thin texture, though many 8ves; some big stretches; a few awkward rhythmic combinations.

Comment: Strangely effective in spite of its lack of harmonic variety. Note: page 21, bar 5: LH 2nd and 3rd f°s quavers not crotchets.

(6) Is my team ploughing, that I was used to drive? Comp. Gloucester, 1908, revised High Wycombe, 1921.

> D minor, a°(b°)-e″, [d′-e″b]. 4/4, Allegro. 3′45″. V/m, P/md.

Subject: What is life like for you now I am dead? Fine, but do not question me too closely.

Voice: Steps, small skips; much modulation; rhythm mostly straightforward, with many paired semiquavers; some melismas; free unaccompanied recitative in sixth stanza.

Piano: Strongly rhythmic, basically in quavers, but many semiquaver figures, often in 8ves; many leaps; highly chromatic.

Comment: Dramatic, though there is little contrast between the two voices.

(7) **The far country**. Into my heart an air that kills. Comp. Crickley Hill, London, 1920.

F# major, c′#-d″#, [f′#-d″#]. 4/8, Adagio quasi andante. 2′45″. V/m, P/m.

Subject: Homesickness.

Voice: Steps, 3rds, broken chords; highly chromatic, with enharmonic notation; fairly continuous semiquavers, triplets and some melismas.

Piano: Thick chromatic writing throughout; many parallel 6ths in both hands; some widely spread arpeggios; however, it is more difficult to read than to play.

Comment: The harmonic complexity makes this hard to bring off, but it can be made rather lovely.

(8) **March**. The sun at noon to higher air. Comp. High Wycombe, 1921.

F major, c′-f ″, [e′b-e″b]. 4/4, Allegro con moto – poco andante – tempo I. 4′45″. V/m, P/m.

Subject: It is spring, and boys and girls gather flowers; it should be the time for love.

Voice: Steps, 3rds, broken chords; 7th drops; some modulation; rhythm straightforward, but many crotchet triplets; long phrases and big climaxes.

Piano: Widespread arpeggios in both hands, quaver triplets; parallel chords in middle section; many accidentals; twelve-bar coda.

Comment: A big finish for the cycle, rather spoilt by the piano coda, which even in the short form given here has little sense of direction. Verse 1 refers to astrology – the sun moves from Pisces to Aries in mid-March.

8 FIVE ELIZABETHAN SONGS. Pub. W.R., 1920. Published separately but now re-issued by B & H in one volume. The early copies of this volume have 'Low Voice' on the cover, but this is incorrect. On 5 July 1912 Gurney wrote to his friend F.W. Harvey as follows: 'I have done 5 of the most delightful and beautiful songs you ever cast your beaming eyes upon. They are all Elizabethan – the words – and blister my kidneys, bisurate my magnesia if the music is not as English, as joyful, as tender as any lyric of all that noble host. Technique all right, and as to word setting – models'. Gurney then gives the titles in their present order. 'How did such an undigested clod as I make them? That, Willy, I cannot say. But there they are – Five Songs for Mezzo-Soprano – 2 flutes, 2 clarinets, a harp and 2 bassoons.' The score may never have been completed; only the piano versions were ever published. However, the original instrumental conception explains the rather awkward piano writing to be found in places in this set. On 21 June 1916 Gurney wrote to Herbert Howells: 'They need a String Quartett or Quintett very badly, and should it be 1 flute, 1 clar., 1 bassoon and a harp? – the piano accompaniment is perfectly adequate.'

(1) **Orpheus** with his lute made trees. (Shakespeare, *Henry VIII*, 1613, Act III, Scene i.)

        E major, d'#-g'', [e'-e'']. 2/4, Andante con moto. 2'. V/me, P/e.

For:	Sop, Ten.
Subject:	Orpheus made all things listen to his music.
Voice:	Mostly by steps; many skips of 6ths and 5ths; many triplets against fours in the piano.
Piano:	Semiquavers, some in 8ves, above chordal crotchets; ends of each stanza chords only; coda semiquaver arpeggio; top notes of some chords must go in RH, and awkward fingering is involved.
Comment:	A well-shaped vocal line and a nicely patterned accompaniment seem slightly divorced from one another.

(2) **Tears**. Weep you no more, sad fountains. (Anon, from John Dowland's *Third and Last Book of Songs or Airs*, 1603.)

        C# minor, c'#-e'', [e'-e'']. 3/4, Adagio. 3'. V/me, P/me.

For:	Sop, Ten; Mezzo, C-Ten, Bar.
Subject:	Do not weep; your love will be reconciled on waking.
Voice:	Steps, small skips; sequences, many descending phrases; simple rhythms.
Piano:	Moving 6ths over slow bass, becoming more chordal later in each stanza; 2nd stanza has the 6ths in both hands.
Comment:	A lovely song, with touches of Elgar in the modulations. Bar 9: *gently* = *quickly* in poem. Bar 19, beat 1, RH: e' not g'#. The poem is attributed to John Fletcher in the score, in error.

(3) **Under the greenwood tree** who loves to lie with me. (Shakespeare, *As You Like It*, 1599, Act II, Scene v.)

        A minor, c'-f''#, [e'-e'']. 2/4, Andante con moto. 1'30". V/me, P/e.

For:	Sop, Ten; Mezzo, Bar.
Subject:	Come and live in the forest, where there is no enemy but winter.
Voice:	Steps, small skips; 7th drop, sequences; short melismas; a variety of phrasing and dynamics.
Piano:	Fairly contrapuntal, and not always convenient for the hands; much variety in rhythm and phrasing.
Comment:	A good atmosphere, though there is rather much sequential writing.

(4) **Sleep**. Come, sleep, and with thy sweet deceiving. (Beaumont and Fletcher, *The Woman-Hater*, 1606, Act III, Scene i.) High and *Low* [*Heritage 1*].

> D♭ major, d'*b*-a"*b*, [e'*b*-f "]. B♭ *major*, 3/8, Adagio. 3'. V/m, P/m.

For: Sop, Ten; *Mezzo, Bar.*
Subject: Let me sleep, if only for a little while.
Voice: Mostly by step, some skips; long curving phrases with several melismas; fairly simple rhythms; good breath control needed.
Piano: Semiquaver broken chords over slow-moving bass; considerable variety of texture.
Comment: A great song. The sense of continuity is amazing: musically speaking there are only four phrases, two in each stanza, the last taking eighteen bars to complete. The necessary breaths, even when rests are provided, must not be allowed to interrupt the flow; for example, the crescendo on *influence* must lead to *powers*. Try playing the opening bar with pedalling in quavers. Gurney wrote to Marion Scott, 11 January 1918: 'play it *almost* slurred' and drew three slurs, as printed, with another slur over the whole bar. The play is now considered to be by Francis Beaumont alone, though John Fletcher may have contributed a few scenes, including possibly this song. It is sung by the heroine, Oriana, while attempting to convince Gondarino, the woman-hater, that his hatred is unreasonable.

(5) **Spring**, the sweet spring, is the year's pleasant king. (Thomas Nashe, *Summer's Last Will and Testament*, 1600.) [*Heritage 1*].

> E major, c'-g"#, [e'-e"]. 2/4, Andante con moto. 2'30". V/m, P/md.

For: Sop; Ten.
Subject: Spring is the best time of the year.
Voice: Many broken chords, some steps and skips; 6th drops and 8ve leaps; three different verses with similar refrains of bird-calls, and a coda of pp e"s; much variety of phrasing, including some actual staccato; some long legato lines; a curving legato allargando up to g"# and down again.
Piano: A dancing semiquaver figure surrounded by short chords, sometimes needing a big stretch; rhythmic repeated chords, chains of 3rds, staccato basses, much 8ve work; awkward pp arpeggio to end.
Comment: Another fine song, the happiest Gurney ever wrote. Many of the piano chords must be spread or re-arranged between the hands. The RH 8ves in bars 63-65 are difficult, and arise no

doubt from the original conception for instrumental ensemble; there is something to be said for omitting the lower notes except for the e's and g's. A slight ritenuto is permissible on the top of the last page to allow for the wide-spread LH chords. The song occurs near the beginning of the play, sung by Ver, the personification of spring.

9 LIGHTS OUT. A Song-Cycle to Poems of Edward Thomas. Pub. S & B, 1926. Though clearly best suited to a baritone there is a note attached to the third song applying to occasions when it is sung by a soprano; the cycle is not high enough for a soprano to be comfortable, but certainly most if not all the songs could be sung by a mezzo. There are a number of verbal problems; since Gurney was unable to proof-read the work, having already been in a mental asylum for two years, suggestions are here made as to ways of restoring Thomas's poems to their original form. As this is not a true cycle, there is no reason why the songs should not be sung separately; however, sung as a whole this may well rank as Gurney's finest work.

(1) **The penny whistle.** The new moon hangs like an ivory bugle. (Poems, 1917 [Steep, 5 January 1915].) Comp. Army, St. Albans, 1918.

D minor, c'#-f ", [d'-e"b]. 2/4, Poco andante. 3'. V/m, P/m.

Subject: A picture of a charcoal-burner's camp in a wood, with a girl reading a letter, and her brother playing a whistle.

Voice: Steps, 3rds, broken chords; held e"b, f; speech rhythms in continuous quavers, with semiquaver pairs and triplets.

Piano: RH broken chords and 6ths in semiquavers over mostly slower LH; some leaping chords and big stretches; many short trills.

Comment: A well drawn pastoral picture. Page 1, bar 9: below *leaves* add *ghylls* (= ravines). Page 4, bar 11: below *hidden* add *who hides*. *Ghylls* can be used easily, but to restore *who hides* it is necessary to change the rhythm of the first crotchet beat into triplet quavers, g' g' d", with *who* on the third, and to give *hides* to the following d" and c". Page 5, bar 15: first b° in LH should be b°b. Pianist must watch for 8ve signs.

(2) **Scents.** Today I think only of scents. (*Last Poems*, 1918 [Steep, 4 April 1915].) Comp. London, 1920.

Db major, d'b-e", [e'b-d"b]. 2/4, Andante. 2'15". V/m, P/m.

Subject: The pleasure of Autumn scents.

Voice: Steps, repeated notes, small skips; 7th drops, 6th leaps; many accidentals; two held e"bs; melisma; varied speech rhythms.

Piano: Continuous semiquaver patterns in RH over quaver bass; many 8ves; much modulation.

Comment: Warmly romantic. There are many differences of detail in the words, and the starts of lines are wrongly shown. The original poem runs as follows:

'Today I think / Only with scents, – scents dead leaves yield, / And bracken, and wild carrot's seed, / And the square mustard field; / Odours that rise / When the spade wounds the roots of tree, / Rose, currant, raspberry, or goutweed, / Rhubarb or celery; / The smoke's smell, too, / Flowing from where a bonfire burns / The dead, the waste, the dangerous, / And all to sweetness turns. / It is enough / To smell, to crumble the dark earth, / While the robin sings over again / Sad songs of Autumn mirth.'

The original words can be used, though a few adjustments are required: Page 6, bar 7: add quaver e'*b* at end of bar for *and*; bar 8: change the last quaver into two semiquavers for *and wild*. Page 7, bar 8: sing *raspberry* as two syllables, and use the third note for *or*; bar 10; add semiquaver f' at end of first crotchet beat, for *or*.

(3) **Bright clouds** of may shade half the pond. (*Poems*, 1917 [Hare Hall, 4-5 June 1916].) Comp. High Wycombe, 1920.

        G major, d'-f ", [f'#-e"]. 2/4, Andante. 2'. V/m, P/md.

Subject: May blossom falls on the pond; no one notices.

Voice: Steps, simple skips, broken chords; sustained f ", pp; long pp phrase to end; simple modulation; simple rhythms.

Piano: Fast broken chords descending through both hands, throughout; many accidentals; long fast arpeggio to finish (use both hands).

Comment: A most delightful song. There is a note at the bottom of the first page: 'If Soprano the accompaniment in parts may be an octave higher.' It is difficult to know what parts are meant, and in any case this lies a little low for a soprano; it would suit a mezzo very well, though. Page 13, bar 3: there should be no punctuation mark after *again*; the sentence runs from *Till* to *men*.

(4) **Lights out**. I have come to the borders of sleep. (Poems, 1917 [Trowbridge, November 1916].) Comp. Hucclecote, Christmas 1919. D*b* major, d'*b*-e", [e'*b*-d"*b*]. 3/8, Adagio. 3'30". V/m, P/m.

Subject: I must leave all, to meet inevitable death.

Voice: 3rds, steps, skips; 8ve drops and leap; much modulation; melisma; extended speech rhythms, with long phrases.

Piano: Continuous flow of semiquavers in both hands; broken chords and parallel chords; rich chromatic harmony.

Comment: A fine setting of a great poem. Thomas wrote to Eleanor
             Farjeon, 6 November 1916: 'Now I have actually done still
             another piece which I call "Lights Out". It sums up what I
             have often thought at that call. I wish it were as brief – 2
             pairs of long notes. I wonder is it nearly as good as it might
             be.' Similar in style to 'Sleep', 8 (3), but musically more
             ambitious; though not so immediately attractive it is
             perhaps the finer song. Thomas's second and last stanzas
             are omitted. They run: 'Many a road and track / That, since
             the dawn's first crack, / Up to the forest brink, / Deceived the
             travellers, / Suddenly now blurs, / And in they sink. // The
             tall forest towers; / Its cloudy foliage lowers / Ahead, shelf
             above shelf; / Its silence I hear and obey / That I may lose my
             way / And myself.' Punctuation from Thomas's fair copy
             clarifies the sense: page 15, bar 8: comma after *forest*; bar
             11: no comma after *straight*; page 17, bar 3: comma after
             ends; page 19, bar 5: commas after *enter* and *leave*. Page 16,
             bar 6: b′ in voice needs a double flat.

(5) Will you come? Will you come? Will you ride so late at my side?
     (*Poems*, 1917 [Steep, 25 March 1915].) Comp. Gloucester, 1922.
             F major, c′-e″, [e′-d″]. 2/4, Andante con moto. 2′. V/m, P/md.

Subject: Come and ride with me, beloved.
Voice: Steps, small skips; much modulation; dancing rhythms,
             with a few tricky melismas at the ends of phrases.
Piano: Continuous semiquavers running in 8ves, with occasional
             chords attached; becomes more elaborate, with some four
             against three; very chromatic.
Comment: Never rising above mf, this is a delightful song. Page 22, bar
             5: second note in voice should have natural, not sharp.

(6) The trumpet. Rise up, rise up, and, as the trumpet blowing. (*Poems*,
     1917 [Royal Artillery Barracks, Trowbridge, 26-28 September 1915].)
     Comp. Dartford, Kent, 1925.
             A♭ major, d′b-f″, [f′-e″]. 4/8, Allegro. 2′15″. V/d, P/d.

Subject: Rise up, scatter the past; open your eyes and go to war.
Voice: Skips, steps; 6th and 7th leaps and drops; some high-lying
             phrases, p and ff; many short melismas, awkwardly placed
             at the ends of phrases; varied rhythms with many paired
             quavers and semi-quavers; long phrases; fairly chromatic.
Piano: Continuous semi-quavers; broken chords, parallel chords,
             much 8ve work; big stretches; very chromatic.
Comment: Written while in the Asylum at Dartford, in order to provide
             a suitable end to the cycle. A valiant attempt, but not really

a success. However, it is possible that a sympathetic performance could make it convincing. A line of the poem is missing at
the top of page 25, where it should read: 'Rise up and scatter /
The dew that covers / The print of last night's lovers – /.' Its
absence means that the following *scatter it* is hard to understand. It might be possible to restore the line with careful
adjustment of note values, or sing *scatter them*, though this
spoils the rhyme with *unlit*. Page 26, bar 8: add *Except* below
Save; to use this change the minim e" to dotted crotchet
quaver. Page 27, bar 7: add *Through* between *stars* and *all*; it
can be sung on the second quaver of the bar. No indication is
given of Thomas's short lines, five to seven syllables.

Note: The remaining songs were issued singly during Gurney's lifetime;
they are all out of print, apart from 10 and 11, which are in *Heritage 1*.

10 Carol of the Skiddaw yowes. The shepherds on the fellside that is by
Bethany. (Ernest Casson.) Comp. 1919. Pub. Boosey, 1920. [*Heritage 1;
50 Modern*].

	A minor, d'-e", [e'-d"]. 2/4, Quasi andante. 1'45". V/e, P/e.
For:	[Mezzo], C-Ten, Bar.
Subject:	Shepherds on Skiddaw in the Lake District pray for warmth and protection in the cold of Christmas-tide.
Voice:	Steps, small skips; no accidentals; simple but varied rhythms.
Piano:	RH crotchet chords over staccato quaver bass; some legato parallel chord passages; no accidentals.
Comment:	A haunting modal melody, with three similar stanzas, this song is well suited to Christmas use. Yowes = ewes. Bar 9; blains = sores, blisters. 9 bars from the end: gird = surround, with a 'fold', as with a sheep-fold, which protects the sheep.

11 I will go with my father a-ploughing. (Seosamh mac Cathmhaoil
[Joseph Campbell].) Pub. Boosey, 1921. [*Heritage 1; 50 Modern*].

	E minor, d'-e", [e'-e"]. 2/4, Allegro. 2'. V/m, P/md.
For:	Mezzo, C-Ten, Bar.
Subject:	I will go with my father, who will sing the songs for ploughing, sowing and reaping.
Voice:	Steps, skips; 8ve drop; modulation for third stanza; straightforward rhythms, though many triplets and short melismas; last page needs a fairly strong voice.
Piano:	Mixture of crotchet chords and semiquaver patterns; some big stretches; many accidentals in 3rd stanza.
Comment:	A warmly romantic setting, with a fine dramatic finish.

12 Since thou, O fondest and truest. (Robert Bridges, *Shorter Poems*,
Book III, 1880]. Comp. 1921. Pub. Boosey, 1921.
E major, d'#-e", [f'#-d"#]. 4/4, Andante. 2'45". V/me, P/me.

For: Mezzo, C-Ten, Bar.
Subject: May heaven reward you for having loved me so well.
Voice: Nearly all by step, a few 3rds and broken chords; 8ve drop
               from held e"; little modulation; one or two longish phrases;
               simple rhythm.
Piano: Chordal, with repeated crotchets off the beat, as in 3 (8),
               another setting of a poem by Bridges; occasional counter-
               melodies; moderately chromatic.
Comment: A romantic love-song, verging on the sentimental. Page 4,
               line 2, bar 2: fourth chord in RH needs quaver tail.

13 Come, O come, my life's delight. (Thomas Campion, *3rd Book of Airs*,
1617.) Comp. 1921. Pub. Boosey, 1922.
Ab major, b°b-f"#, [e"-eb]. 3/4, Adagio. 2'30". V/m, P/m.

For: [Mezzo], Bar.
Subject: Come to me quickly, for I love you.
Voice: Steps, some chromatic, many 3rds; 8ve drops; enharmonic
               notation; sustained f" and e"bs on last page; rhythms some-
               what unexpected in places.
Piano: Broken chord quavers; 8ve work; many accidentals.
Comment: Romantic, with some curious harmony and word setting
               which become more convincing with study. Page 3, bar 4:
               fourth quaver f' needs a flat.

14 The bonnie Earl of Murray. Ye Hielands and ye Lawlands. (Scots
ballad.) Comp. 1918. Pub. W.R., 1921.
D minor, d'-f", [d'-d"]. 4/4, Allegro. 1'30". V/me, P/m.

For: Mezzo, Bar.
Subject: The Earl of Murray is slain, and he might have been a king.
Voice: Steps, many skips, broken chords; 8ve leap; climax on sus-
               tained f"; simple rhythm with many Scotch snaps.
Piano: Chordal; quaver horn-calls in both hands; much 8ve work.
Comment: Folksong style; two similar stanzas.

15 The County Mayo. Now with the coming of the spring. (James
Stephens, after Raftery, *Reincarnations*, 1918.) Comp. 1918. Pub.
W.R., 1921.
E minor, c'-f", [e'-e"]. 2/4, Andante con moto. 3'. V/m, P/m.

For: Bar.
Subject: Now it is spring I would like to go home to County Mayo, with
               many visits on the way.
Voice: Steps, many skips, some broken chords; 9th leap, 7th drops,

6th leap and drops; almost a patter song, with many triplets.

Piano: RH semiquavers over crotchet bass; middle section in C minor with 8ves in both hands, agitato; much modulation.

Comment: An attractive song, though the agitato section seems a little contrived; would suit an Irish singer very well. Page 6, bar 4: *Rising like* = *Rising up like* in poem. Stephens made a number of revisions to the poem in his *Collected Poems* of 1926.

16 West Sussex drinking song. They brew good ale at Haslemere. (Hilaire Belloc, *Verses*, 1910.) Comp. 1921. Pub. Chappell, 1921.

F major, c'-f ", [d'-d"]. 4/4, Allegro. 1'45". V/me, P/me.

For: Bar.
Subject: Beer, where to get it and how to enjoy it.
Voice: Skips, broken chords, steps; 8ve leap, to f "; melisma; very straightforward rhythms.
Piano: Crotchet chords with quaver decorations; much 8ve work.
Comment: Good rhythmic piece, much like Warlock's drinking songs. A good encore. Published as one of Chappell's 'Concert Ballad Successes'! It is interesting to note that there are many small verbal changes from Belloc's original, made deliberately for singing purposes, and accepted by Belloc.

17 Captain Stratton's fancy. O some are fond of red wine and some are fond of white. (John Masefield, *Ballads and Poems*, 1910.) Comp. 1917. Pub. S & B, 1920.

G major, c'-e", [d'-d"]. 4/4, In march time. 2'. V/me, P/me.

For: Bar.
Subject: The virtues of drink, but it must be rum!
Voice: Mostly by step; 6th leap to e"; sustained e" to finish; simple rhythms with many dotted notes and Scotch snaps.
Piano: Chordal, mostly in crotchets, but many dotted rhythms; much 8ve work.
Comment: Similar to Warlock's setting, but slightly simpler, particularly for the piano. Gurney sets verses 1, 3 and 7 from Masefield's original 7-stanza poem, and adds choruses by repeating some of the words; Warlock set verses 1, 2, 3, 4 and 6, without using choruses. Stanza 5 runs: 'Oh some are fond of dancing, and some are fond of dice, / And some are all for red lips, and pretty lasses' eyes; / But a right Jamaica puncheon is a finer prize / To the old bold mate of Henry Morgan.' A good encore. The song was clearly composed by request, since Gurney wrote to Marion Scott on 15 July 1917: 'It has been a grind to write it – The whole thing was more distasteful to me as it might have been the writing of something I loved.'

18 **Edward, Edward**. Why does your brand sae drop with blood. (Border
   ballad from *Percy's Reliques*, 1765.) Comp. 1913. Pub. S & B, 1922.
           D minor – F# minor – F minor – D minor, c'-f ", [d'-d"]. 4/4,
           Allegretto con moto – Poco meno mosso – Tempo I. 5'15". V/m,
           P/m.

For: Mezzo; Bar.
Subject: What is that blood, Edward my son? I have killed my hawk –
                my horse – my father! What will you do? Leave you all. What
                will you leave me? The curse of hell for your evil council.
Voice: Steps and broken chords, mostly in crotchets, folk-song style;
                some dramatic interjections; some recit. sections; a 10th drop
                f "b to d'b at the climax.
Piano: Pattern changes for each stanza: minim and crotchet chords,
                quaver broken chords, quaver triplets in 8ves, recit. sections.
Comment: A magnificent song, clearly related to Stanford's 'La Belle
                Dame Sans Merci', but with much more scope for drama; an
                absolute gift to the imaginative performer. There are a
                number of verbal alterations, many of which make for clarity
                or better singing and are probably intentional: bar 12: *slain* =
                killed; the same at page 6, bar 3; page 7, bars 7-8 and 11-12:
                upon a boat = *in yonder boat*; bar 13: *gang o'er* = *fare over*; and
                here a stanza is omitted. In two places however the change is
                clearly a mistake, for it destroys the sense and must be
                corrected: page 7, bars 4-5, and page 10, bars 7-8 should read
                now tell me, O, not *I tell thee O*. Page 5, end of bar 8: dule ye
                dree, = grief you suffer. Page 6, bars 1 and 2: flats are needed
                for e', d', e'.

19 **Sowing**. It was a perfect day for sowing. (Edward Thomas, *Poems*, 1917
   [Steep, 23 March 1915].) Comp. Summer 1918. Pub. S & B, 1925.
           C minor, c'-e", [e'b-c"]. 6/8, Andante con moto. 2'45". V/m,
           P/md.

For: Mezzo, C-Ten, Bar.
Subject: Contentment, that a gentle rain has begun after sowing has
                been completed.
Voice: Skips and broken chords; 9th leap to e"; very long legato
                phrases; fairly simple rhythms.
Piano: Quaver melody over two-part semiquaver accompaniment;
                changes to flowing quavers, mostly in three or four parts;
                semiquaver sections become more elaborate in places, with
                many accidentals; some big stretches.
Comment: Nearly a very beautiful song, but the harmonic complications
                are not always convincing. No indication is given of the short
                lines of this poem, alternating six and four syllables. Tho-
                mas's MS had a final stanza, which, though he rejected it, is of

interest: 'A kiss for all the seeds' / Dry multitude, / A tear at
ending this / March interlude.'

20 Star-talk. 'Are you awake, Gemelli, this frosty night?' (Robert Graves,
Over the Brazier, 1916.) Comp. 1920, revised July 1925. Pub. S & B,
1927.

	D major, b'-f"#, [d'-d"]. 4/4, Allegro con moto. 1'45". V/md, P/m.
For:	Mezzo, Bar.
Subject:	The stars complain of the cold on a frosty night.
Voice:	3rds, steps, repeated notes; broken chord sequences; 8ve leap, 7th leaps and drops; wide-ranging phrases; accidentals and modulation; rhythms fairly simple if treated as 2/2 rather than 4/4, since there are many crotchet triplets.
Piano:	Simple chords, in minims and crotchets with decorations; in the third stanza changes become more rapid, and there are some rather violent modulations.
Comment:	A most attractive song, though the third stanza raises some problems and may be hard to bring off. On page 5 it is possible, but by no means certain, that there are some errors among the array of c sharps and c naturals. Remembering that Aquarius is the water-carrier will help make sense of the third and last stanza. Gurney has omitted stanzas three and four as published in *Georgian 1916-1917*, which run: ' "What do you hunt, Orion, / This starry night?" / "The Ram, the Bull and the Lion, / And the Great Bear," says Orion, / "With my starry quiver and beautiful belt / I am trying to find a good thick pelt / To warm my shoulders tonight, / To warm my shoulders tonight." // "Did you hear that, Great She-bear, / This frosty night?" / "Yes, he's talking of stripping me bare / Of my own big fur," says the She-bear, / "I'm afraid of the man and his terrible arrow: / The thought of it chills my bones to the marrow, / And the frost so cruel tonight! / And the frost so cruel tonight!" ' Page 3, bar 8: *We'll* = *We* in poem. Page 5, bar 4: no *the* in poem.

JOHN IRELAND
1879-1962

Ireland's songs are set out in the order given in the five volumes of the *Complete Works for Voice and Piano*, published by S & B in 1981. The **Tonality** is the one in *Complete Works*, even when not original; similarly the first voices printed as **For** are those for the *Complete Works* version. In both cases they are printed in italics if known not to be original. Collections are referred to as follows:

Coll 1 = *The Land of Lost Content, and other songs* S & B, 1976.
Coll 2 = *Eleven Songs*, S & B, 1970.
Heritage 2 = *A Heritage of English Song*, vol. 2, B & H, 1977.

Colls 1 and 2 have valuable prefaces by John Longmire.

JOHN IRELAND

COMPLETE WORKS FOR VOICE AND PIANO. Volume 1.

1 THE LAND OF LOST CONTENT. (A.E. Housman, *A Shropshire Lad*, 1896.) Comp. October 1920 – January 1921. Pub. Augener 1921. High [Coll 1], and *Low*. Though a cycle, the songs were all published separately in both keys as well as together; though composed for the tenor Gervase Elwes, no particular voice is specified in the score, and some could well be sung by women. There is much valuable information in the Preface to Coll 1. This is a fine cycle, capturing better than almost any other the complicated emotions underlying Housman's apparently simple verse. Ireland's MS is in BL (Add. 52898); it contains no MM markings.

(1) The Lent lily. 'Tis spring, come out to ramble.
   E minor, g'-f"#, [a'-f"]; *D minor*. 3/4,2/4, Andantino con moto, crotchet = 66-72. 2'15". V/me, P/me.

For: Sop, Ten; *Mezzo, Bar*; *C-Ten*.
Subject: Spring is here; it does not last long, so gather your flowers now.
Voice: Steps, small skips; slightly modal; flowing quavers with occasional longer notes; some long phrases.
Piano: LH ostinato broken chord figures; RH continuous flow of thirds in quavers, with occasional thicker texture; chromatic.
Comment: An enjoyable song. Fourteen bars from the end: smaller hands are advised to omit g's at bottom of RH harmony.

(2) Ladslove. Look not in my eyes.
   Ab major, f'-a"b; *F major*. 4/4, Poco sostenuto, crotchet = 80-84. 2'10". V/m, P/m.

For: [Sop], Ten; *[Mezzo]*, Bar.
Subject: If you look in my eyes you may see yourself, and love and suffer as I do, and as Narcissus did.
Voice: Steps, simple skips; some high-lying phrases with sustained high climax in both stanzas; rhythms simple.
Piano: Thick chordal writing with much internal counterpoint; a big stretch is almost essential.

Comment: Warm and romantic. Last line: jonquil = type of narcissus.

(3) **Goal and wicket**. Twice a week the winter through. Comp. 22
    November 1920.
        E minor, e'-g″, [g'-f″#]; *C# minor*. 4/4,3/4,2/4, Vivace,
        crotchet = 96-100. 1′05″. V/me, P/m.
For: Ten; *Bar*; *C-Ten*.
Subject: I play football in winter and cricket in summer; it is better
        than dying.
Voice: Steps, simple skips; strong rhythms; sustained finish.
Piano: Strongly rhythmic, with many 8ves in both hands.
Comment: Lively, with good climax, dies away at end.

(4) **The vain desire**. If truth in hearts that perish.
        A minor, e'-a″b, [g'-g″]; *F# minor*. 3/4,2/4, In tempo
        moderato, crotchet = 56-60. 2′15″. V/m, P/m.
For: [Sop], Ten; *[Mezzo], Bar*.
Subject: My love is so strong it should prevent you from dying; since
        it cannot, be kind to me before going to a lonelier place.
Voice: Steps, skips; chromatic; free speech rhythms; sustained
        high phrases.
Piano: Chordal; some inner counterpoint; thick, sustained,
        chromatic.
Comment: A song of great emotional intensity, one of Ireland's finest.
        Third page, bar 1; notes 3-5 of RH should have triplet sign
        above. At the end of Ireland's MS are the words 'Dies Irae.
        Jan 8. 1921'.

(5) **The encounter**. The street sounds to the soldiers' tread.
        C major, g'-g″, [a'-e″]; *A major*. 2/2,3/2, Allegro alla marcia,
        minim = 76-80. 1′15″. V/me, P/m.
For: [Sop], Ten; *[Mezzo], Bar*; *C-Ten*.
Subject: Hallo, soldier; we do not know each other, but I wish you
        well.
Voice: Steps, simple skips; straightforward march rhythms.
Piano: Bass crotchet ostinato in 8ves; RH two-part counterpoint, to
        be played without pedal, and needing careful fingering.
Comment: Tonality somewhat obscure; a rather mysterious march,
        fading out at the end with an eight-bar piano coda.

(6) **Epilogue**. You smile upon your friend today.
        D*b* major, f'-a″b, [b'*b*-g″*b*]; *Bb major*. 4/4,3/2, Allegretto con
        moto, crotchet = 96-100. 1′25″. V/m, P/m.
For: [Sop], Ten; *[Mezzo], Bar*.
Subject: You smile on me today; 'tis late, but better late than never.

Voice:	Steps, leaps, repeated g″bs in sustained phrase; simple speech rhythms.
Piano:	Chordal, quaver arpeggios; highly chromatic, many double flats.
Comment:	An essentially contented end to the cycle, it does not stand well as a single song. MS tempo mark: Sostenuto, con moto moderato.

2 The heart's desire. The boys are up the wood with day. (A.E. Housman, *A Shropshire Lad*, 1896.) Comp. 1917. Pub. W.R. 1917, High [Coll 3], Medium, Low.

D*b* major, f′-a″*b*, [f′-g″*b*]; B major, B*b* major. 3/4, Allegretto con moto, crotchet = 108. 2′. V/me, P/m.

For:	Sop, Ten; Mezzo, Bar.
Subject:	The boys collect their daffodils, and the girls their willow-branches; all obtain their heart's desire, let me have mine.
Voice:	Steps, skips; some modal notes; long flowing legato phrases.
Piano:	LH quaver arpeggios, RH chordal, sometimes overlapping; some big leaps and stretches.
Comment:	Romantic and immediately attractive; well worth singing. These are the last three stanzas of the poem 'March', which has five stanzas, the first beginning 'The sun at noon to higher air'. Gurney sets the complete poem in *The Western Playland*. B*b* major copy, 9 bars from end; voice 2nd note e′*b*.

3 Hawthorn time. 'Tis time, I think, by Wenlock town. (A.E. Housman, *A Shropshire Lad*, 1896.) Comp. 1919. Pub. W.R., 1919. High and *Medium*. C major, d′-g″, [a′-f ″]; B*b major*. 4/4, Moderato ed espressivo. 1′30″. V/me, P/me.

For:	Sop, Ten; *Mezzo, Bar.*
Subject:	It must be spring in Wenlock, but those who stay away will miss it; let it last long, though I am not there.
Voice:	Steps; many skips of 5ths and 6ths; rhythms simple, but phrasing needs care to make the verbal sense clear.
Piano:	Gently moving chords, fairly thick texture at times.
Comment:	A pleasantly nostalgic song. Ten bars from the end: *long* refers to time not space. The note at the bottom of page 22 of the *Complete Works* is incorrect, being copied from the previous song; this is No XXXIX of *A Shropshire Lad*.

4 SONGS SACRED AND PROFANE. Comp. 1929-1931. Pub. Schott, 1934. Six songs published together, with words by different poets. This is a well contrasted group needing a mezzo or baritone with a good top register for some of the songs. They can of course be sung separately.

Ireland's MSS of all but 4 (4) are in BL (Add. 52898).

(1) The advent. No sudden thing of glory or fear. (Alice Meynell, *Preludes*,
1875.) Comp. Christmas 1931.

> D minor/major, d'-g", [f'-f ″]. 4/4,3/4, Rather slowly, crotchet =
> 50-52. 3'10″. V/me, P/me.

For:	Sop, Ten; Mezzo, Bar.
Subject:	A meditation on the birth of Jesus, and his dependence on the natural things around him.
Voice:	Steps, simple skips; 8ve drop; one 5th leap to brief g″ needs care; simple speech rhythms, several triplets.
Piano:	Slow chordal; substantial interlude provides climax of song, with heavy chords subsiding to a rocking bass.
Comment:	An unusual and rather haunting song; possibly usable at Christmas, though in no way a carol. The MS has a number of differences from the published version, and no tempo mark. The poem, entitled 'Meditation', is headed with the following Latin couplet: 'Rorate Coeli desuper, et nubes pluent Justum / Aperietur Terra, et germinet Salutorem' (Isaiah 45:8).

(2) Hymn for a child. Flocking to the Temple. (Sylvia Townsend Warner,
The Espalier, 1924.)

> A major, c'#-f ″, [e'-e″]. 3/4,2/4, With movement, crotchet =
> 80-84. 2'. V/me, P/me.

For:	Mezzo, Bar.
Subject:	Jesus speaking in the Temple at twelve years old; he amazes the elders and then obeys his mother; may we all be as good as he. But the tone of the words is somewhat sardonic.
Voice:	Steps, small skips; 7th leap; repetitive simple rhythm, almost dance-like; middle section more legato with freer rhythm.
Piano:	Steady rhythmic chords; occasional RH flourishes; chromatic.
Comment:	A strange but effective song; both words and music have an air of mockery. Bar 21, voice, note 2: g' needs a sharp; in Ireland's MS bar 20 was 3/4 and bar 21 2/4, so the sharp was not then needed. Other differences in MS –bar 9: *dogs-eared* = *dog-eared* in MS, *dog's-eared* in poem. MS tempo mark: Not too slowly.

(3) My fair. Fair, no beauty of thine will last. (Alice Meynell, *Preludes*,
1875.) Comp. July 1929.

> B major, e'-g″. 3/4, With breadth, generally about crotchet =
> 50. 3'10″. V/md, P/md.

For:	Sop, Ten; Mezzo, Bar.
Subject:	Your beauties will only last in my love; hide what you would

keep, within my heart.

Voice: Steps, skips; 6th leaps and drops; much modulation and chromaticism; very free rhythm, some long phrases; sustained legato alternating with more spoken passages.

Piano: Chordal, with much decoration; thick texture with wide stretches; many quick melismas for both hands; highly chromatic.

Comment: A difficult song; the tonality is very uncertain, and ensemble may cause problems. The poem is not easy either; however, there are rewards here for ambitious performers. The poem is headed: 'Song. The Lover urges the better Thrift.' Bar 23: *the* = *thy* in poem; bar 35: *are* = *art* in poem. No tempo mark in MS.

(4) **The salley gardens**. Down by the salley gardens. (W.B. Yeats, *Crossways*, 1889.) Published separately, High and *Low*.
E minor, e'-e''; *D minor*. 3/4,2/4, At speaking pace. 2'. V/me, P/me.

For: Sop, Ten; Mezzo, Bar; *Cont, C-Ten, Bass*.
Subject: My love bid me take life easy, but I would not, and now weep.
Voice: Steps, simple skips; detailed speech rhythms.
Piano: Chordal, occasional melodic phrases; slightly chromatic.
Comment: Slightly falls between art-song and folk-song, but a nice change from more familiar settings. Yeats's original title – 'An Old Song Resung' – derives from the poem's source, an old woman's memory of a stanza from a broadside ballad, 'The Rambling Boys of Pleasure'.

(5) **The soldier's return**. Jump through the hedge, lass! (Sylvia Townsend Warner, *The Espalier*, 1924.) Comp. St Andrew's Day 1931.
G minor, d'-e'', [g'-d'']. 4/4, Alla marcia, crotchet = 112. 1'. V/me, P/me.

For: Mezzo, Bar; C-Ten.
Subject: Your soldier is home; he may be black and breathless now, but wait until sunset! [The soldier is dead, this is his ghost.]
Voice: Steps, a few small skips; 8ve drop; strongly rhythmic, with occasional legato phrases.
Piano: March-like chords; one legato chromatic passage.
Comment: The rather dissonant harmony helps to make this apparently straightforward song quite sinister in its effect. Bar 8: *hills* = *hill* in poem. The MS is headed 'The Return', and dedicated to Edward Clark. MS tempo mark: Tempo di marcia.

(6) **The scapegoat**. See the scapegoat, happy beast. (Sylvia Townsend Warner, *The Espalier*, 1924.) Comp. 7 December 1931.

G major, e'-f ", [f'#-e"]. 2/4,3/4, Animated, crotchet = 104-108. 1'20". V/me, P/md.

For: Mezzo, Bar.
Subject: The scapegoat is happy; carrying other's sins does not bother him, his own no longer count; in town righteous men rejoice.
Voice: Steps, many skips; held f " at end; lively dance rhythm; short parody waltz in the middle.
Piano: Sharp bouncy rhythmic chords; many accidentals; fast finish.
Comment: Lots of life; sardonic; a good finisher. MS tempo mark: Animato.

5 The sacred flame. Thy hand in mine. (Mary Coleridge, 'Song', *Poems*, 1907, edited posthumously by Newbolt [1888].) Comp. 1918. Pub. W.R., 1918. High and Low.

C major, d'b-a"b, [f'-g"b]; Bb major. 3/4,4/4,2/4, Moderato con moto, 1'45". V/m, P/m.

For: Sop, Ten; Mezzo, Bar.
Subject: We will go through life together, always together.
Voice: Steps, small skips; much modulation; free rhythms; wide range of pitch and dynamics; legato lines.
Piano: Broken chord patterns; some two against three; much modulation.
Comment: A passionate song, much more complex musically than Frank Bridge's well-known setting. High key copy, last bar but one: rest in RH should be quaver, not crotchet.

6 Remember. Time brought me many another friend. (Mary Coleridge, 'Not Yet', *Fancy's Following*, 1896 [1885].) Comp. 1918. Pub. W.R., 1918. High, *Medium, Low*.

D major, e'b-g", [f'#-e"]; *C major, Bb major*. 4/4, Moderato. 1'35". V/me, P/me.

For: Sop, Ten; *Mezzo, Bar*; *C-Ten*.
Subject: I have made many new friends, but cannot forget my old love.
Voice: Steps, simple skips; 8ve drop; climax on held g" in both verses; simple rhythms.
Piano: Simple chordal; a few leaps and modulations.
Comment: Pleasant song, if slightly sentimental.

7 TWO SONGS. In spite of the different publication dates these two songs are listed under this heading in *Cat*. This is certainly correct, since there is a clear musical connection between the two – compare bar 16 of 7 (1) with the first bar of 7 (2). Also, the high key was original in both cases, in spite of the *Complete Works* giving the low key version of 7 (2), as Ireland's MS in BL (Add. 52899) and the original Augener edition make clear. They can, of course, be sung separately, since they were published separately.

(1) **The trellis**. Thick-flowered is the trellis. (Aldous Huxley, in *Oxford Poetry*, 1918.) Comp. 1920. Augener, 1920. High [Coll. 2] and *Low*.

A♭ major, c'-g'', [f'-f '']; *F major*. 3/4,2/4, Moderato, crotchet = 63-66. 3'. V/md, P/md

For: Sop, Ten; *Mezzo, Bar*; *C-Ten*.

Subject: The trellis hides our happy love from all but the birds and flowers, through the long summer days.

Voice: Steps; several leaps and drops of 8ves, 7ths, and 6ths; varied rhythms, with long sustained legato phrases; soft held f ''s.

Piano: Broken and sustained chords; leaps; thickly scored; highly chromatic; much colour variation required.

Comment: A wonderful atmospheric song, well worth the effort involved; good understanding between voice and piano essential. Ireland's MS has no MM mark.

(2) **My true love hath my heart**. (Sir Philip Sidney, *The Countess of Pembroke's Arcadia*, 1580.) Comp. 1920. Pub. Augener, 1921. High and *Low* [Coll 2].

E major, d' #-f ''#(f ''), [e'-e'']; G major. 3/4,2/4,4/4, Con anima, ma non troppo mosso, crotchet = 76-80. 1'40''. V/m, P/d.

For: *Mezzo*; Sop.

Subject: My love and I have exchanged hearts, and this makes us one.

Voice: Steps, skips, some chromatics; long phrases; the heavy accompaniment requires a big voice; some very free rhythms; the alternative to f ''#, though given by Ireland, is disappointing, and should be avoided if possible.

Piano: Highly chromatic, with fast-moving thick chords, needing a big stretch; many rows of 8ves, mostly filled-in; and in spite of these technical problems the rhythm must remain fluid.

Comment: With the right performers a most exciting song, thoroughly worth the effort involved. A good finisher. Low key copy: bar 15 should have 3/4 at the beginning. The MS, in G major, has no MM, and the tempo mark is Con anima ma non troppo allegro. The poem is sung by the shepherdess Charita to Dametus, who is lying with his head in her lap.

8 The East Riding. Salt-laden, sad with cry of ships. (Eric Chilman.) Comp. c. 1920. Pub. Enoch, 1920. High, Medium, Low.

C minor, e'♭-g'', [g'-g'']; A minor, G minor. 2/2, With

movement and breadth, minim = 48-50. 1'30". V/me, P/me.

For: Sop, Ten; Mezzo, Bar; C-Ten; Cont, Bass.

Subject: Winds from the four quarters shake the East Riding, and shake my soul.

Voice: Steps, a few skips; 6th drops; slightly modal; simple rhythm.

Piano: Chordal; not too thick, though many 8ves; slightly chromatic.

Comment: A rather trite poem with uninspired music, though containing some characteristic harmonic colouring.

9 Love is a sickness full of woes. (Samuel Daniel, *Hymen's Triumph*, 1615, Act I, Scene v.) Comp. July 1921. Pub. W.R., 1921. *High* [Coll 3], *Medium*, Low.

    Gb major, e'*b*-g", [g'*b*-g"*b*]; *F major*, E*b* major, 3/4,2/4, Allegretto con moto, crotchet = 72-76. 1'45". V/m, P/m.

For: *Sop, Ten*; *Mezzo, Bar*; Cont, C-Ten, Bass.

Subject: Love is a torment, whether or not we have it.

Voice: Steps, many skips; 6th drop, 8ve leap; lies high; ends on soft held g"*b* rhythms quite straightforward.

Piano: Chordal, fairly thick; very chromatic; some decoration.

Comment: The chromatic dissonances appear slightly forced, but this can be an effective song if well performed. Ireland's MS in BL (Add. 52898) is in E*b* major.

COMPLETE WORKS FOR VOICE AND PIANO. Volume 2.

10 Sea fever. I must go down to the seas again. (John Masefield, *Saltwater Ballads*, 1902.) Comp. Chelsea, October 1913. Pub. Augener, 1915. High, Medium High, Medium Low, Low [Coll 2].

    E minor, b°-d", [e'-d"]; A minor, G minor, F minor. 4/4, Lento, crotchet = about 52-56. 2'30". V/e, P/me.

For: C-Ten, Bass; Ten; Bar.

Subject: An old sailor's desire to return to the sea.

Voice: Steps, simple skips, broken chords; regular speech rhythms.

Piano: Chordal, with some chromatics.

Comment: Ireland's best known song. It is not a recit., the rhythms should be carefully followed.

11 The bells of San Marie. It's pleasant in Holy Mary. (John Masefield, *Ballads and Poems*, 1910.) Comp. 1918. Pub. Augener, 1919. High, Medium, Low [Coll 2].

    G minor, c'-d"; C minor, A minor. 6/8, Rather slowly, dotted crotchet = 50. 2'40". V/me, P/m.

For: Cont, Bass; C-Ten; Sop, Ten; Mezzo, Bar.

Subject: At San Marie the bells ring, rung by the sailors who come there; it is pleasant to hear them.

Voice: Steps, skips, broken chords; 7th drop; rocking rhythm.
Piano: Basically chordal; many 8ves; some ostinati.
Comment: A surprisingly sad setting of these words; did Ireland perhaps imagine drowned sailors and a sunken cathedral? Stanza 2, line 2: sonsie = good-looking and good-natured.

12 The vagabond. Dunno a heap about the what and why. (John Masefield, *Saltwater Ballads*, 1902.) Comp. February 1922. Pub. Augener, 1922. *High* [Coll 2] Medium High, *Medium Low, Low.*
                Bb major, f'-f''; *Ab* major, *G major, F major.* 4/4, Tempo moderato, crotchet = 66-72. 1'45". V/me, P/me.
For: *Ten*; Bar; *C-Ten*; *Bass.*
Subject: A tramp's philosophy of life and death.
Voice: Steps, a few simple skips; speech rhythms.
Piano: Chordal.
Comment: Some authorities have described this song in glowing terms, praising its poetic sensitivity; others may find it almost impossibly condescending and 'imitation folk', complete with slang and dialect. MS in BL (Add. 52899).

13 THREE SONGS to Poems by Arthur Symons. These three songs, although grouped under this title in the *Complete Works*, have different copyright dates and are unrelated in subject. *Cat.* lists them separately, but has a note suggesting they may be considered a set, and that they are 'specially suitable for contralto'. They would seem a little high for most contraltos, but make an excellent set for mezzo or baritone; only the first was published in more than one key. Ireland's MS of the set is in BL (Add. 52899). There are no MM marks.

(1) The adoration. Why have you brought me myrrh? (*The Loom of Dreams*, 1901.) Comp. October 1918. Pub. Chester, 1919. *High*, Medium, *Low*.
                A*b* minor, d'b-f'', [d'b-d''b]; *B minor, F# minor.* 3/2,2/2, Allegretto con moto, minim = 44-48. 2'30". V/m, P/m.
For: Mezzo, Bar; *Sop, Ten*; *C-Ten*; *Cont, Bass.*
Subject: A dialogue: the first speaker rejects the gifts of myrrh, frankincense and gold that the second has travelled far to bring; it is too late, the gifts should be made to 'her' whom the second speaker has followed so long.
Voice: Steps, a few skips; some modulation which through enharmonic notation looks more extreme than it is; almost entirely in crotchets; sustained legato line required.
Piano: Chordal; much use of ostinati; many accidentals.
Comment: A mysterious song. The two speakers are not named, nor are

we told who 'her' refers to. The first speaker is probably Jesus, the second may be an orthodox churchman with 'her' the established church, or perhaps a philosopher with 'her' as Sophia, goddess of wisdom. A close friend of Ireland's has suggested he took the first of these alternatives. Whatever it means it is a rather beautiful song.

(2) **The rat**. Pain gnaws at my heart. (*Amoris Victima*, 1897.) Comp. October 1918. Pub. Chester, 1919.

> B minor, b°-e″, [c′-c″]. 4/4,3/4, Lento, crotchet = 48. 1′40″. V/m, P/m.

For: Mezzo, Bar; C-Ten.
Subject: The pain of long-lost love.
Voice: Steps, skips; 8ve leaps and drops; some chromatics; speech rhythms, with many triplets.
Piano: Chordal with rhythmic decoration; highly chromatic; fairly large stretch desirable.
Comment: A strongly emotional song, well worth performing.

(3) **Rest**. The peace of a wandering sky. (*The Loom of Dreams*, 1901.) Comp. July 1919. Pub. Chester, 1920.

> D*b* major, e′*b*-f ″, [f′-e″*b*]. 4/4,3/2, Tranquillo e sostenuto. 2′30″. V/m, P/m.

For: Mezzo, Bar.
Subject: Peace is all around, but will only reach my heart when it ceases to beat.
Voice: Steps, skips; 8ve, 7th and 6th drops; very varied phrase-lengths, recit. style passage near end; some chromatics.
Piano: Chordal ostinati in LH with decorative ostinati in RH; some widely spread arpeggios; some big stretches.
Comment: It is significant that the publishers give a French text, by Jean-Aubry; the music is highly atmospheric, reminiscent of Debussy in romantic mood. MS tempo mark: Tranquillo.

14 **Santa Chiara (Palm Sunday; Naples)**. Because it is the day of Palms. (Arthur Symons, *Images of Good and Evil*, 1899.) Comp. 1925. Pub. Augener, 1925. *High*, Medium, *Low*, [Coll 2].

> *G minor*, c′-e″*b*(d), [f′-d″]; *C minor*, A minor. 3/4,4/4, Moderato e poco largamente, crotchet = 60. 2′35″. V/m, P/m.

For: *Cont, C-Ten; Bass; Sop, Ten*; Mezzo, Bar.
Subject: Since it is Palm Sunday carry a palm for me, though I can no longer do so myself, having lost all belief.
Voice: Steps, some skips; 8ve drop; speech rhythms, many triplets.
Piano: Chordal; some ostinati, some two against three; fairly thick chromatic texture; some important melodic phrases.

Comment: Strongly conveys the sense of despair following on loss of faith; the little boats under the blue sky are beautiful but irrelevant, 'I have grown tired of all these things'. Ireland's MS in BL (Add. 52898), tempo mark: Moderato.

15 TWO SONGS. Comp. April 1928. Pub. OUP, 1929. Given this heading in both the *Complete Works* and *Cat.*, they were published separately and have words by different poets.

(1) **Tryst (In Fountain Court)**. The fountain murmuring of sleep. (Arthur Symons, *Silhouettes*, 1892.)
No key signature, d'-f"#, [g'-e"b]. 3/4,2/4, Very slow and sustained. 3'30". V/m, P/m.

For: Mezzo, Bar.
Subject: This peaceful afternoon seems to be waiting, as I am for you.
Voice: Steps, skips; slightly chromatic; speech rhythms with some long phrases; one brief climax with the only f"#.
Piano: Chords, some rather complex, with a treble line in continuous quavers above much of the time; vague tonality.
Comment: Atmospheric; the enjoyment of the peaceful afternoon outweighs the sense of expectation, which, though aroused strongly for a moment quickly subsides, suggesting perhaps that the singer has dropped off to sleep in the heat. Arthur Symons lived in Fountain Court at the Temple.

(2) **During music**. O cool unto the sense of pain. (D.G. Rossetti, 1886 [1851].)
Eb major, b°b-g"b, [d'-e"b]. 3/2,2/2, Moderato. 2'45". V/m, P/m.

For: Mezzo, Bar.
Subject: Music, though its written form means no more to me than Egyptian hieroglyphs, when played by your small hands can cure my pain and shake my soul.
Voice: Steps, many skips; 7th drop, 6th drop and leap; chromatic; a strong climax on the one g"b; speech rhythms, but drawn out, with some long phrases.
Piano: LH mostly chordal, occasional wide-ranging arpeggios; RH quaver broken chord pattern; chromatic.
Comment: A peaceful atmosphere broken twice; once by the piano describing Egypt in a slightly sinister interlude, and again by the dramatic climax in the middle of the second half.

16 **When I am dead, my dearest**. (Christina Rossetti, 'Song', *Goblin Market and Other Poems*, 1862 [12 December 1848].) Comp. 16 July 1924. Pub. OUP, 1928. String quartet accompaniment on hire from OUP.

F major, d'-d". 2/4, At speaking pace. 2'. V/e, P/e.

For: Mezzo, Bar; C-Ten.
Subject: Do not mourn me when I die; remember me if you will, I may
             or may not remember you.
Voice: Steps, a few skips and broken chords; simple speech rhythm,
             mostly in quavers.
Piano: Chordal, with a few passing notes.
Comment: Perfect simplicity, hauntingly memorable. Ireland arranged
             the accompaniment for string quartet himself.

17 MOTHER AND CHILD. (Christina Rossetti, *Sing-Song: A Nursery
Rhyme Book*, 1873.) Comp. 1918. Pub. W.R., 1918. This set of eight
short songs, dedicated to Ireland's married sister, is not a true cycle, in
that there is no continuous story. However, all the songs relate to
children; the first is about a new-born baby and the last two concern
death. Christina Rossetti's book contains a large number of short
verses – 'Rhymes dedicated without permission to the baby who
suggested them'. Several different shorter groups could be formed. The
songs are very simple but have great charm. V/e, P/e.

For: Mezzo; but songs 17 (3-5, 7, 8) could be sung by Bar or C-Ten.
Voice: Steps and many small skips; occasional chromatics; rhythms
             simple. Songs 17 (1) and 17 (5) lie slightly high for a beginner.
Piano: Mostly chordal; some rocking figures and decoration.

(1) Newborn. Your brother has a falcon. Published separately.
             C major, d'-f ", [e'-d"]. 2/2, Moderato, minim = 58. 1'.
Comment: Voice has one f " and four e"s in three bars. A cradle song.

(2) The only child. Crying, my little one?
             C major, e'-f ", [f'-d"]. 2/2, Moderato, minim = 54. 1'30".
Comment: Mother hurrying through the snow sings to comfort her tired
             child. Bar 13, piano RH, beat 1: # to f' not a".

(3) Hope. I dug and dug amongst the snow.
             A minor, d'-d", [e'-d"]. 6/8, Allegretto, dotted crotchet = 44.
             50".
Comment: Flowers will grow from beneath snow, but nothing will come
             from sand. Slightly modal.

(4) Skylark and nightingale. When a mounting skylark sings.
             Eb major, e'b-e"b. 2/4, Allegretto, crotchet = 58. 50".
Comment: A happy child finding heaven on earth.

(5) **The blind boy**. Blind from my birth.

A minor, e'-e", [a'-e"]. 3/4, Andante moderato, crotchet =
84-88. 1'.

Comment: Introductory bar for use only when sung separately. A blind
boy dreams of being able to see nature in heaven. This poem
was added to the collection between 1873 and 1894.

(6) **Baby**. Love me, I love you.

D major, e'-e", [f'#-d"]. 4/4, Allegretto, crotchet = 92. 1'.

Comment: A happy cradle song; slightly modal.

(7) **Death-parting**. Goodbye in fear, goodbye in sorrow.

E minor, e'-e", [f'#-d"]. 6/8, Moderato con moto, dotted
crotchet = 52. 1'50".

Comment: A dialogue as mother bids sad farewell to her dying child,
who replies, 'never to part again'.

(8) **The garland**. Roses blushing red and white.

F major, d'-f ", [d'-d"]. 3/4, Poco andante, crotchet = 50. 1'10".

Comment: The meanings of flowers; roses for delight, violets for death.

18 **What art thou thinking of?** (Christina Rossetti, 'Mother and Child',
first published 1896 [10 January 1846].) Comp. September 1924. Pub.
S & B, 1976. [Coll 1].

Ab major, e'b-g"b, [f'-f "]. 3/4, No tempo mark. 3'. V/m, P/m.

For: Sop.

Subject: 'What are you thinking of?' said the mother; 'Of heaven,'
replied the child. 'Would you like to go there?' 'Yes, now,
wouldn't you?'

Voice: Steps, simple skips; few accidentals; one phrase lies
between d"b and g"b for six bars; needs considerable control.

Piano: Varied rhythmic patterns, with many broken chords and
arpeggios; generally thin texture; some chromatic passages.

Comment: The contrast between the child's simple view of heaven and
the mother's knowledge that death must come first is very
clear in this strange and rather haunting song. Bar 11: *am* =
was in poem. Ireland's MS in BL (Add. 52899).

COMPLETE WORKS FOR VOICE AND PIANO. Volume 3.

19 **FIVE POEMS BY THOMAS HARDY**. Comp. 1926. Pub. OUP, 1927.
A genuine cycle, describing the singer's relationship with a particular
woman over a period of years. The songs are numbered, not titled, and
there is a musical connection between the first and last. This may well

be considered Ireland's finest, if musically most difficult cycle, though many think his Housman settings more typical. Both singer and accompanist must be technically accomplished and imaginatively sensitive to Hardy's very individual view of life.

b°*b*-g″*b*(e″), [d′-e″*b*]. 10′30″. V/md, P/d.

For: Bar.

(1) **Beckon to me to come**. ('Lover to Mistress', *Human Shows*, 1925.)
          3/4,2/4, With moderate movement. 2′.

Subject: One sign would bring me to you, whatever the difficulty.

Comment: Note the fluttering handkerchief in the accompaniment. A generally gentle introduction to this tough cycle, though the congested harmony hints at troubles to come. The poem is noted as being 'from an old copy', and may well refer to Tryphena Sparks, with whom Hardy was in love before he met Emma Gifford, his future wife. Between her house and his there were two fields, a wood, and several lone trees. Bar 9: forecasts = prospects. Ireland's MS in BL (Add. 52897).

(2) **In my sage moments**. ('Come not; yet come!', *Human Shows*, 1925.)
          3/4,2/4, Deliberate. 3′05″.

Subject: At times I can say, stay away and leave me in peace; but no! Come, even though your presence may destroy me.

Comment: Slow and hesitant; speech rhythms; thick chromatic harmony; a powerful climax at the moment of decision, ending in despair. This may have been addressed to Mrs Arthur Henniker, a close friend of Hardy's for thirty years. She was living in Ireland when they first met, but moved to England soon afterwards. Ireland's MS (incomplete) in BL (Add. 52897).

(3) **It was what you bore with you, Woman**. ('Without, not within her', *Late Lyrics and Earlier*, 1922.)
          9/8,6/8, With gracious movement. 1′10″.

Subject: What you brought with you saved a soul, though you never knew.

Comment: Elaborately pianistic accompaniment with a powerful climax. The poem seems to be about Emma – ' "She was so *living*, he used to say", *The Early Life*' (Bailey). She was, however, more interested in social life than Hardy's writing. Bar 18: Hardy's MS has *his* for *my*, which would suit this cycle better. 'The final stanza suggests that at last Hardy hurt Emma through scorning her' (Bailey).

(4) The tragedy of that moment. ('That moment', *Human Shows*, 1925.)
2/2,3/2, Slow. 2'.

Subject: When I came in and you spoke to me I was overwhelmed by sorrow.

Comment: A slow and intense recit., with low and very congested harmony. It ends with a short drum-roll; as of a funeral? A strange poem, which the commentators seem to feel refers to Emma's jealousy of Mrs Henniker. However, the context of the cycle suggests that the woman is dying, and does not know it, whereas the singer does.

(5) Dear, think not that they will forget you. ('Her Temple', *Late Lyrics and Earlier*, 1922.)
3/2, Deliberate. 2'15".

Subject: I will build you such a shrine as all men will wonder at it, and you will be remembered, though I shall not.

Comment: The opening refers back to the first bars of the cycle. The first stanza is strong, as befits the building of a temple; the second is loving, wistful, accepting the singer was never of importance in her life in the way she has been in his. The poem probably refers to Emma, and the 'Poems of 1912-13' (*Satires of Circumstance*) which Hardy wrote immediately after her death.

20 THREE SONGS to poems by Thomas Hardy. (*Late Lyrics and Earlier*, 1922.) Comp. 1925. Pub. Cramer, 1925. Not a cycle, the songs were published separately in various keys, but a good group for mezzo or contralto.

(1) Summer schemes. When friendly summer calls again.
A♭ major, c'-f ", [f'-e"b]; *G major*. 4/4,3/2, Comodo, minim = 66. 2'. V/me, P/m.

For: Mezzo, Bar; *Cont, C-Ten.*

Subject: When summer comes we will go out and enjoy the countryside; so I say, but who can foretell the future?

Voice: Steps, simple skips; some modulation; long legato lines.

Piano: RH chordal, LH broken chords; second stanza the reverse; some chromatics; quick chord changes and arpeggios.

Comment: A lively rhythmic piece. Bar 11: fane = temple. *Moon* in the last line was Hardy's 'symbol of cold reality' (Bailey).

(2) Her song. I sang that song on Sunday.
D minor, c'-d", [d'-c"]; *F# minor*, E minor. 4/4, Rather slowly, crotchet = 60. 2'25". V/me, P/me.

For: *Cont*; *Sop*; Mezzo.

Subject: I sang that song before I knew him, and to him when he came here; does he sing it now he has left me to sorrow?

Voice: Steps, simple skips; folksong style till the broad climax of the last stanza.

Piano: Chordal; simple, though with some chromatics, and the climax is filled out with passing notes and a thicker texture.

Comment: The poem can cause problems. The singer has a favourite song she has sung all her life. Years ago she met a stranger from a place she did not know, who no doubt fascinated her for that very reason; he came in to her at night, as is told in the climax on the last page. At that time (stanza 3) she was untouched by despair. Since then, 'in after years', he left her (beginning of stanza 3) to weeping and fear (stanza 2). The final mood of the song is reflective, not despairing; it all happened a long time ago. Bailey gives the following explanation: ' "Her Song" seems a soliloquy by the ghost of Hardy's first wife. Then the Monday when the song was chosen as "fittest to beguile" would be the evening of Monday, March 7, 1870, when Hardy first met Emma Gifford at St. Juliot Rectory. The summer would be August of that year, when he paid his second visit to Cornwall. The "afteryears" would refer to the period of "The Last Performance". (When near the end of her life Emma tried to regain Hardy's affection by playing old songs on the piano). In the final stanza, Emma's ghost wonders whether Hardy, yet alive in "some dim land afar", sings the song, perhaps in memory of her.' Modal in flavour. A fine song. Bar 18; cup-eyed = tears enough to fill a cup.

(3) Weathers. This is the weather the cuckoo likes.

  C major, c'-d"; *E major*, D major. 6/8,9/8, Allegretto pastorale, crotchet = 69-72. 2'. V/me, P/me.

For: *Cont, Bass*; *Sop, Ten*; Mezzo, Bar; C-Ten;

Subject: The cuckoo likes summer, so do I; the shepherd shuns winter, so do I. Both seasons are described in detail.

Voice: Steps, simple skips; a generally lilting triplet rhythm with some surprises.

Piano: Basically chordal, with a dotted triplet rhythm added almost throughout, sometimes RH, sometimes LH, occasionally both.

Comment: C major edition, third page, bar 5: RH second note g" not a". D major edition, third page, bar 5: RH first note needs a dot after it. E major edition, three bars from the end: LH first beat, natural to d° not f°. Bar 15: bills = sings; bar 39: hill-hid tides = the sea, beyond the hills.

21 Great things. Sweet cyder is a great thing. (Thomas Hardy, *Moments of Vision*, 1917.) Sketch made January 1925. Pub. Augener, 1935. Medium High, *Medium*.

> *C major*, c'-e''(d''), [d'-c'']; D major. 2/2, Lively, minim = 92-96 approx. 2'. V/me, P/m.

For: *Bar, C-Ten*; Ten, Bar.

Subject: Drinking, dancing and loving have always been great things to me. What when death comes? They will still have been great things to me.

Voice: Steps, many skips, some modulation; strong dance rhythms; more legato section for love, and a short recit-style section for death.

Piano: Bouncy chords; rhythmic figuration; a good grasp of the keyboard is needed.

Comment: Great fun, rather like a Warlock drinking song. Bar 9: spinning down to Weymouth town – Hardy was a cyclist and must have often ridden the seven miles from Dorchester to Weymouth, pausing at the Ship Inn on Ridgeway. Last two stanzas: Hardy seems to have been uncertain about his refrain: St. 3, line 8: *Aye, greatest* (1919) = *A great* (1917, 1923); St. 4, line 2: *Greatest* (1919) = *Great* (1917, 1923); line 8: *Greatest* (1919) = *Great* (1917, 1923). Ireland uses the 1919 version of the poem, but 1917 and 1923 agree, and might be better for singing. Ireland's MS in BL (Add. 52897), with no MM mark.

22 FIVE XVIth CENTURY POEMS. Comp. Deal, 1938. Pub. Hawkes, 1938. These are independent songs, though they all relate to spring and make an excellent recital group for baritone (or c-tenor). They are clear in tonality, tuneful, and immediately attractive to any audience. Ireland's MS in BL (Add. 52897).

(1) A thanksgiving. Pleasure it is to hear, iwis, the birdes sing. (William Cornish, in *Bassus*, 1530.) Published separately.

> D major, b°-e'', [d'-d'']. 3/4, With impulse and warmth, crotchet = 69-72. 1'35''. V/m, P/m.

For: Mezzo; Bar; C-Ten.

Subject: Spring is a pleasure; it is given by God, so thank Him.

Voice: Steps, skips, sequences; 7th leap, broken chords; a strong legato line; fairly simple rhythm, several triplets and short melismas.

Piano: Rich chords with decorations; some quick arpeggios across both hands; wide stretches.

Comment: A fine song of praise, suitable for church use. Bars 3-4: iwis

= indeed. MS title: 'To Him give praise'; MM crotchet =
66-69.

(2) **All in a garden green**. Whenas the mildest month of jolly June.
(Thomas Howell, or Richard Edwardes, in *A Paradyse of Daynty
Devises*, 1576.)

        F major, d'-e". 4/4, Leisurely and smooth, crotchet = 54-56.
        1'40". V/me, P/me.

For: Mezzo; Bar; C-Ten.
Subject: Spring brings fruit, flowers, and love.
Voice: Steps, broken chords, sequences; 7th drop, 6th drop and
              leap; modulation; long flowing legato lines.
Piano: Flowing sequence of changing harmonies, almost in Quilter
              style; some chromatics.
Comment: Warm and charming. MS title: 'The Red Rose'. Bar 8: eke =
              also.

(3) **An aside**. These women all both great and small. (Anon, temp. Henry
VIII; BL Harleian MS 7578.)

        Bb major, b°b-e"b, [b°b-d"]. 2/4,3/4, Light and lively, crotchet
        = 112-116. 1'05". V/m, P/m.

For: [Mezzo]; Bar; C-Ten.
Subject: Women are always changing, but I will not say so.
Voice: Steps, many skips, broken chords; 8ve leaps, 7th drop; a
              lively patter-song, with frequently changing rhythms.
Piano: Bouncing chords, with changing rhythmic patterns for each
              stanza; neat fingers required.
Comment: One of Ireland's few really light-hearted songs. Bar 9, beat
              2: e' in RH should have natural sign. MS title: 'These
              women'. In *OB 16* the poem is attributed to Heath, though
              nothing is known of him, not even his first name.

(4) **A report song**. Shall we go dance the hay, the hay? (Nicholas Breton,
in *England's Helicon*, 1600.)

        Eb major, e'b-e"b. 6/8, Liltingly, dotted crotchet = 76. 1'30".
        V/me, P/m.

For: [Mezzo]; Bar; C-Ten.
Subject: Shall we dance, sing, woo, kiss, – but then I woke up!
Voice: Steps, small skips in sequences; 8ve leaps; fairly regular
              crotchet-quaver rhythm throughout.
Piano: LH crotchet-quaver, RH dotted triplets, throughout;
              occasional melodic phrases in LH need bringing out, and the
              little chromatic coda is not easy to play cleanly.
Comment: A pleasant pastoral, but it can easily lose interest unless
              performed with some imagination. 'Report' was a term in

Rhetoric for the repetition of words or phrases. The title in *England's Helicon* reads 'A Report Song in an dreame, betweene a Sheepheard and his Nimph'; the repeated words of each first line are ranged separately on the right of the page. St. 1, line 3: the hay = a type of dance, cf. Shepherd's Hay. St. 3, lines 2 and 3: it is always better to act than merely to think. St. 5, line 1: refers to the old game of prisoner's base, where players chase each other; but *base* was also used at this time for a type of skirt! MS tempo mark: With lilt.

(5) **The sweet season.** When May is in his prime. (Richard Edwardes, in *A Paradyse of Daynty Devises*, 1576.)

        D major, d'-e", [e'-e"]. 4/4, With movement, but not fast, crotchet = 126 approx. 3'. V/m, P/m.

For:	Mezzo; Bar; C-Ten.
Subject:	Compares the May of the year with youth and its joys; 'when May is gone, of all the year the pleasant time is past'.
Voice:	Steps, skips, broken chords; 8ve and 7th drops; chromatics; much rhythmic variety and contrast of legato and marcato.
Piano:	March-like, with running quaver bass attached to LH chords, some chromatic contrapuntal writing; much rhythmic variety; many different touches required; despite these problems it lies well under the hands.
Comment:	Three similar stanzas, with some increase in intensity from first to last; each one is cheerful and lively till the last line; the song, and the set, end on a note of regret. MS title: 'Rejoice in May'. Ireland was 59 when he wrote these songs.

23 WE'LL TO THE WOODS NO MORE. (A.E. Housman, *Last Poems*, 1922.) Comp. 1927. Pub. OUP, 1928. A unique work consisting of two songs and a piano solo. Both songs are slow-moving, with speech rhythms in the voice, and slowly changing chords in the piano. Chromatic, with steps, skips, and repeated notes for the voice, and a thick piano texture. The piano solo has more movement, in flowing semiquavers. It is dedicated 'To Arthur [G. Miller], in memory of the darkest days'. Ireland's MS in BL (Add. 52899). V/m, P/m.

For:	Bar.

(1) **We'll to the woods no more.**

        D minor, c'b-f ", [d'-d"]. 5/4,3/4,2/4,4/4, Rather slowly. 2'05".

Subject:	It is autumn, and we will go to the woods no more.
Comment:	MS tempo mark – Poco lento. This is the introductory poem to Housman's *Last Poems*.

(2) **In boyhood**. When I would muse in boyhood.
> No key signature. c'#-f", [d'-f"]. 2/4,3/4, At speaking pace.
> 1'35".

Subject: In boyhood I looked for friends worth dying for; I found them, and they died for me.

(3) **Spring will not wait** the loiterer's time, who keeps so long away.
> Piano solo. 4'. See the *Collected Piano Works*, vol. 3, S & B.
> At the end the MS has: 'for A.G. Feb 12 1927. J.I. Feb 1927.'

COMPLETE WORKS FOR VOICE AND PIANO. Volume 4.

24 SONGS OF A WAYFARER. Pub. Boosey, 1912. Though published as a set these are independent songs. They do, however, make a reasonable group of well-contrasted songs for baritone (or counter-tenor).

(1) **Memory**, hither come, and tune your merry note. (William Blake, *Poetical Sketches*, 1783.) Comp. before 1905.
> D major, b°-d", [c'#-d"]. 3/2,2/2, Con moto, minim = 72. 1'45".
> V/e, P/me.

For: Mezzo, Bar; C-Ten; Cont, Bass.
Subject: I will walk by the stream and dream of my memories, and at night go through the darkened valley with melancholy.
Voice: Steps, a few skips, scale; 6th leap and drop; simple rhythms, mostly continuous crotchets; longish legato phrases.
Piano: Chordal, with gently moving decoration.
Comment: Pleasant, though not as memorable as Quilter's setting.

(2) **When daffodils begin to peer**. (Shakespeare, *A Winter's Tale*, 1611; Act III, Scene iv.) Comp. c. 1905.
> C major, b°-e"(e"b), [c'-d"]. 3/4,2/4, Allegro con moto, crotchet
> = 132. 1'45". V/me, P/m.

For: Bar; C-Ten.
Subject: Spring and summer are cheerful times, but what matters is to travel the country with a cheerful heart.
Voice: Steps, many skips and broken chords; 8ve leaps, 7th and 8ve drops; mostly exuberant marcato, some quiet legato passages.
Piano: Bouncing chords ranging up and down the keyboard, with passages of additional decoration.
Comment: This is Autolycus' song. In the play it has one more stanza and is broken up by dialogue. This alters the meaning of 'But shall I go mourn for that, my dear', bars 39-40, which does not refer to the previous verse, but to the intervening

spoken line: 'But now I am out of service', i.e. out of a job. Bar 3: peer = appear. Bar 5; doxy = a female beggar or prostitute. Bars 10-11; replaces winter's pallor, or, reigns in winter's domain. Bar 20: pugging = thieving? (meaning uncertain, *OED*). However, according to the Appendix to Alexander Schmidt's *Shakespeare Lexicon*, 'Pugging means (not as the glossary explains it, thievish) but pegging, pegtooth, i.e. the canine or dogtooth. "The child hasn't its pegging teeth" old women will say. J. Walter, *Shakespeare's True Life*.' Bar 34: aunts = whores. Bar 36: tumbling = making love. Bar 57; hent = grasp.

(3) **English May**. Would God your health were as this month of May. (Dante Gabriel Rossetti, first published 1886 [?1854].) Comp. c. 1905.

E*b* major, b°*b*-e″*b*, [e′*b*-c″]. 2/4,3/2, Allegretto, crotchet = 68. 2′45″. V/m, P/me.

For:	[Mezzo], Bar; C-Ten; [Cont], Bass.
Subject:	Would God we were abroad, for your health's sake; if my life could give you the breath of Italy I would give it you, and my spirit would see you recover.
Voice:	Steps, broken chords, scales; repeated notes; 7th drop; speech rhythms; some long legato phrases.
Piano:	Chordal with decorations; chromatic passages.
Comment:	A warmly romantic piece. Rossetti's younger brother William believes the poem to be addressed to Elizabeth Siddal, whom Rossetti met in 1850 and married in 1860. She was tubercular, and died in 1861.

(4) **I was not sorrowful**. (Ernest Dowson, 'Spleen', *Verses*, 1896. For Arthur Symons.) Comp. 1903.

C major, c′-e″*b*, [d′-d″]. 6/8,9/8, Andante moderato, quaver = 100-108. 3′. V/m, P/m.

For:	[Mezzo], Bar; C-Ten; [Cont], Bass.
Subject:	'I was not sorrowful, but only tired of everything that ever I desired.'
Voice:	Many repeated notes, occasional skips, a few steps; 7th drop; speech rhythms, nearly all on a monotone.
Piano:	Chords in one hand and arpeggios in the other almost throughout; some very complex harmonies.
Comment:	A strange song, somewhat French in atmosphere; highly convincing in its depiction of this mood.

(5) **I will walk the earth**. Up to the top of the trees. (James Vila Blake.) Comp. 22 May 1911.

C major, c′-e″(g″). 3/4, Allegro, crotchet = 100. 1′30″. V/me, P/me.

For: [Mezzo], Bar; C-Ten.

Subject: To the top of the trees, to the peaks o' the cloud! Nay, I will walk on the earth.

Voice: Broken chords, steps, skips, sequences; straightforward rhythm with some triplets; big climax on e″, ending on sustained e″, optionally g″.

Piano: Full chordal writing in both hands, like a 'Royalty ballad'.

Comment: Composed at the request of the publishers to complete the set with something popular; the words are trite in the extreme, but the music has plenty of life and vigour. Ireland's MS in BL (Add. 52898).

25 MARIGOLD: AN IMPRESSION. Comp. May-June 1913. Pub. as a set by W.R., 1916. Three strange songs, advanced for their time; though a close-knit group each could stand alone. Ireland's MS in BL (Add. 52898).

For: Bar, with wide range.

(1) Youth's spring-tribute. On this sweet bank. (Dante Gabriel Rossetti, Sonnet 14 from *The House of Life*, 1881 [1870-1881].)

Eb major, b°b-g″(f ″), [d′-e″b]. 3/4,5/4,2/4, Allegretto, crotchet = 60. 3′45″. V/m, P/m.

For: Bar.

Subject: Lie on this bank in the April sun, and feel my kisses, for this is the hour of love.

Voice: Steps, skips, short scale, sequences; chromatics; the climax on g″ can be avoided, but is followed by sustained f ″, forte; speech rhythms; variety of colour needed.

Piano: Wide-ranging chromatic chord progressions; many quick arpeggios; uncertain tonality.

Comment: Not easy, but remarkably sensual and sensuous. Six bars from the end: suit-service = service rendered by attendance at a lord's court, a feudal term; love must be obeyed. Ireland started an orchestral version, but did not complete it.

(2) Penumbra. I did not look upon her eyes. (Dante Gabriel Rossetti, 1870.)

No key signature, a°-f ″, [c′#-d″#]. 2/4,3/4, Poco andante, crotchet = 66. 5′. V/md, P/md.

For: Bar.

Subject: I did not look at her, though no one would have noticed; I did not touch her, though any friend might do so; I did not listen to her, though all might enjoy her voice. Told of her sadness,

though I knew it and wept, I did not speak, so that the sea
and wind shall speak more strongly in memory.

Voice: Mostly by step, occasional wide-ranging phrases; 7th leaps
and drops, 8ve and 10th drops; highly chromatic, with little
sense of tonality; long legato phrases in final section.

Piano: Parallel chords, arpeggios, patches of counterpoint; highly
chromatic; two against three and five against six; wide
dynamic range.

Comment: A demanding setting of a mysterious poem. Penumbra = a
partly shadowed area round a complete shadow, the lighter
outer border of a sun-spot. Ireland omitted the fourth
stanza: 'I did not cross her shadow once, / (Though from the
hollow west the sun's / Last shadow runs along so far,) /
Because in June it should not bar / My ways, at noon when
fevers are.'

(3) **Spleen**. Around were all the roses red. (Ernest Dowson, after
Verlaine, *Decorations: in Verse and Prose*, 1899.)
No key signature, a°-d'', [c'#-c''#]. 3/4, Con moto moderato,
crotchet = 78-82. 3'05". V/m, P/m.

For: [Mezzo], Bar; C-Ten; [Cont], Bass.

Subject: Nature around us is too perfect; I fear separation, yet am
tired of everything, alas, save thee.

Voice: Almost all by step; at end 7th and 8ve leaps, 7th drops; very
chromatic; rhythms simple till near end, then very free.

Piano: Suggestions of a waltz, with chords on second and third
beats in LH, quaver broken chords in RH, often with nothing
on the first beat; some solo melismas for RH.

Comment: Easier, but somewhat less interesting than the first two
songs. At the end there is a musical reference to the opening
of the first song, though coming nearly twelve minutes later
it is easy to miss it! The poem is one of four translations from
Verlaine, the original being 'Les roses étaient toutes rouges',
Aquarelles No 2 from *Romances sans paroles*, 1874.

26 **Earth's call (A Sylvan Rhapsody)**. The fresh air moves like water
round a boat. (Harold Munro, 'Weekend', *Collected Poems*, 1933.)
Comp. February 1918. Pub. W.R., 1918.
Eb major, b°-f''#, [f'-e'']. 3/4,2/4, Con moto moderato. 4'45".
V/md, P/d.

For: Mezzo; Bar. Though *Cat*. says 'For Contralto'.

Subject: A walk in the country, seeing the birds, finding a bank to lie
on together, listening to all the sounds of nature, though all
that can be heard today is 'cuckoo'.

Voice: Steps, skips; chromatic; long legato lines varied by speech
                rhythm sections; an extended climax involving sustained e″,
                f″#, e″#, all within a few bars, followed shortly by a two-bar
                e″, pp.
Piano: In Ireland's personal elaborate keyboard style; much use of
                measured tremolos in both hands, contrasting meters in
                broken chords building to the fully-scored climax, followed by
                eighteen bars piano solo before the short concluding stanza.
Comment: A scena rather than a song, needing a big voice and a fine
                pianist. It could be very exciting for all concerned. This is one
                stanza from a long narrative poem.

27 TWO SONGS TO POEMS BY RUPERT BROOKE. (*1914 and Other
Poems*, 1915.) These songs in fact bear different dates; they are
separate treatments of similar subjects, and not meant to be sung
together. It is interesting to note that in both songs, bars 14-15 and
32-33 of the first and bars 44-45 of the second, Ireland uses an idea that
became part of the main largamente tune of his Epic march of 1942.

(1) **The soldier**. If I should die, think only this of me. Comp. 1917. Pub.
    W.R., 1917. High, Medium, Low.
                F major, d′-f″, [f′-f″]; Gb major, Eb major. 3/2,4/4, Moderato.
                2′30″. V/me, P/me.
For: Bar; Ten; C-Ten, Bass.
Subject: If I die, and am buried in a foreign field, think that there lies
                some English earth, raised in England, and that a purified
                heart will somewhere give back the thoughts engendered by
                this peaceful land.
Voice: Steps, a few small skips; some high-lying phrases; simple
                rhythms; legato throughout.
Piano: Chordal, with many melodic phrases in treble and bass; rich
                but not thick texture.
Comment: This may seem a dated patriotic song, but it is surely convinc-
                ing in a way that the second song is not. There is real feeling
                here in both words and music, and it is a true description of
                the mood in which men went to war in 1914. We may no
                longer share these ideas, but we should be able to understand
                them, and perhaps even be moved by them.

(2) **Blow out, ye bugles**, over the rich dead. Comp. January 1918. Pub.
    W.R., 1918.
                Eb major, c′-f″, [e′b-e″b]. 4/4,3/2, Con moto, crotchet = 80.
                2′35″. V/m, P/m.
For: Bar.

Subject: However poor or lonely, in death these gave their lives for us, and in so doing, brought back honour and nobility.
Voice: Steps, skips; long legato phrases; a marcato climax in the middle with sustained f ″s.
Piano: Marching crotchet bass in 8ves with changing chords above; parallel triads with two against three at climax; strong modulation for last stanza.
Comment: This seems more contrived, as if both poet and composer, at different times and perhaps for different reasons, were trying to create emotions they felt appropriate for the time, but did not really feel themselves.

28 **Spring sorrow**. All suddenly the wind comes soft. (Rupert Brooke, *Poems 1911-14*, 1914 [1912].) Comp. April 1918. Pub. W.R., 1918. High and Low [Coll 3].
            F major, c′-d″; Ab major. 3/4, Poco andante. 1′45″. V/me, P/me.
For: Mezzo, Bar; Cont, C-Ten, Bass; Sop, Ten.
Subject: It is spring; the hawthorn buds appear. My heart, frozen all winter, thaws and puts out its own buds, though they are buds of painful memories.
Voice: Steps, skips, broken chords; 7th drop; legato line throughout, with simple rhythms modified by the words.
Piano: Gently moving harmonies in four or five parts, as if designed for string quartet; a few very carefully placed chromatics.
Comment: Perhaps Ireland's most perfect miniature; the line is exquisitely shaped to match the subtle emotions of the poem, both saying much more than appears on the surface. Bar 4: frore = frozen.

THE COMPLETE WORKS FOR VOICE AND PIANO. Volume 5.

29 **Hope the hornblower**. Hark ye, hark to the winding horn. (Henry Newbolt, *Poems New and Old*, 1912.) Comp. before 1911. Pub. Boosey, 1921, *High, Medium High, Medium Low*, Low. Original edition pub. Boosey, 1911.
            Bb major, f′-g″, [f′-f ″]; C major, A major, G major. 2/2, Allegro. 1′40″. V/me, P/me.
For: *Ten*; Bar; C-Ten.
Subject: The huntsman calls to his hearers to follow him. They ask what he is hunting; he tells them not to ask; it may be an echo or a shadow, but 'we ride'.
Voice: Repeated notes, many 4th skips; 8ve leap; many sustained f ″s, only one short g″; straightforward rhythms.
Piano: Rhythmic figures in RH over crotchet broken chord bass.

Comment: Full of energy and drive, would end a group well. The
             original edition was published in G major and A major only,
             with alternative simplified accompaniment in both keys.
             This simplified version became the new edition in 1921, and
             is the one printed in *Complete Works*.

30 **When lights go rolling round the sky**. (James Vila Blake.) Comp.
    1911. Pub. Chappell, 1911. High and Low [Coll 1].
                 D major, d'-f''#(e''), [e'-e'']; C major. 3/2, Allegro con brio,
                 minim = 104-112. 2'45". V/me, P/me.
For: Ten; Bar; C-Ten.
Subject: Away with melancholy! We have our loves and lives to enjoy.
Voice: Steps, skips; bouncing rhythms with occasional sustained
             e''s, alternating with sequential legato section.
Piano: Strongly rhythmic; chords and repeated notes; legato
             sections.
Comment: A 'Royalty ballad', but first-class of its kind, which should be
             in every baritone's repertoire. Good finisher.

31 **A song from o'er the hill**. A song came over the hill to me. (P.J.
    O'Reilly.) Comp. 1913. Pub. Leonard, 1913. High, Medium, Low.
                 Ab major, d'-e''b, [e'b-d''b]; C major, Bb major. 2/4, Andante.
                 1'45". V/e, P/me.
For: Cont, C-Ten, Bass; Sop, Ten; Mezzo, Bar.
Subject: Years ago I heard a haunting melody; I think I hear it still.
Voice: Steps and skips; 8ve leap, 7th leap and fall; simple rhythms.
Piano: Chordal, some times broken; some melodic fragments in
             8ves.
Comment: A 'Royalty ballad', sentimental and unconvincing.

32 **Bed in summer**. In winter I get up at night. (Robert Louis Stevenson,
    A Child's Garden of Verses, 1885.) Comp. 1912-13. Pub. Curwen,
    1915.
                 F major, c'-d'', [d'-c'']. 6/8, Allegretto e semplice. 1'10". V/e,
                 P/e.
For: Mezzo, Bar; C-Ten.
Subject: In winter I get up in the dark, but in summer I have to go to
             bed while it is still light and I would rather play.
Voice: Almost all by step; one 6th leap; continuous crotchet-quaver
             rhythm.
Piano: RH dotted 6/8 rhythms, with sustained and often melodic
             bass.
Comment: Simple and charming. RLS wrote to William Archer, 27
             March 1894: 'Marjorie Fleming I have known, as you
             surmise, for long. She was possibly – no, I take back possibly

– she was one of the greatest works of God. Your note about the resemblance of her verses to mine gave me great joy, though it only proved me a plagiarist'. See Richard Rodney Bennett's *A Garland for Marjorie Fleming*, Novello, 1986. Marjorie Fleming lived from 1803 to 1811.

33 **I have twelve oxen** that be fair and brown. (Anon, Early English, Balliol MS 354.) Comp. July 1918. Pub. W.R., 1919. High and Medium [Coll 3].

	F major, c'-f ", [c'-d"]; G major. 4/4, Allegretto grazioso. 1'45". V/me, P/m.
For:	Mezzo, Bar; Sop, Ten.
Subject:	I have four lots of twelve oxen grazing in different places; have you seen them?
Voice:	Steps, skips; simple rhythms; final phrases extended, and include the one f ", which should be slightly lengthened.
Piano:	Chordal, but with different rhythmic arrangements for each of the four stanzas; some thick jumping chords; 8ve passages; and a quick finish.
Comment:	A most enjoyable song, for performers and audience. Excellent end to a group. Note that in the *Complete Works* page 22 should be page 21 and vice versa!

34 **SONGS OF A GREAT WAR**. (Eric Thirkell Cooper.) Comp. November 1916. Pub. W.R., 1917. These two wartime songs are settings of verse that is poetically weak and expresses sentiments which do not stand close examination. The settings suggest that Ireland was not wholly convinced by them, but was trying to respond to the mood of the time.

(1) **Blind**. God, who gave the world its fairness.

	D minor, d'-d". 4/4, Steady and sustained. 1'30". V/e, P/me.
For:	Mezzo; Bar; C-Ten.
Subject:	'God, who took my sight away, help me do without it, pray.'
Voice:	Almost all by step; crotchets with some paired quavers.
Piano:	Chordal, with 8ves and moving inner parts.
Comment:	Foursquare, serious and dull, though some have found it moving.

(2) **The cost**. Take back the honour and the fame.

	F minor, c'-f ", [f'-e"]. 3/4,4/4, Hurried and impassioned. 1'15". V/me, P/m.
For:	Bar.
Subject:	Take away the victory, give me back my friend.
Voice:	Steps, skips; sustained e"s and f"s; rhythmic opening followed

by legato descent from climax in both stanzas.

Piano: Much 8ve work, some filled in; first half of stanzas rhythmic and energetic; second half broad and emotional.

Comment: Emotional and dramatic, too much so for conviction. This is what non-combatants thought combatants ought to feel, not the real thing.

35 The merry month of May. O, the month of May. (Thomas Dekker, *The Shoemaker's Holiday*, 1600. The First Three-man's Song.) Comp. July 1921. Pub. W.R., 1921. High, Medium, Low.

E major, c'#-f"#, [d'#-e"]; G major, D major. 2/4, Allegro con anima, crotchet = 116-120. 1'30". V/m, P/md.

For: Bar; Ten; C-Ten.

Subject: In May I made Peg my summer's queen; we hear the nightingale sing of true love, and see the cuckoo – come away! We do not want him near when we kiss.

Voice: Many 3rds, widening to 4ths, 5ths and 6ths at the ends of each stanza; quick lively patter, the same melody for each of the four stanzas, with changes of detail to fit the words; only one f"# per verse, but a sustained one.

Piano: Rapidly changing chords over LH rhythmic figures; very little pedal; it needs considerable dexterity.

Comment: Marvellous fun, and an absolute model of word-setting. G major edition, bar 13: voice first note should be dotted. Bar 40: the nightingale sings from the pain of the thorn at her breast; bar 45: the cuckoo sings of cuckolds.

36 The three ravens. There were three ravens sat on a tree. (Words and melody traditional.) Comp. c. 1920. Pub. W.R., 1920. Medium and Low.

F minor, c'-e"b, [f'-c"]; G minor. 2/4, In free time, (moderato). 3'30". V/e, P/me.

For: Mezzo, Bar; Sop, Ten.

Subject: The ballad of a dead knight watched by his hound and hawks, and buried by a fallow doe, who then died herself.

Voice: Almost entirely by step, with simple rhythms.

Piano: Chordal, with some variation of lay-out and harmony for each stanza, including some parallels and decoration; modal flavour.

Comment: A basically simple but moving song. Last line: leman = sweetheart.

37 The journey. Do you see the road awinding? (Ernest Blake.) Comp. c. 1920? Pub. Enoch, 1920. High, Medium, Low.

C major, d'-f", [e'-d"]; D major, Bb major. 2/2, With movement, minim = 96-100. 1'. V/e, P/me.

For: Mezzo, Bar; Sop, Ten; C-Ten.

Subject: Can you see the road and hear the bridle bells? Past rivers, down the slopes, the journey ends in sunlight on the hill.

Voice: Steps, a few skips; a modulation; one short f ″ in final phrase; simple rhythms.

Piano: Quaver broken chords in RH over LH crotchet ostinati; some parallel chords.

Comment: Lively, with some carefully worked detail, but essentially a 'Royalty ballad'.

38 If we must part. (Ernest Dowson, 'A Valediction', *Verses*, 1896 [1893].) Comp. 1929? Pub. S & B, 1976. [Coll 1]. 'For July 25th, 1929.'
G major, d′-e″, [e′-e″]. 2/4,3/4, No tempo mark. 1′50″. V/m, P/m.

For: Mezzo; Bar; C-Ten.

Subject: If we must part, just touch my hand and say, 'until some other day'. Life is short, love is long, but words are weak.

Voice: Steps, skips, repeated notes; chromatic; free speech rhythms.

Piano: Chordal, with some decoration; chromatic.

Comment: A restrained but deeply emotional song, only published after Ireland's death. Ireland's MS in BL (Add. 52898).

39 THREE SONGS. Comp. July, 1926. Pub. Augener, 1928. 'For Feb 22, 1926'. Ireland thought of this as a trilogy, but certainly the first two can stand as single songs. Ireland's MS in BL (Add. 52899). They were published together and separately.

For: Mezzo; Bar.

(1) Love and friendship. Love is like the wild rose-briar. (Emily Brontë, first published 1850 [1839].)
No key signature, c′-g″, [d′-e″]. 3/4,2/4, With moderate movement. 2′15″. V/me, P/m.

Subject: Love, like the rose, is sweet but fading; friendship, like holly, may not be so fair, but lasts.

Voice: Steps, skips; climax on sustained g″; 8ve leap to d″, piano, held, at end; fairly simple speech-influenced rhythms.

Piano: Fairly thick-textured rhythmic patterns; chromatic scales in 3rds and 4ths in RH; some wide jumps in LH.

Comment: Comparatively straightforward; D major/minor tonality in spite of lack of key signature.

(2) Friendship in misfortune. Give me the depth of love. (Anon.)
Db major, d′b-f ″, [f′-e″b]. 3/4,2/4, Sustained and fervent. 1′55″. V/m, P/m.

Subject: Give me the love which can survive misfortune, and only ends
            with death.
Voice: Steps, skips, broken chords; sustained f ″ for climax; chroma-
            tic; speech rhythms.
Piano: Slow-moving, thick, and highly chromatic chords. Final
            chord in RH should have *b* to d‴ not f ‴.
Comment: A deeply felt and moving song.

(3) **The one hope**. When vain desire at last. (Dante Gabriel Rossetti,
    Sonnet 101, the last in *The House of Life*, 1881, first published 1870.)
            No key signature, b°*b*-f ″#, [e′-e″]. 3/4,2/4, Rather slowly.
            4′15″. V/md, P/md.
Subject: When we die shall we be able to forget our vain desires? If we
            receive any grace in heaven, give me only the one Hope, that
            word alone.
Voice: Steps, skips, semi-monotone; e″*b*s sustained over three bars;
            f ″# over two bars; 8ve and 7th drop, augmented 5th leap;
            highly chromatic; slow speech rhythm; long legato phrases.
Piano: Thick, slow-moving, and highly chromatic chords, with con-
            siderable variety of lay-out.
Comment: This is a real challenge for sensitive and musical performers;
            for a sympathetic audience it provides a fittingly intense
            conclusion to the trilogy. Rossetti told Alice Boyd that the
            poem 'refers to the longing for accomplishment of individual
            desires after death'. Line 10: the Cumaean sibyl inscribed her
            prophecies on leaves; Hyacinth was accidentally killed by
            Apollo – from his blood sprang a flower whose petals bore the
            word 'Alas'.

40 **If there were dreams to sell**. (Thomas Lovell Beddoes, 1851.) Comp.
   1918. Pub. W.R., 1918. High, Medium, Low.
            E*b* major, c′-f ″, [e′*b*-e″*b*]; F major, D*b* major. 2/2, Moderato.
            1′50″. V/me, P/e.
For: Mezzo, Bar; Sop, Ten; C-Ten.
Subject: Dreams make different demands; if you could choose what
            would you buy? Peace in a lonely cottage, to heal my ills.
Voice: Steps, skips; a few chromatic notes; much use of d″*b* and e″*b*,
            but only one f ″; simple speech rhythms.
Piano: Slow chords, simple harmonies, occasional melodic moments.
Comment: One of Ireland's most attractive songs, but the fact that he
            omitted the remaining three very disturbing stanzas of the
            original poem testifies to a restricted aim. However, Ireland
            may not have known the rest of the poem, *OB* only printed the
            first two verses, whereas *NOB* gives all five.

41 Tutto e sciolto. A birdless heaven. (James Joyce, *Pomes Penyeach*, 1927.) Comp. c. 1931. Pub. OUP, 1932. Written for *The Joyce Book*, edited by Herbert Hughes.

	No key signature, e'-e". 3/4,2/4, Rather slowly. 2'. V/m, P/m.
For:	[Mezzo], Bar.
Subject:	In this evening scene remember her who was once almost thine.
Voice:	Steps, skips; 7th drop, 6th drop and leap; sustained e"s; very free rhythm needing a sustained legato line; somewhat chromatic.
Piano:	Rather spare texture for Ireland; slow chords with a few leisurely arpeggios; highly chromatic.
Comment:	Pure magic in the right hands. The title is taken from an aria in La Sonambula (Bellini): 'All is lost now, / By all hope and joy am I forsaken / Nevermore can love awaken / Past enchantment, no nevermore.'

*

42 The holy boy. Lowly, laid in a manger. (Herbert S. Brown.) Arranged 1938; see Comment. Pub. B & H, 1938. High and Medium. Not in *Complete Works*.

	F major (modal) d'-g"(a"), [f'-e"b], Eb major. 6/8, Andante tranquillo, dotted crotchet = 44-46. 2'30". V/e, P/me.
For:	Sop, Ten; Mezzo, Bar.
Subject:	Christmas carol.
Voice:	Mostly by step, a few 4ths, simple rhythm.
Piano:	Chordal, occasional jumps and stretches.
Comment:	Composed in 1913 as No. 3 of (4) Preludes for Piano, 'The Holy Boy (A Carol of the Nativity)'. It proved immensely popular, and Ireland made arrangements for violin and piano and cello and piano in 1919. When making the song version in 1938 Ireland added two bars introduction, and modified the cadence at bar 8 of stanza 2, which was an F major chord in the piano solo; the song has G minor, and remains a tone higher than the original to the end. In 1941 he arranged the song version for SATB, and made a version for string quartet or string orchestra which can be used as an accompaniment for this if desired. Now printed in *Sing Solo Christmas*, ed. John Carol Case, OUP 1987; High in F major, Low in D major.

ROGER QUILTER
1877-1953

Quilter's songs are set out in order of publication. Only those songs to which he gave an opus number have been included. The **Tonality** is the original key, other published keys being given in italics. Note that the original keys of **22** are not known. Collections are referred to as follows:

Heritage 2 = A Heritage of English Song, vol. 2, B & H, 1977.
50 Modern = Fifty Modern English Songs, B & H, ?1927.

ROGER QUILTER

1 **FOUR SONGS OF THE SEA**. Op 1. (Roger Quilter.) Comp. 1900. Pub. Forsyth, 1901. Songs 1 (2-4) were re-issued in 1911 as *Three Songs of the Sea*, considerably revised, and with added metronome marks. Both versions were published in *High* and Low keys. At a later date Forsyth re-issued the original 1901 version of *Four Songs*, although Quilter had rejected them.

(1) **I have a friend**, a true, true friend.
C major, c'-d"; *Eb major*. 4/4, Allegro moderato. 1'15". V/e, P/e.

For: *Sop, Ten*; Mezzo, Bar; Cont, C-Ten, Bass.
Subject: My friend is as true as the ocean.
Voice: Steps, a few 3rds and 4ths; no accidentals; rhythms easy.
Piano: Chordal.
Comment: Simple and hymn-like; omitted from the 1911 revision.

(2) **The sea-bird**. I watched a sea-bird flying.
E minor, e'-e" [e'-c"]; *G minor*. 3/4, Poco andante, crotchet = 66. 1'45". V/m, P/me.

For: *Sop, Ten*; Mezzo, Bar; C-Ten.
Subject: At evening I watched a sea-bird, and heard his cry, before he flew away into the unknown.
Voice: Steps, 3rds, repeated notes; sustained forte e" at climax of second stanza; simple rhythms with a few quick decorations.
Piano: Chordal, with some counterpoint; middle stanza re-written for 1911, with RH chords over LH broken chords replacing simple broken chords between the hands. Slightly chromatic.
Comment: The dynamics were also revised for 1911, and Quilter rewrote several lines of the poem.

(3) **Moonlight**. Under the silver moonlight.
D major, c'#-d" [f'#-d"]; *F major*. 4/4, Moderato, crotchet = 88. 1'30". V/e, P/e.

For: *Sop, Ten*; Mezzo, Bar; Cont, C-Ten, Bass.

Subject: A description of white wings in the moonlight.
Voice: Broken chords, with some repeated notes; very simple rhythms.
Piano: Chordal, with a little decoration; a couple of bass notes must be treated as grace-notes.
Comment: The dynamics of the three stanzas are mf, pp, mf, in the original; and p, mp, pp, in the revision.

(4) **By the sea**. I stood today by the shimm'ring sea.
              D minor, d'-e" [d'-d"]; *F minor*. 9/8, Poco allegro con moto, dotted crotchet = 72. 1'15". V/me, P/e.
For: *Sop, Ten*; Mezzo, Bar; C-Ten.
Subject: The beauty of the sea made me whole.
Voice: Steps and 3rds, several rising phrases, with climax on sustained forte d", and two firm e"s. Rhythms simple.
Piano: Decorated chords over LH arpeggios; fairly thick texture and some 8ve work; a few rather awkward moments.
Comment: Words of second stanza changed in 1911, and the accompaniment was somewhat simpler in the original version.

2 **FOUR SONGS OF MIRZA SCHAFFY**. Op 2. (Friedrich Bodenstedt, *Die Lieder des Mirza Schaffy*, 1851.) Pub. Elkin, 1903. Translations by Walter Creighton. Re-issued in 1911 as *Four Songs*, with a new translation by R.H. Elkin, in *High* and Low keys, and somewhat revised, particularly as regards the layout of the accompaniment. These notes refer to the revised version. Schaffy (Mirza merely means 'man of letters') was a schoolmaster in Tiflis, Georgia, with whom Bodenstedt studied languages. In later years Bodenstedt confessed that the poems were in fact his own work; they were immensely popular, reaching their 26th edition in 1869. The collection has several subsections, given below after the song title. In 1931 Quilter published, without opus number, 'My heart adorned with thee', as being his own translation from Mirza Schaffy, which suggests some confusion somewhere!

(1) **Neig' schöne Knospe! Dich zu mir!** (Come tender bud, lean close to me). Hafifa, 4.
              G major, d'-e" [e'-d"]; *Bb major*. 3/4, Poco andante con moto, crotchet = 69. 1'45". V/me, P/m.
For: *Sop, Ten*; Mezzo, Bar; C-Ten.
Subject: Come tender bud, let me warm thee into flower.
Voice: Repeated notes, simple skips; 8ve leap, 7th and 6th drops; simple rhythms.

Piano: Gently moving harmonies, some broken chord and 8ve work; leaping chords at climax; some chromatics.

Comment: Original tempo mark: Andante moderato.

(2) **Und was die Sonne glüht**. (The glow of summer sun). Nachklänge aus der Schule der Weisheit, 6.

G minor. d'-e"b [d'-d"]; *Bb minor*. 2/4, Moderato ma con spirito, crotchet = 76. 1'. V/me, P/m.

For: *Sop, Ten*; Mezzo, Bar; C-Ten.

Subject: I have woven nature into my singing.

Voice: Steps, 3rds, many 5ths and 8ves, diminished 7th drop; fairly simple rhythms.

Piano: Crotchet bass line with off-beat chords, some 8ves and LH skips.

Comment: Original tempo mark: Allegro con spirito e marcato. The rather angular voice part is interesting.

(3) **Ich fühle deinen Odem**. (The magic of thy presence). Nachklänge aus der Schule der Weisheit, 3.

Db major. c'-f"(d"b) [d'b-d"b]; *F major*. 4/4, Andante moderato, crotchet = 72. 1'45". V/e, P/e. Both keys issued separately.

For: *Sop, Ten*; Mezzo, Bar; C-Ten.

Subject: I feel your presence everywhere.

Voice: Steps, simple skips; no accidentals; very simple rhythms.

Piano: Chordal, mostly minims and crotchets.

Comment: A romantic 'Royalty ballad', and would go well in a group of such songs.

(4) **Die helle Sonne leuchtet**. (The golden sunlight's glory). Nachklänge aus der Schule der Weisheit, 2.

F major. c'-f " [f'-d"]; *Ab major*. 6/8, Moderato con moto, dotted crotchet = 54. 1'15". V/me, P/e.

For: *Sop, Ten*; Mezzo, Bar.

Subject: As the sun shines on the sea, so shines your image in my dreams and my songs.

Voice: Steps, simple skips, repeated notes; 8ve leap; modulation; simple crotchet-quaver rhythms; fairly big climax at end.

Piano: Semiquaver broken chords between the hands, with counter-melodies in various parts; some 8ves and leaping chords at end; chromatic in places.

Comment: Original tempo mark: Moderato. The effective modulation for the second stanza and a good climax, though more for the piano than the voice, makes this quite an exciting song; a finisher for a light group.

3 THREE SONGS. Op 3. Independent songs, Comp. 1904-5. Pub. separately in several keys by Boosey: 3 (2) pub. 1904; **3 (1)** and (2) pub. 1905.

(1) **Love's philosophy**. The fountains mingle with the river. (Shelley, *Posthumous Poems*, 1824 [1819].)

> F major [*Heritage 2, 50 Modern*], d'-a", [f'-g"]; *D major, C Major*. 3/4, Molto allegro con moto, crotchet = 112. 1'20". V/m, P/md.

For: Sop, Ten; *Mezzo, C-Ten, Bar*.
Subject: Everything in nature combines, why not you and I? The mountains kiss heaven, why don't you kiss me?
Voice: Broken chords, steps, repeated notes; 8ve drops, 6th leaps; big final climax with sustained a".
Piano: Toccata-style semiquavers, mostly in RH, but LH has them in wide-ranging arpeggios at climax; bravura finish in 8ves.
Comment: Deserves its reputation as a good finisher. Often taken too fast, crotchet = 112 allows for the agitato in the second stanza, where the singer's attempt at logical argument starts to break down, being carried away by desire. The piano postlude surely describes the response of the previously reluctant lover.

(2) **Now sleeps the crimson petal** now the white. (Tennyson, *The Princess*, VII, 1847.)

> E♭ major, c'-e"♭, [e'♭-c"]; *G♭ major, F major, D major*. 3/4-5/4, Moderato quasi andantino, tempo rubato, crotchet = 60. 2'. V/me, P/e.

For: *Sop, Ten*; Mezzo, Bar; C-Ten; *Cont, Bass*.
Subject: All sleeps, so waken thou with me.
Voice: Steps and broken chords, 8ve, 7th and 6th drops; three phrases start on e"♭, none sustained; nearly all quavers, recit.-style.
Piano: Gently moving harmony with many parallel 6ths.
Comment: Words from 'The Princess, A Medley'; six lines are omitted between the two stanzas set here: 'Now droops the milkwhite peacock like a ghost, / And like a ghost she glimmers on to me. // Now lies the earth all Danaë to the stars. / And all thy heart lies open unto me. // Now slides the silent meteor on, and leaves / A shining furrow, as thy thoughts in me.' Six bars from the end Quilter originally wrote *slip into my* to four semiquavers (ad lib); later changing this to *into my* to three triplet quavers, perhaps because *slip* is not repeated in the poem. He also made many changes in the accompaniment: bars 5/16, old bass: crotchet

G, crotchet F, crotchet {f °/c'}; new bass: crotchet G, crotchet A, quaver F, quaver c°, quaver a°, triplets. Bars 6/17, old bass: beat 1, minim f ° tied from previous bar, and crotchet c', which should perhaps also be tied; new bass: crotchet c', no f °. Bar 13, old bass: beat 3, acciaccatura F tied to crotchet {F/a° natural}; new bass: crotchet {F/C/a° natural} chord with arpeggio sign. Bar 18, new editions: g° missing on 3rd quaver. Bar 19, 3rd crotchet, old RH: {c'/b°*b*}, part of crotchet chord; new RH: quaver c', quaver b°*b*. In most cases Quilter's first thoughts appear to be the better.

(3) **Fill a glass with golden wine** (W.E. Henley, *Echoes*, 1875.)
C major, c'-e", [c'-c"]; *E major, Eb major, Db major.* 4/4, Allegro maestoso e appassionato, crotchet = 104. 2'. V/me, P/me.

For:	*Sop, Ten*; Mezzo, Bar; C-Ten.
Subject:	Let us drink and kiss, and not regret the passing of time.
Voice:	Steps, 4th, 5th and 6th skips; climb to sustained e"*b*; steady crotchet rhythms and a short agitato section in quavers; big final phrase with e", less effective alternative given.
Piano:	Solid crotchet chords, often jumping the 8ve; some off-beat quaver chords in the agitato section.
Comment:	Sounds like a try-out for 'Fair House of Joy', 8 (7), but with a much plainer piano part. Quilter appears to have taken the poem as being about love and wine, and ignored the remainder; the result is a 'Royalty ballad' with a good tune.

4 FOUR CHILD SONGS. Op 5. (Robert Louis Stevenson, *A Child's Garden of Verses*, 1885.) Pub. Chappell, 1914; revised edition 1945. High and *Low*. Not up to Edward German's excellent *Just So Song-book*, but the publication of a revised edition after thirty years suggests many found these songs attractive. See Ireland **32** for further comment on the poems.

(1) **A good child**. I wake before the morning.
F major, d'-a", [f'-f "]; *D major.* 3/4, Allegro con grazia, crotchet = 120. 1'30". V/me, P/. Published separately in both keys.

For:	Sop, Ten; *Mezzo, Bar*.
Subject:	I am happy, for I have been good today.
Voice:	Skips and steps, 7th drop; simple rhythms.
Piano:	Chords, broken chords, counter-melodies; some chromatics.
Comment:	A pleasant waltz, but the words may be found embarrassing.

A letter from Stevenson to Henrietta Milne, November 1885, reads: 'see A Good Boy – much of the sentiment of which is taken direct from one evening at B[ridge] of A[llen], when we had a great play with the little Glasgow girl.' 'A Good Boy' was Stevenson's title. St. 3, line 2: *sleep again = sleepsin-by* in poem.

(2) **The lamplighter**. My tea is nearly ready.
      E*b* major, e'*b*-b"*b*(g"); *C major*. 4/4, Allegro semplice, crotchet = 112. 1'30". V/me, P/me.

For: Sop, Ten; *Mezzo, Bar*.
Subject: I want to be a lamplighter when I grow up.
Voice: Steps, skips, 8ve leaps; continuous quavers.
Piano: Chordal, with some quaver passages, and a fairly wide range.
Comment: Almost a patter-song.

(3) **Where go the boats?** Dark brown is the river.
      A major, e'-g#(f"#), [a'-f"#]; *F major*. 2/4, Andantino quasi allegretto, crotchet = 58. 1'45". V/me, P/me. Published separately in both keys.

For: Sop, Ten; *Mezzo, Bar*; *C-Ten*.
Subject: My boats go down the river, where others will find them.
Voice: Steps, simple skips; high phrase at end, but alternative given; very simple rhythms.
Piano: Gently moving harmonies.
Comment: Rather a charming song, if a little sentimental.

(4) **Foreign children**. Little Indian, Sioux or Crow.
      E minor, e'-a", [a'-e"]; *C minor*. 2/4,3/4, Allegro, crotchet = 100. 1'30". V/me, P/m.

For: Sop, Ten; *Mezzo, Bar*.
Subject: Don't all you foreign children wish you were me?
Voice: Steps, simple skips; mostly quavers; no accidentals.
Piano: Chordal, with occasional rather awkward semiquaver figures.
Comment: Words politically impossible today, though perhaps valid from a child's view-point when written.

5 **THREE SHAKESPEARE SONGS.** Op 6. Comp. 1905. Pub. Boosey, 1905; new edition 1906. *High, Medium*, Low. Much the best of Quilter's four groups of Shakespeare songs, and the only one designed to be sung as a set.

(1) **Come away, death.** (*Twelfth Night*, 1601, Act II, Scene iv.)

C minor, c'-e"b, [d'-c"]; *E minor, Eb minor.* 4/4, Poco andante, crotchet = 63. 3'. V/m, P/me.

For: *[Sop], Ten*; [Mezzo], Bar; C-Ten.

Subject: Let me die for love, and be buried where no true lover shall find my grave.

Voice: Steps, broken chords; 7th drops, 8ve leaps; melisma at end; simple rhythms with a few triplets.

Piano: Broken chords, repeated chords; some counter-melodies.

Comment: Not only is this a beautiful setting, but it is excellent training in phrasing and manipulation of breathing places, particularly in verse 2. Note the MM, not too slow.

(2) **O mistress mine** where are you roaming. (*Twelfth Night*, 1601, Act II, Scene iii.)

Eb major, b°b-e"b, [c'- c"]; *G major, Gb major [Heritage 2].* 3/4, Allegro moderato, crotchet = 80. 1'30". V/me, P/me.

For: *Ten*; Bar; C-Ten.

Subject: Don't run away – stay and kiss me, we will not always be young.

Voice: Broken chords and simple skips; steps; 6th leap followed by 7th drop; 7th leap and drop; simple rhythms.

Piano: Introductory parallel chords with dotted rhythms; then simple chordal accompaniment in crotchets and quavers.

Comment: A lively 'gather ye rose-buds while ye may' song. The crotchet = 80 seems a little slow, at least for the introduction to each stanza. The slower repeat of the first line at the end can be justified by using it to show the singer's realisation that his light-hearted remarks are only too true; thus strengthening the song rather than weakening it.

(3) **Blow, blow, thou winter wind.** (*As You Like It*, 1599, Act II, Scene vii.)

C minor/major, c'-e", [e'b-c"]; *E minor/major, Eb minor/major.* 3/4, Non troppo allegro ma vigoroso e con moto, crotchet = 76. 2'30". V/m, P/m.

For: *[Sop], Ten*; [Mezzo], Bar; C-Ten.

Subject: Winter is not as cruel as friend's ingratitude.

Voice: Steps, simple skips; phrases start high, and e'b is jumped to and sustained; held e" at end; rhythms: varied, minor; simple, major; singers have been known to take the final g' as g"!

Piano: Wide-ranging chords, particularly in minor section, with some semiquaver figures attached; LH has leaping quaver chords in major section.

Comment: Catches the bitter satisfaction of the words very successfully.
              Wind should be rhymed with *kind*. Again the crotchet = 76
              seems on the slow side; the Italian seems very precise, and
              the last two words – con moto – should not be forgotten.

6 TO JULIA. Op 8. (Robert Herrick, *Hesperides*, 1648.) Comp. 1905; Pub.
Boosey, 1906. A cycle of six songs. High (d'b-a"), and *Low* (a°-f "#). This is
a true cycle, with short introduction for piano solo, and a brief interlude
before the final song. Though the poems do not tell any kind of story they
are all on the one subject, Herrick's love for Julia. The theme of the
opening bars, representing Julia, runs right through the work. All the
songs, except perhaps **6 (5)**, can be sung separately; however, it is a fine
cycle, and deserves far more performances.
For: Ten, Bar.

(1) The bracelet. Why I tie about thy wrist.
              D minor, e'-a", [g'-f "]; *B minor*. 3/4, Allegro con moto, crotchet
              = 84. 1'45". V/m, P/md.
Subject: I tie this ribbon round your wrist to show you are my captive;
              but in reality it is I that am your bond-slave.
Voice: Steps, broken chords; some chromatics; last phrase has leaps
              to g"# and then to sustained a", ff; some melismas; rhythms
              simple but varied.
Piano: Toccata-style continuous semiquavers; much 8ve work;
              requires considerable keyboard facility.
Comment: A good lively opening song. The crotchet = 84 may seem slow
              to start with, but a faster tempo cannot be maintained
              convincingly.

(2) The maiden blush. So look the mornings when the sun.
              F major [*50 Modern*], f'-g", [g'-e"]; *D major*, once published
              separately. 4/4, Moderato semplice, crotchet = 80. 1'45". V/m,
              P/me.
Subject: Nature blushes beautifully; so does my Julia.
Voice: Steps and 3rds, some 6th leaps; flowing speech rhythms; a
              long last phrase with f " for five beats out of fourteen.
Piano: Gently flowing harmonies divided between the hands.
Comment: Quilter at his most seductive. Much rubato is needed; the
              crotchet = 80 works for the introduction, but this tempo
              cannot be sustained.

(3) To daisies. Shut not so soon, the dull-eyed night.
              Db major [*Heritage 2*], e'b-a"b, [f'-f "]; *Bb major*. Published
              separately in both keys. 3/4, Andante sostenuto, crotchet =

48. 2'. V/me, P/me.

Subject: Daisies, do not shut so soon; wait till Julia sleeps, then the whole world may follow her example.

Voice: Steps, 6th drops, many other skips; slightly chromatic; ends with 6th leap to sustained f″, piano; smooth quaver movement.

Piano: Parallel chordal movement in quavers, many 8ves; no problems.

Comment: Deservedly popular; a wonderfully shapely melodic line, richly accompanied.

(4) The night piece. Her eyes the glow-worm lend thee.

C# minor/Db major [*50 Modern*], c'#-g″#, [f'-f ″]; *A minor/ major*. Once published separately in both keys. 2/4, Molto allegro e leggiero, crotchet = 100. 1'45″. V/m, P/md.

Subject: Do not fear the dark, come to me.

Voice: Quick patter, mostly by step in first two verses; third verse modulates, with many 4ths; last verse slower, more legato; long final melisma descending from g″ needs plenty of breath.

Piano: Another toccata, but with more varied rhythms than 6 (1) and a barer texture; the slower fourth verse is chordal with LH arpeggios; the coda has an accelerando and uses the full range of the keyboard – it must be memorised.

Comment: Though it has its difficulties this is an original and effective song; the slower climax is based on the opening 'Julia' theme of the cycle.

(5) Julia's hair. Dew sat on Julia's hair, and spangled there.

F minor, e'b-a″b, [f'-f ″]; *D minor*. 3/4,4/4, Adagio misterioso, crotchet = 40. 1'45″. V/me, P/e.

Subject: A description of dew on Julia's hair.

Voice: Mostly by step; one phrase starts on a″b but falls at once; easy speech rhythms.

Piano: Slow parallel chords and arpeggios.

Comment: A beautiful and atmospheric song, but would not stand alone.

(6) Cherry ripe. 'Cherry ripe, ripe', I cry.

F major, e'-a″, [g'-g″]; *D major*. 3/4, Allegro con brio, crotchet = 96. 2'. V/m, P/d.

Subject: Cherries are my Julia's lips.

Voice: Skips, steps, sequences; many 8ve drops; fairly chromatic; ending needs power in middle of range.

Piano: Another toccata, very spread between the hands, covering a fairly wide range; middle section slower, triplet broken chords; all somewhat chromatic; a bravura ending.

Comment: Intended as a show-off ending this song is unfortunately more difficult than it sounds, rather than the reverse. However, though perhaps not worth the effort as a single song it does bring the cycle to a triumphant conclusion.

7 SONGS OF SORROW. Op 10. (Ernest Dowson). Comp. 1907-8. Pub. Boosey, 1908. *High* and Low. A deeply felt group of songs written after a period of illness. They are all slow, which makes them more satisfactory as single songs than as a set; they are nevertheless individually well worth performing.

For: *Sop, Ten*; Mezzo, Bar.

(1) A coronal. Violets and leaves of vine. (*Verses*, 1896.)

Bb major, b°b-f ", [d'-e"b]; *Db major*. 4/4, Poco andante, crotchet = 56. 3'. V/me, P/m.

Subject: We gather violets to crown Love, when living, while dying, and as a wreath after Love is dead.

Voice: Steps and 3rds, one 8ve drop; moderately chromatic for a few bars; almost continuous quavers.

Piano: Smoothly flowing harmony, with a rather thick texture; chromatic passages.

Comment: Some attractive phrases, but not altogether convincing. Dowson's subtitle reads: 'With His songs and Her days to His Lady and to Love.'

(2) Passing dreams. They are not long, the weeping and the laughter. (Prologue to *Verses*, 1896.)

Eb minor, b°b-f ", [e'b-d"b]; *F# minor*. 4/4, Andante serioso, crotchet = 58. 1'45". V/me, P/me.

Subject: Emotions do not last long, and have no meaning after death.

Voice: Steps, broken chords; fairly simple rhythms.

Piano: Chordal, with occasional arpeggios and counter-melodies.

Comment: Containing the famous line about 'the days of wine and roses', this is a moving expression of regret. Dowson adds 'Vitae summa brevis spem nos vetat incohare longam' - 'Life's brief span forbids long enduring hope' (Horace, *Odes* I iv).

(3) A land of silence. What land of silence, where pale stars shine. (*Verses*, 1896.)

Db major, b°b-g"b(e"b), [e'b-d"b]; *E major*. 3/4, Andante moderato, crotchet = 54. 2'30". V/me, P/m. Once published separately in both keys.

Subject: We will rest in a land of silence, forsaking the world.
Voice: Steps and 3rds; slightly chromatic; simple rhythms.
Piano: Gently flowing harmony, in fairly thick texture; chromatic at times; some counter-melodies.
Comment: A beautiful song, expressing resignation with conviction. Dowson's title: 'Beata Solitudo'.

(4) In spring. See how the trees and the Osiers lithe. (*Decorations: in Verse and Prose*, 1899.)

E major, b°-e′, [d′#-d″#]; *G major*. 4/4, Lento non troppo, crotchet = 58. 2′45″. V/me, P/me.

Subject: Look at spring and its beauty; our spring will come no more.
Voice: Steps, simple skips; broken chords, 6th leaps; simple rhythms; pp e″ near end.
Piano: Rather static harmony, with repeated chords and some counter-melodies; moderately chromatic.
Comment: A successful mixture of pleasure and sadness.

8 SEVEN ELIZABETHAN LYRICS. Op 12. Comp. 1907-8. Pub. Boosey 1908. High and *Medium*. This is not a cycle, but a well-contrasted set of excellent songs. In view of the popularity of 'Fair House of Joy' it is hard to understand why the others are so seldom sung.

(1) Weep you no more, sad fountains. (Anon, from John Dowland's *Third Book of Ayres*, 1603.) Comp. July 1907.

F minor [*Heritage 2*], e′b-g″, [g′-e″b]; *D minor*. 3/4, Poco andante, crotchet = 56. 2′30″. V/e, P/e. Published separately in both keys.

For: [Sop], Ten; *[Mezzo], Bar; C-Ten*.
Subject: Do not weep; your love will be reconciled on waking.
Voice: Steps and 3rds; very simple rhythms.
Piano: Gently moving harmonies, with occasional melodic phrases.
Comment: Simple but haunting. Original MS title: 'A Dirge'.

(2) My life's delight. Come, O come, my life's delight. (Thomas Campion, *Third Book of Ayres*, 1618.) Comp. December 1907.

G major, g′-a″, [g′-e″]; *E major*. 4/4, Molto allegro con moto, crotchet = 132. 1′30″. V/me, P/m. Published separately in both keys.

For: [Sop], Ten; *[Mezzo], Bar*.
Subject: Come to me quickly, for I love you.
Voice: Steps, broken chords, 6th leap and drop, 7th leap; rhythms fairly simple; some phrases are stretched; held g″ at end.
Piano: Crotchet chords in RH against LH quaver arpeggios; no real

problems, but speed must be maintained.

Comment: Conveys the enthusiasm of the poem with great success; extremely enjoyable to perform.

(3) **Damask roses**. Lady, when I behold the roses sprouting. (Anon, from an Italian original; set (twice) by John Wilbye, *The First Set of Madrigals*, 1598.) Comp. July 1907, in D major.

Eb major, f'-a"(g"), [g'b-e"b]; *C major*. 3/4, Andante moderato, crotchet = 52. 1'15". V/m, P/me.

For: Ten, Bar.
Subject: Seeing roses, and your lips, I can hardly tell them apart.
Voice: Steps, broken chords, repeated notes; 8ve leap, 5th leap to the short a", with an alternative given which badly weakens the phrase; rhythms simple, with some triplets.
Piano: Chordal, with some inner movement, and rhythmic repetition for a few bars.
Comment: Short and sweet, a lovely little song. MS title: 'Roses'. The words are a translation from the Italian, 'Quand'io miro le rose', from Angelo Grillo's *Parte prima delle rime*, 1589.

(4) **The faithless shepherdess**. While that the sun with his beams hot. (Anon, set as a madrigal by William Byrd in *Songs of Sundrie Natures*, 1589, and published in *England's Helicon*, 1600.)

Bb minor, f'-a"b, [a'b-f"]; *G minor*. 3/4,5/4,3/2, Allegro capriccioso, crotchet = 84. 1'45". V/m, P/m.

For: Sop, Ten; *Mezzo, Bar*.
Subject: I heard a shepherd singing about his faithless love.
Voice: Steps and 3rds; 8ve leaps, 6th leaps and drops; 7th leap to a"b at end; rhythmic, a legato middle section to each verse.
Piano: Quaver chords, many semi-quaver figures above; some 8ves.
Comment: The changes of time signature should cause no problems. A good contrasting item for the middle of the set, but it is a pity Quilter did not include the other two stanzas of the original: 'Another shepherd you did see, / To whom your heart was soon enchained. / Full soon your love was leapt from me, / Full soon my place he had obtained. / Soon came a third your love to win, / And we were out and he was in. // Sure you have made me passing glad / That you your mind so soon removed, / Before that I the leisure had / To choose you for my best beloved. / For all my love was past and done / Two days before it was begun.'

(5) **Brown is my love**, but graceful. (Anon, from Yonge's *Musica Transalpina*, Book 2, 1597.) Comp. December 1907.

Bb major, f'-g", [g'-f"]; *G major*. 3/4, Poco andante grazioso con tenerezza, crotchet = 58. 1'15". V/me, P/me.

For: Ten; *Bar*; *C-Ten*.
Subject: My love is beautiful, but scornful.
Voice: Starts with 8ve drop, g″-g′; 6th drop, and two more 8ve drops; steps and simple skips; modulation; simple rhythms, some triplets.
Piano: Gently moving harmonies, some accidentals.
Comment: Another gem, similar to 8 (3). Bar 7: the original poem has *thy*, for *her*.

(6) **By a fountainside**. Slow, slow, fresh fount. (Ben Jonson, *Cynthia's Revels*, 1600, Act I, Scene ii; set by Henry Youll, *Canzonets to Three Voices*, 1608.) Comp. November 1907.

       C# minor/Db major, c′#-g″#, [f′#-f″]; *Bb minor/major*. 4/4, Moderato tristamente ma con moto, crotchet = 88. 3'. V/m, P/m. Published separately in both keys.
For: Sop, Ten; *Mezzo, Bar*.
Subject: Nature should weep with me to see her pride withered.
Voice: Steps and 3rds; 6th and 7th leaps, 6th drop; long melismatic phrase near end; some modulation; mostly crotchets, but considerable variety in phrase length.
Piano: Chordal, and broken chords between the hands; many accidentals; some crotchet triplets.
Comment: The most elaborate of the set. The move to the major is magical; a fine song.

(7) **Fair house of joy**. Fain would I change that note. (Anon, set by Tobias Hume in *The First Part of Ayres*, 1605.)

       Db major [*Heritage 2*], f′-a″b, [a′b-g″b]; *Bb major*. 3/4, Moderato ma con moto ed appassionato, crotchet = 66. 2'. V/m, P/m. Published separately in Db major, *Bb major*, *Ab major*.
For: Sop, Ten; *Mezzo, Bar*; *C-Ten*.
Subject: I can sing of nothing but love.
Voice: Steps and simple skips, repeated notes; 6th leap and drop; mostly quavers, with some extended phrases; big finish, 8ve leap to final sustained a″b.
Piano: Chordal, with much internal movement; fairly thick texture; much 8ve work, some 9th stretches. Note by Quilter in low key editions: 'The piano part in this transposed key has been slightly altered'; there are in fact quite considerable changes in layout.
Comment: Original tempo mark in MS: Moderato sostenuto, crotchet = 56. This appears in some printed copies, though Quilter clearly found it too slow and altered it. The instruction 'con

moto ed appassionato' should not be forgotten. The first sentence is often misunderstood, and might be paraphrased thus: 'I wish I could sing according to the rules, for I think singing love-songs is harmful.' This song deserves its popularity, and makes a fine end to a group, but why not sing some of the others in the set?

9 FOUR SONGS. Op 14. Comp. 1909-10. Pub. Boosey, 1910. Although published together, these are independent songs. *High* and Low.

(1) Autumn evening. The yellow poplar leaves have strewn. (Arthur Maquarie, *The Wheel of Life*, 1909.)

> G minor, c'-e'', [e'b-d'']; *Bb minor*. 4/4, moderato tranquillo, crotchet = 58. 2'45". V/me, P/me.

For:	*Sop, Ten*; Mezzo, Bar.
Subject:	A gentle elegy over the loved one's grave.
Voice:	Mostly by step, some simple skips; mf climax on e''b, and more quietly on e''. A few chromatics; rhythm mostly quavers, with some slower and more extended phrases, but many commas.
Piano:	Gently moving harmonies over a fairly static bass line, slightly chromatic at times.
Comment:	There is a haunting melancholy about this song, very moving. Title of poem: 'Allerseelen'.

(2) April, April, laugh thy girlish laughter. (William Watson, *The Hope of the World and other Poems*, 1898.)

> Ab major, d'-f'', [e'b-e''b]; *Bb major*. 3/4, Allegro scherzoso e leggiero, crotchet = 126. 1'. V/me, P/m.

For:	*Sop, Ten*; Mezzo, Bar.
Subject:	Laugh thy girlish laughter, then weep thy girlish tears.
Voice:	4ths, 5ths, and steps; 6th and 7th leap, 8ve drops; two-bar crescendo on e''b; fairly simple rhythms.
Piano:	Waltz LH, with two-part tunes in RH.
Comment:	A trite waltz, quite up to the standard of the 'poem'.

(3) A last year's rose. From the brake the nightingale. (W.E. Henley, *Echoes*, 1872-1889.)

> Db major, e'b-f'', [f'-d''b]; *Eb major*. 4/4, Andante moderato poco con moto, crotchet = 63. 2'15". V/me, P/m. Published separately in both keys.

For:	*Sop, Ten*; Mezzo, Bar.
Subject:	The nightingale sings to the rose, though both know last year's rose and nightingale are dead; 'love and life shall still prevail'.

Voice: Steps and 3rds, a few skips; some chromatics; mostly quavers.

Piano: Freely moving and somewhat chromatic harmonies; much two against three; fairly thick texture.

Comment: More interesting than 9 (2), but still rather routine stuff.

(4) **Song of the blackbird**. The nightingale has a lyre of gold. (W.E. Henley, *Echoes*, 1876.)

Bb major, d'-f ", [g'-d"]; *C major*. 3/4, Molto allegro giocoso, crotchet = 132. 1'30". V/m, P/md. Published separately in both keys.

For: *Sop, Ten*; Mezzo, Bar.

Subject: I prefer the blackbird to the nightingale, for he sings of life and love.

Voice: Broken chords, steps and simple skips; starts semi-recit.; long final phrase with sustained f " and e"b, all forte.

Piano: Toccata style, chromatic in places.

Comment: A good bravura finisher. The crotchet 132, although strictly only relevant to the introduction, implies a fast tempo for the rest of the song, which requires a pianist with some facility; however it is often performed more slowly.

10 THREE SONGS. Op 15. Independent songs, published separately by Boosey, Pub. 1914.

(1) **Cuckoo song**. Blow, blow, winds of May. (Alfred Williams.) Comp. 1913.

D major, f'-a", [g'-f "#]; *B major*. 2/4, Molto allegro, crotchet = 96, middle page crotchet = 80. 2'15". V/m, P/md.

For: [Sop], Ten; *[Mezzo]*, Bar.

Subject: I love May and the cuckoo, and dream of them in the winter.

Voice: Steps, skips, 8ve drop, 6th leap; sustained f " forte, and a" and g" ff; some chromatics; varied rhythm and tempo.

Piano: Toccata style, with groups of three, four and five per beat; broken chords between the hands; many accidentals; it is surprisingly awkward to play as the runs are frequently interrupted, making it hard to obtain a rhythmic flow.

Comment: In spite of the line 'all the world is my wife', dedicated to and sung by Melba! With more variety than most of Quilter's songs it makes a good finisher.

(2) **Amaryllis at the fountain**. Crowned with flowers I saw fair Amaryllis. (Anon, set by Byrd in *Psalms, Songs and Sonnets*, 1611, and by Pilkington, *The Second Set of Madrigals*, 1624.) Comp. 1914.

G major, d'-a", [g'-g"]; *E major*. 4/4, Allegretto delicato, crotchet = 100. 1'. V/m, P/me.

For:	Sop, Ten; *Mezzo, Bar*.
Subject:	Amaryllis wrote of her faith on the sand, and it blew away.
Voice:	Broken chords, 4ths and 5ths, 8ve drops; two sustained g"s; fairly wide dynamic range; variety of easy rhythms.
Piano:	Chords, some broken, with decorations; some modulation.
Comment:	A delightful song, good as an encore or a finisher. The poem is a free translation from Girolamo Amelonghi's 'Sedendo in su l'arena d'un bel rio' in *Scelta di rime*, 1579.

(3) **Blossom time**. Blossom on the plum, wild wind and merry. (Nora Hopper.) Comp. 1914.

G major, g'-a", [b'-g"]; *E major*. 2/4, Allegro, crotchet = 104. 1'15". V/m, P/m. Also issued as a duet, in F major.

For:	Sop, Ten; *Mezzo, Bar*.
Subject:	Early spring; sun, showers, and wind; blossoms and a single swallow.
Voice:	Simple skips, steps and repeated notes; sustained a" forte for three and a half bars of a seven-bar phrase; rhythms simple.
Piano:	Rhythmic chordal, not too thick, but with many small skips.
Comment:	A pleasantly light-hearted 'Royalty ballad'.

11 THREE SONGS FOR BARITONE OR TENOR. Op 18, Nos 1-3. Pub. Elkin, 1914, as separate songs, reissued under this title in 1920 in one volume and separately. *High* and Low.

(1) **To wine and beauty**. Vulcan! provide me such a cup. (John Wilmot, Earl of Rochester, *Poems on Several Occasions*, 1680.)

E♭ major, b°b(c')-f"(e"♭), [e'b-e"♭]; *F major*. 3/4, Moderato ma con moto ed appassionato, crotchet = 90. 1'30". V/m, P/m.

Subject:	Let us have plenty to drink, and then make love again.
Voice:	Broken chords, steps, 8ve leap; sustained e"♭s, ff, and (optional) f"; straightforward rhythms with many triplets; some accidentals.
Piano:	Chordal, often broken; fairly thick texture; many triplets, some two against three.
Comment:	Similar in style to 'Fair House of Joy', 8 (7); enthusiastic and loud, it makes a good finisher. The poem has been heavily bowdlerised; the original version had the title 'Upon his Drinking a Bowl', and ran as follows: '*Vulcan* contrive me such a Cup, / As *Nestor* us'd of old; / Shew all thy skill to trim it up, / Damask it round with Gold. // Make it so large that

fill'd with Sack, / Up to the swelling brim; / Vast Toasts, on the delicious Lake, / Like Ships at Sea may swim. // Engrave not Battail on his Cheek, / With War, I've nought to do; / I'm none of those that took *Mastrich*, / Nor *Yarmouth* Leager knew. // Let it no name of Planets tell, / Fixt Stars or Constellations; / For I am no Sir *Sydrophel*, / Nor none of his Relations. // But carve thereon a spreading Vine, / Then add Two lovely Boys; / Their Limbs in Amorous folds intwine, / The Type of future joys. // *Cupid* and *Bacchus* my Saints are, / May drink and Love still reign, / With Wine I wash away my cares, / And then to Cunt again.'

(2) **Where be you going,** you Devon maid. (John Keats, first published 1853 [14 March 1818, sent in a letter to B.R. Haydon a week later].)

> D major, c'#-d", [d'-b']; *F major*. 4/8, Moderato semplice, crotchet = 60. 1'15". V/m, P/me.

Subject: I love Devon but love you more; let's lie on the grass and kiss.
Voice: Steps, simple skips; 8th drop, 7th drop; varied rhythms.
Piano: Chordal, with decorative figures attached; slightly chromatic.
Comment: An effective flirtation song. St. 2 has been omitted: 'I love your meads, and I love your flowers, / And I love your junkets mainly, / But 'hind the door I love kissing more, / O look not so disdainly.' Page 10, bar 1: *hang on a* = *hang up on the*, in poem.

(3) **The jocund dance.** I love the jocund dance. (William Blake, *Poetical Sketches*, 1783.)

> G major, e'-e", [f'#-d"]; *Bb major*. 2/4, Allegro, crotchet = 88. 1'30". V/m, P/md.

Subject: I love country life, and all our neighbours; but I love Kitty above all.
Voice: 3rds, 4ths, steps; sustained e"s, twice; the varied rhythms need precise diction.
Piano: Basically chordal, but considerable use of ornamental figures requires a good facility at the indicated tempo,
Comment: There are occasional touches of modality in this thoroughly cheerful song, completing a very useful group for male voices.

12 Spring is at the door. Op 18, No 4. (Nora Hopper.) Pub. Elkin, 1914. *High* and Low.

> D major, a°(c'#)-f"#(d"), [e'-c"#]; *F major*. 4/4, Allegro moderato, crotchet = 92. 1'30". V/me, P/m.

For: *Sop, Ten*; Mezzo, Bar; C-Ten.

Subject: Spring brings all kinds of flowers, and delight.
Voice: Steps and 3rds; sustained f″# (or c″#); a few accidentals;
              mostly quavers with a few triplets.
Piano: Chordal, quite quickly broken at times, and with one rather
              elaborate interlude.
Comment: Pretty music to somewhat uninspired verse. Bar 5: maund =
              a wicker basket with handles; bar 13: mullein = a herbaceous
              plant with yellow flowers; mallow = a reddish-purple wild
              flower; bar 15: sallow = willow.

13 TWO SEPTEMBER SONGS. Op 18, Nos 5 and 6. (Mary Coleridge,
Poems, 1907.) Pub. Elkin, 1916. *High* and Low. The poems were
published posthumously, edited by Henry Newbolt. These are the first
two of a set of three poems under the title 'Chillingham'. Chillingham is
in Northumberland.

(1) Through the sunny garden. (1903.)
              E major, b°-e″, [c′#-c″#]; *G major*. 2/4, Andante moderato,
              crotchet = 42. 2′. V/me, P/me.
For: *Sop, Ten*; Mezzo, Bar; C-Ten.
Subject: Describes the view from a garden of the hills beyond.
Voice: Steps, simple skips, repeated notes, 8ve drop, some chroma-
              tics, ends on a sustained b°.
Piano: Gently moving harmony with many repeated chords; some
              triplets; many accidentals.
Comment: An atmospheric song, with more adventurous harmony than
              is usual with Quilter. The repeat of the opening two lines does
              not appear in the poem.

(2) The valley and the hill. O the high valley, the little low hill. (1905.)
              D minor, c′-e″, [f′#-d″]; *E minor*. 4/4, Allegro con moto e poco
              appassionato, crotchet = 138. 1′15″. V/me, P/m.
For: *Sop, Ten*; Mezzo, Bar; C-Ten.
Subject: Describes the beauty of a landscape that would be missed
              even in heaven.
Voice: Steps, simple skips, repeated notes; 6th drop; simple
              rhythms; but the tempo requires fast clear diction.
Piano: Chordal crotchets with quaver patterning, chromatics.
Comment: An effective contrast to the previous song. There is a strong
              Dorian Mode flavour to the 1st and 3rd stanzas, while stanza
              2 is in D major. A useful pair of songs for the young singer.
              Quilter has left out the third stanza: 'O the red heather on the
              moss-wrought rock, / And the fir-tree stiff and straight, / The
              shaggy old sheep-dog barking at the flock, / And the rotten old
              five-barred gate.'

14 THREE SONGS OF WILLIAM BLAKE. Op 20. Comp. 1916. Pub. W.R. 1917. *High* and Low keys.

For: *Sop, Ten*; Mezzo, Bar; Cont, C-Ten, Bass.

(1) **Dream valley**. Memory, hither come, and tune your merry notes. (*Poetical Sketches*, 1783.)

             D major, b°-d″, [d′-b′]; *Gb major*. 4/4, Moderato, poco andante, crotchet = 58. 2′. V/me, P/me.

Subject: Memory, come and stir my fancies, and when night comes I will walk with Melancholy.

Voice: Steps, broken chords; short melisma in last rather long phrase; mostly quavers, some triplets.

Piano: Gently moving harmony; some 8ves; somewhat chromatic coda.

Comment: The nostalgia of the words is well matched by the music.

(2) **The wild flower's song**. As I wandered in the forest. (From Blake's MS sketchbook used from 1793-1811, first published 1905.)

             G major, b°-d″, [d′-c″]; *Bb major*. 4/4,3/2, Allegro semplice ma con moto, crotchet = 90. 1′45″. V/m, P/m.

Subject: In the forest I heard a wild flower sing: 'I dreamt of delights and looked for joy, but met with scorn.'

Voice: Steps and skips; fairly chromatic; varied but simple rhythms.

Piano: Harmony moving in quavers; some broken chords; chromatic.

Comment: Musically enjoyable, but the poem is weakened since Quilter, having made something of *scorn* by his harmony, repeats the opening stanza as though nothing had occurred. Variants from Blake's MS: St. 1, line 1: *the = in the*; St. 2, line 1: *earth = dark*; line 3: *thoughts = fears*.

(3) **Daybreak**. To find the western path. (From Blake's MS notebook, 1800-1803, first published 1874.)

             Eb minor, d′b-e″b, [e′b-d″b]; *F# minor*. 3/4, Tempo moderato, ma con moto e poco rubato, crotchet = 72. 1′30″. V/m, P/md.

Subject: I search for morning through the gates of wrath; the war is over and the sun rises.

Voice: Steps and 3rds, repeated notes; 6th drops; fairly chromatic; climax reaches four beats on d″b followed by seven beats on e″b, f to ff; fairly varied rhythms.

Piano: Elaborately laid out, semiquaver triplet decorations over chordal arpeggios; chromatic, thick texture with many 8ves.

Comment: A strange poem and strange music. In trying to match the mood of each individual line Quilter tends to weaken the flow; however, this has more real speed and drive than most of his songs, and could be a good finisher, given a good pianist. Variants from Blake's MS: Title = 'Morning'; St. 1, line 4: *morning = Mercy*.

15 THREE PASTORAL SONGS. Op 22. (Joseph Campbell [Seosamh MacCathmhaoil].) Comp. 1920. Pub. Elkin, 1921. Original version with violin, cello, and piano accompaniment, but issued simultaneously for voice and piano solo. In fact, everything in the string parts is doubled on the piano, and the piano part is unchanged in the second version. *High* and Low.

For: *Sop, Ten*; Mezzo, Bar.

(1) I will go with my father a-ploughing.
        A*b* major, c′-f ″(e″*b*), [f′-c″]; *Bb major*. 6/8, Allegretto con moto, dotted crotchet = 76. 2′. V/me, P/me. Piano accompaniment version published separately in both keys.

Subject: I will go with my father, who will sing the songs for ploughing, sowing and reaping.

Voice: Steps and 3rds; 8ve drop (optional); very simple rhythms.

Piano: Chordal, sometimes broken, and a few passing notes.

Comment: Well written, as always, but not very memorable.

(2) Cherry valley. In Cherry Valley the cherries blow.
        E major, b°-e″, [c′-c″]; *G major*. 4/4, Moderato un poco andante, crotchet = 60. 2′30″ V/m, P/m.

Subject: Description of Cherry Valley in moonlight, with the fairies.

Voice: Steps, skips, broken chords; sustained forte e″ and 8ve drop; long low b° to finish; fairly chromatic; almost speech rhythm; some long phrases.

Piano: Slowly changing chromatic harmony, sometimes spread between the hands; some decoration; quite congested at times.

Comment: An interesting song, atmospheric and effective, though the poem is a little trite. Low key full score, one bar from the end, piano LH: bass clef missing at half bar.

(3) I wish and I wish.
        C minor, c′-g″(e″*b*), [f′-c″]; *D minor*. 9/8,6/8, Allegro moderato ma con moto, dotted crotchet = 84. 2′ V/me, P/m.

Subject: I wish I could be a bee or a swan, and be living in Ireland; if the fairies came for me I would go.

Voice: Steps, 3rds, repeated notes, broken chords; some accidentals; simple rhythms, but neat diction is required.

Piano: Broken chords in quavers, both hands; much parallel
             movement; many accidentals.
Comment: Tempo is important; this song can easily settle into a jog-trot
             and become even duller than it really is. Poem weak.

16 FIVE SHAKESPEARE SONGS. Op 23. Pub. Boosey, 1921. **16 (2)**
published separately, 1919; **16 (3)** published, also 1919, as a duet. *High*
and Low.

(1) **Fear no more the heat of the sun.** (*Cymbeline*, 1610, Act IV, Scene ii.)
     Comp. 1921.
                 F minor, c'-e''b, [f'-d''b]; *G# minor*. 4/4, Andante moderato,
                 crotchet = 92. 3'. V/me, P/me.
For: *Sop, Ten*; Mezzo, Bar; C-Ten.
Subject: An elegy: death comes to all, and solves all problems.
Voice: Steps, 3rds, occasional skips; slightly modal, but several
             modulations and a few chromatics; very simple rhythms.
Piano: Chordal, with some decoration and occasional arpeggios;
             moderately chromatic.
Comment: Pleasant enough, though hardly worthy of the words. Page 4,
             bar 11: consign to thee = sign the same contract with you.
             Page 5, bar 3: exorcisor = one who can conjure up evil spirits;
             bars 11-12: consummation = fulfilment, as of life by death;
             second syllable as in 'sum', not as in 'consume'.

(2) **Under the greenwood tree.** (*As You Like It*, 1599, Act II, Scene v.)
     Comp. 1919.
                 D major, d'-d'', [e'-d'']; *F major*. 2/4, Allegro moderato ma
                 giocoso, crotchet = 96. 1'. V/me, P/m.
For: *[Sop], Ten*; [Mezzo], Bar; [Cont], C-Ten, Bass.
Subject: Come live in the forest, where there is no enemy but winter.
Voice: Steps, 3rds, broken chords in sequence, slightly extended
             final phrase; rhythms simple; the tempo requires some neat
             diction.
Piano: Chordal; with decorative semiquavers, often two parts in one
             hand; a few wide LH leaps; some accidentals.
Comment: Nice and lively, it could end a group, for there is little sign of
             winter in this cheerful song! Bar 9: turn = attune, adjust to fit.

(3) **It was a lover and his lass.** (*As You Like It*, 1599, Act V, Scene iii.)
     Comp. 1921.
                 E major, c'#-e'', [e'-b']; *Ab major*. 2/4, Allegro moderato,
                 crotchet = 74. 2'. V/me, P/m.
For: *Sop, Ten*; Mezzo, Bar; C-Ten.

Subject: Spring is the time for lovers.
Voice: Steps and simple skips; short sequences; some accidentals; simple rhythms; one e″, short and quiet, at end.
Piano: Some counterpoint; rhythmically decorative chords; semiquaver RH broken chord patterns; some accidentals.
Comment: An enjoyable setting, with no problems. Page 13, bar 1: a carol was a song for dancing, with no necessary religious connotation. Page 14, bar 10: prime = the first part of the day, the year (spring), or life (youth).

(4) Take O take those lips away. (*Measure For Measure*, 1604, Act IV, Scene i.) Comp. 1921.
              D*b* major, e′*b*-d″*b*, [f′-c″]; *E major*. 3/4, Andante espressivo, crotchet = 60. 1′15″. V/e, P/me.
For: *Sop, Ten*; Mezzo, Bar; Cont, C-Ten, Bass.
Subject: Go, but give me back my kisses.
Voice: Steps and 3rds; simple though varied rhythms.
Piano: Gently moving harmony; slightly chromatic; fairly thick texture.
Comment: Has charm, but little passion.

(5) Hey, ho, the wind and the rain. When that I was and a little tiny boy. (*Twelfth Night*, 1601, Act V, Scene i.) Comp. 1921.
              C major, d′-f ″(d″), [e′-d″]; *Eb major*. 2/4, Allegretto marcato, crotchet = 96. 1′30″. V/me, P/m.
For: *[Sop], Ten*; [Mezzo], Bar; C-Ten.
Subject: Nothing in life matters very much; nor did this play!
Voice: Steps, repeated notes, simple skips; the f ″ at the end is really essential, in spite of the given alternative; bouncy rhythms, simple but varied.
Piano: Quaver chords with decorated top line; some LH leaps.
Comment: Another reasonable finisher, particularly in view of the words, though there is no sign of wind or rain in this setting! In fact Quilter has omitted the fourth stanza, perhaps as being too realistic! It runs: 'But when I came unto my beds, / With hey, ho, the wind and the rain, / With tosspots still had drunken heads, / For the rain it raineth every day.'

17 FIVE ENGLISH LOVE LYRICS. Op 24. Independent songs, and published separately. This would in fact make an excellent group for tenor or baritone, though some transposed versions would have to be used, and it might be advisable to re-arrange the order.

(1) **There be none of beauty's daughters**. (Lord Byron, *Poems*, 1816 [28 March 1816].) Comp. 1922. Pub. Chappell, 1922. High, *Medium, Low*.
Eb major, e'b-g", [g'-e"b]; *C major, B major*. 4/4, Poco andante con moto, crotchet = 88. 2'. V/me, P/me.

For: Ten; Bar; *C-Ten*.
Subject: You and your voice have a magic that can calm the seas.
Voice: Broken chords, steps; 6th leap; sequences; modulation; simple rhythms.
Piano: Broken chords with many snatches of counter-melody; some modulation.
Comment: Beautiful; calm, warm and loving, with no artificial climax to spoil the mood.

(2) **Morning song**. Pack, clouds, away! and welcome, day. (Thomas Heywood, *The Rape of Lucrece*, 1608, Act IV, Scene vi.) Comp. 1922. Pub. Chappell, 1922; revised and re-issued 1927. High, *Medium, Low*.
E major, f'#-a", [g'#-e"]; *D major, C major*. 3/4, Allegretto non troppo, ma con spirito, crotchet = 112. 1'45". V/m, P/md.

For: Sop, Ten; *Mezzo, Bar*.
Subject: Let all the birds come and 'give my love good-morrow'.
Voice: Steps, simple skips; some modulation; big climax with sustained a" followed by four bars e", all forte; rhythms simple, though some surprises, and neat diction is needed.
Piano: Toccata style, much two against three; chords spread between the hands in a variety of rhythms; many accidentals.
Comment: Similar in style to 'Love's Philosophy', **3** (1), and would make a welcome alternative as a finisher.

(3) **Go, lovely rose**. (Edmund Waller, *Poems*, 1686.) Comp. 1922. Pub. Chappell, 1923. High, *Medium, Low*.
Gb major, f'-g"b, [a'b-e"b]; *F major, Eb major [The English Recital Song*, Chappell, 1979]. 4/4,3/2, Moderato, poco con moto, 2'30". V/m, P/m.

For: Ten; *Bar*; *C-Ten*.
Subject: Go, rose, tell my love she is as fair as you, and like you must be seen to be admired; by thy death show the fate common to all rare things.
Voice: Steps, small skips; 6th drop; some accidentals; sustained g"b; fluid speech rhythms and some long phrases, though these can be divided.
Piano: Gently moving harmonies, slightly chromatic; some two against three; rich texture.
Comment: Quilter's masterpiece; a wonderful love-song, both words and music continue to yield new beauties over the years.

(4) O, the month of May. (Thomas Dekker, *The Shoemaker's Holiday*, 1600. The First Three-man's Song.) Comp. 1926. Pub. Chappell, 1928. *High* and Low.

D major, d'-e"(d"), [f'-d"]; *F major*. 2/4, Allegretto con amore, crotchet = 96. 1'45". V/me, P/m.

For: *Ten*; Bar; C-Ten.
Subject: In May I said to my true-love, 'Be my Summer's Queen.'
Voice: Steps, small skips; some modulation; sustained d"s and (optional) held e"; bouncy but straightforward rhythms.
Piano: Light, chordal; some LH jumps; fairly chromatic; considerable variety of phrasing.
Comment: A delightful song, full of life and enthusiasm. In St. 3 the cuckoo is not wanted because of his association with 'cuckold'.

(5) The time of roses. It was not in the winter. (Thomas Hood, *Poems*, 1846.) Comp. 1928. Pub. Chappell, 1928. *High*, Medium, *Low*.

D minor, c'-g"b, [a'-f"]; *E minor, C minor*. 2/2, Con moto, amabile, minim = 66. 1'30". V/m, P/m.

For: *Sop, Ten*; Mezzo, Bar; *C-Ten*.
Subject: We plucked roses when we met – winter is not the time for lovers.
Voice: Steps, simple skips, some chromatics; sustained g"b, forte, and e", piano; long phrasing desirable though not essential; rhythms fairly simple.
Piano: Broken chords very freely divided between the hands; some counter-melodies; fairly chromatic.
Comment: Pleasant flow, with some effective contrasts. The poem was first published in 1827 with two more stanzas, which Hood dropped in 1846.

18 SIX SONGS. Op 25. Independent songs, published separately.

(1) Song of the stream. Flow on! happy stream. (Alfred Williams.) Comp. 1921. Pub. W.R., 1922. High, *Medium*.

E major, c'#(d'#)-f"#, [e'-e"]; *D major*. 4/4, Allegretto moderato con moto, crotchet = 88. 2'45". V/m, P/m. MS in F major.

For: Sop, Ten; Mezzo, Bar; *C-Ten*.
Subject: The river will flow for ever to the sea, but our lives are doomed to wither.
Voice: Steps, small skips, 6th leap and drop; chromatic at times; sustained e" at end; varied rhythms, but mostly quavers.
Piano: Mixture of chords, broken chords, and alternate note figures; much two against three in quavers; chromatic.

Comment: Handicapped by poor words and lack of variety in a rather long song.

(2) **The fuchsia tree**. O' what if the fowler my blackbird has taken? (Old Manx ballad, perhaps by Charles Dalmon.) Comp. 1923. Pub. W.R., 1923. *High*, Medium, *Low*.

        B minor, b°-f″#, [f′#-e″]; *C# minor, A minor*. 6/8, Andante poco con moto, dotted crotchet = 46. 1′30″. V/me, P/e.

For: *Sop, Ten*; Mezzo, Bar; *C-Ten*.
Subject: I must weep for my loss.
Voice: Steps, 3rds, 6th leap; almost continuous quavers; melisma on *ah* at end.
Piano: Chordal, broken for a few bars; fairly rich texture.
Comment: A folksong melody of great beauty, sensitively harmonised.

(3) **An old carol**. I sing of a maiden that is matchless. (Anon, fifteenth century; BL MS Sloane 2593; *EEL*, *EV*, Davies.) Comp. 1923. Pub. W.R., 1924. *High*, Low.

        D major, c′-d″, [e′-b′]; *Gb major*. 2/4, Andante moderato, crotchet = 60. 2′. V/me, P/me.

For: *Sop, Ten*; Mezzo, Bar; Cont, C-Ten, Bass.
Subject: A carol in praise of Mary: 'Well may such a lady Goddes mother be.'
Voice: Steps, a few simple skips; some accidentals; simple rhythms.
Piano: Gently moving chords, somewhat chromatic.
Comment: Slightly modal in flavour, despite the chromatic colouring, this is hauntingly beautiful. The words have been slightly modernised, notably in the first stanza: *matchless* = *makeless* (without a mate, *and* matchless); *choose* = *ches*. See *EEL*, *EV* or Davies, the last two providing some interesting notes on the poem's symbolism.

(4) **Arab love song**. My faint spirit was sitting in the light of thy looks, my love. (Percy Bysshe Shelley, *Posthumous Poems*, 1824 [1821].) Comp. 1927. Pub. W.R., 1927. *High*, Medium, *Low*.

        C minor, f′-f″, [g′-e″b]; *D minor, B minor*. 4/4,3/2, Allegro non troppo, ma sempre con moto, crotchet = 132. 1′30″. V/m, P/md.

For: *Sop*; Mezzo.
Subject: Although you have ridden far from me, my heart is still with you and may comfort you.
Voice: Steps and 3rds; great rhythmic variety, with several crotchet triplets; forte climax on minim g″.
Piano: Continuous quaver triplet broken chords between the

hands, with many floating melodic lines embedded in them; many accidentals; as always it is well written for the keyboard, but needs a good pianist to bring it off.

Comment: An original and exciting song.

(5) **Music, when soft voices die**. (Percy Bysshe Shelley, *Posthumous Poems*, 1824 [1821].) Comp. 1926. Pub. W.R., 1927. *High*, Medium, *Low*.

A♭ major, f'-f", [g'-d"♭]; *B♭ major, G♭ major*. 4/4, Un poco andante, crotchet = 63. 1'45". V/me, P/me.

For: *Sop, Ten*; Mezzo, Bar, *C-Ten*.
Subject: 'And so thy thoughts, when thou art gone, Love itself shall slumber on.'
Voice: Steps, a few simple skips; sustained quiet f" near end; mostly crotchets, but some interesting rhythmic variety.
Piano: Broken chords, quavers between the hands, with some counter-melodies and a few richer-textured bars.
Comment: A simple setting, matching the poem well.

(6) **In the bud of the morning-O**. In the scented bud of the morning-O. (James Stephens, 'The Daisies', *Songs from the Clay*, 1915.) Comp. 1926. Pub. W.R., 1926. *High*, Low.

D major, d'-e", [f'#-d"]; *F major*. 4/4, Poco allegro grazioso, crotchet = 126. 1'15". V/me, P/me.

For: *Sop, Ten*; Mezzo, Bar; C-Ten.
Subject: My love and I walked happily together.
Voice: Steps, simple skips, 8ve drop; sustained e" mf; simple rhythms.
Piano: Broken chords between the hands, with decorations.
Comment: Attractive, though not as memorable as Samuel Barber's setting. In St. 3 ladies should change *she* to *he*.

19 TWO SONGS TO POEMS BY R.L. STEVENSON. Op 26. Published separately in various keys. Comp. 1922. Pub. Elkin, 1922.

(1) **In the highlands,** in the country places. (*Songs of Travel*, 1895.)

E♭ major, b°♭-e"♭, [d'-d"]; *G♭ major*. 4/4, Moderato, crotchet = 80. 2'45". V/m, P/m.

For: *Sop, Ten*; Mezzo, Bar; C-Ten.
Subject: O to be in the quiet hills, at night, and dream of life, and death.
Voice: Steps, small skips; some slightly unusual modulations; longish phrase, middle voice, at end of second stanza; rhythms mostly simple, though varied.

Piano: Decorated chordal writing, becoming fairly elaborate, with two against three and many accidentals in second stanza.

Comment: The harmonically adventurous (for Quilter) second stanza goes well with the description of the enchantments of night in the hills, and the song has much warmth of feeling. *Her*, three bars from the end of verse 1, is in italics in the original poem, being presumably the spirit of the hills.

(2) Over the land is April. (*New Poems*, 1918.)

C major, d'-e″, [e'-d″]; *D major, Bb major.* 4/4, Allegro appassionato, minim = 76. 2'. V/m, P/md.

For: *Sop, Ten*; Mezzo, Bar; C-Ten.

Subject: It is spring – Love, do you hear me sing? It is winter, I will sing of spring.

Voice: Repeated notes, small skips; some accidentals; long final phrase with two and a half bars of forte e″.

Piano: Toccata style with some hand crossing, though the middle section is simpler.

Comment: A weak attempt at a brilliant song, from an incomplete poem of Stevenson's, published after his death with no attempt at editing; the third stanza is a repeat of the first as far as 'Over the high brown mountain', after which four lines are printed in *New Poems* which are clearly alternative last lines, though given as if all were part of the poem: 'I sound the song of spring / I throw the flower of spring / Do you hear the song of spring? / Hear you the song of spring?' Quilter has taken this confusion as licence to invent his own ending.

20 FIVE JACOBEAN LYRICS. Op 28. Comp. 1925. Pub. Boosey, 1926. **20** (1) composed and published separately in 1923. A group, not a cycle, though the first and last songs happen to be in the same key. *High*, Medium, *Low*.

(1) The jealous lover. My dear mistress has a heart. (John Wilmot, Earl of Rochester; *Poems on Several Occasions*, 1680.)

D major, d'-f″#, [f′#-d″]; *F major, C major.* 3/4, Moderato con moto, crotchet = 72. 2'. V/me, P/m.

For: *Ten*; Bar; *C-Ten.*

Subject: My mistress has such charm as all must love her, therefore I dare not let her out of my sight for a day.

Voice: Steps, small skips; simple modulation; sustained f″# forte near end; fairly simple rhythms.

Piano: Chordal with decoration; rich texture, much two against three; crossed hands and rapid arpeggios at climax.

Comment: Similar tune to 'Who is Sylvia', **22** (1), but a much more impassioned accompaniment; very enjoyable. St. 3, line 4: *warm = arm*, in poem.

(2) **Why so pale and wan**, fond lover? (Sir John Suckling, *Aglaura*, 1646, Act IV, Scene ii].

C♯ minor, e'-e", [d'-e"]; *D minor, B minor.* 4/4, Allegro non troppo, ma con spirito, crotchet = 120. 1'. V/me, P/m.

For: *[Sop], Ten*; [Mezzo], Bar; C-Ten; *[Cont], Bass.*

Subject: Will looking ill or keeping silent win your love? No; if she will not love of her own accord 'the devil take her'!

Voice: Steps, small skips; mostly quavers; third stanza broken up by many rests, crotchet triplets, and a snappy finish.

Piano: Strongly rhythmic broken chords; fairly chromatic; not always as expected in rhythm or notes.

Comment: Two rather romantic verses, followed by a dramatic one; this would make a good finisher.

(3) **I dare not ask a kiss**. (Robert Herrick, 'To Electra', *Hesperides*, 1648.)

D♭ major, e'♭-e"♭, [e'♭-d"♭]; *E♭ major, C major.* 2/2, Andantino quasi allegretto, minim = 56. 1'. V/me, P/me.

For: *[Sop], Ten*; [Mezzo], C-Ten, Bar; *[Cont], Bass.*

Subject: I dare not ask a kiss or smile; just let me kiss the air that has touched you.

Voice: Steps, simple skips; mostly simple rhythms, but some crotchet triplets; last phrase starts on f"♯, piano.

Piano: Chordal, with gentle arpeggios.

Comment: Pleasant, but somewhat sentimental.

(4) **To Althea from prison**. When love with unconfined wings. (Richard Lovelace, *Lucasta*, 1649 [written in prison, 1642].)

E♭ major, d'♭-e"♭, [e'♭-d"]; *F major, D major.* 3/4, Allegro moderato con moto, crotchet = 104. 2'. V/me, P/m.

For: *Ten*; Bar; *C-Ten, Bass.*

Subject: Prison is no prison when Althea brings her love and we can drink wine together.

Voice: Steps, simple skips; some modulation; straightforward rhythm.

Piano: Fairly elaborate broken chords; some two against three; fairly chromatic; some leaping chords.

Comment: No sign of prison in this rather routine love-song. Quilter omits the third stanza, in praise of King Charles I: 'When, (like committed Linnets) I / With shriller throat shall sing / The sweetness, mercy, majesty, / And glories of my King; / When I shall voice aloud how good / He is, how great shall

be; / Inlarged winds that curl the flood / Know no such liberty.'
St. 1, line 7: *birds* = *Gods*, in *Lucasta* and one MS, though
most have changed it to *birds*. Clayton gives *Gods*, perhaps
being painted *putti* = Cupids, so popular at this time.

(5) The constant lover. Out upon it, I have loved three whole days
together. (Sir John Suckling, *The Last Remains*, 1659.)

> D major, d'-f ″#, [f' #-d″]; *E major, C major*. 4/4, Allegretto con
> spirito, crotchet = 126. 1'30″. V/me, P/m.

For: *Ten*; Bar; *C-Ten*.

Subject: I have loved for three whole days – what constancy! And I
would not have done that for anyone else.

Voice: Mostly by step, some simple skips; 6th drop; slight
modulation, continuous quaver rhythm; one f ″#, forte, in
final phrase.

Piano: Continuous triplet quaver broken chords, with quaver
melodies above or within; fairly chromatic.

Comment: Quilter repeats the first two of Suckling's four stanzas at the
end, thus removing the point of the verse by treating the vow
as sincere rather than cynical. Quilter gives the poem as
printed in Thompson's edition of 1910, in Grierson's *Metaphysical Lyrics*, 1921, and in *OB*; *NOB* has the following
variants: St. 3, lines 1-2: *But a pox upon't, no praise / There is
due at all to me*; St. 4, line 2: *And that very very face*, following
Clayton in *Cavalier Poets*.

21 I arise from dreams of thee, Op 29. (Percy Bysshe Shelley, 'The Indian
Serenade', *Posthumous Poems*, 1824 [1819].) Composed, for tenor and
orchestra, for the 1929 Harrogate Festival. Pub. Boosey, 1931. High,
Low.

> E♭ minor, g'♭-g″, b'♭-g″♭]; *C minor*. 3/4, Andante con moto,
> crotchet = 58. 4'. V/m, P/md.

For: [Sop], Ten; *[Mezzo], Bar*; *C-Ten*.

Subject: Rising from dreams I have come to your window, I faint with
love and you must revive me.

Voice: Steps, skips, both augmented and diminished in places;
many modulations; varied rhythms, though fairly simple.

Piano: Shows signs of its origins in what must be a fairly elaborate
orchestral score, but being transcribed by an excellent pianist
the difficulties are not so much a matter of technique as of
balancing the different voices; it could be very effective with
an imaginative accompanist.

Comment: Well worth singing; it has atmosphere and variety, and
should prove rewarding for performers and audience alike.

22 FOUR SHAKESPEARE SONGS. Op 30. Comp. 1933. Pub. Boosey, 1933. 22 (1) comp. 1926, pub. Boosey 1927. High and Low keys.

(1) **Who is Sylvia?** What is she? (*Two Gentlemen of Verona*, 1594, Act IV, Scene ii.)

	D major, f'#-d''; F major. 3/4, Moderato un poco con moto, crotchet = 72. 2'. V/me, P/me.
For:	[Sop], Ten; [Mezzo], Bar; C-Ten.
Subject:	Is Sylvia as wonderful as they say? Yes. Then praise her.
Voice:	Steps, 4ths, broken chords; no accidentals; simple rhythms.
Piano:	Chordal with decorations; some arpeggios; few accidentals.
Comment:	Three very similar stanzas; it has charm, but little excitement. Note, in relation to Trevor Hold's invaluable book *The Walled-in Garden*, page 37: the low key copy of the set does not repeat the word 'garlands', maybe the 1927 separate copy does, it is clearly unnecessary. Low key volume, page 5, bar 1, beat 1, RH: d'', delete dot.

(2) **When daffodils begin to peer.** (*The Winter's Tale*, 1611, Act IV, Scene iii.)

	Ab major, e'b-e''b, [f'-c'']; C major. 2/4, Allegretto grazioso, crotchet = 96. 1'. V/me, P/me.
For:	Ten; Bar; C-Ten.
Subject:	Spring is the time for me, with girls and beer to be had.
Voice:	Steps, skips, broken chords; sustained e''b at end; simple bouncy rhythms.
Piano:	Rhythmic figures, sometimes a little awkwardly arranged.
Comment:	A reasonably cheerful spring song, though with no suggestion of Autolycus, the 'snapper-up of unconsidered trifles', about it. Page 7, bar 6: peer = appear; bar 7: doxy = female beggar or prostitute; bars 12/13: replaces winter's pallor, or, reigns in winter's domain. Page 8, bar 5: pugging = ?pilfering – meaning uncertain, *OED*, but see Ireland 24 (2). Page 9, bar 5: aunts = prostitutes; bar 7: tumbling = making love. (Did Quilter actually know what these words meant?) The play has three more stanzas, interspersed with dialogue. Low key volume, page 7, bar 12: last quaver d' should have natural.

(3) **How should I your true love know?** (*Hamlet*, 1602, Act IV, Scene v.)

	G minor, d'-d'', [d'-c'']; B minor. 2/4, Andante moderato, quaver = 76. 1'45''. V/me, P/me.
For:	Sop, Ten; Mezzo, Bar; Cont, C-Ten, Bass.
Subject:	Your true love is dead, lady.
Voice:	Steps, small skips, broken chords; slightly modal; simple rhythms.

Piano: Gently moving harmony, mostly in four parts to start with; some widely spread broken chords in last verse; fairly chromatic.

Comment: Simple and very moving. Page 10, bar 9: hats bearing cockle-shells were worn by pilgrims to the shrine of St James of Compostela. Page 11, bar 2: shoon = shoes. Low key volume, page 11, bar 7, beat 1: natural to b° not g°.

(4) **Sigh no more, ladies**, sigh no more. (*Much Ado About Nothing*, 1598-99, Act II, Scene iii.)

                C major, c'-d", [e'-c"]; E♭ major. 4/4, Allegretto, minim = 72. 1'30". V/me, P/m.

For: Sop, Ten; Mezzo, Bar; Cont, C-Ten, Bass.

Subject: Do not sigh, ladies; men can't be trusted, so let them go, and be happy.

Voice: Steps, skips, sequences; some quaver pairs; fairly simple rhythms.

Piano: Chordal, often skipping, with decorations.

Comment: Many variations of tempo in this otherwise straightforward song. Page 15, bar 6: dumps = sad songs, usually of love.

23 TWO SHAKESPEARE SONGS. Op 32. Comp. 1938. Pub. Boosey, 1939, issued separately. *High*, Low. The published copies do not indicate original key, but Quilter's MS of **23 (2)** is in C major/minor.

(1) **Orpheus with his lute** made trees. (*Henry VIII*, 1613, Act III, Scene i.)

                C major, b°-e", [e'-d"]; *Eb major*. 6/8, Allegretto quasi andantino, dotted crotchet = 42. 2'. V/me, P/me.

For: *Sop, Ten*; Mezzo, Bar; C-Ten.

Subject: All nature responded to the music of Orpheus.

Voice: Skips, steps, 7th drop; slight modulation; simple rhythms.

Piano: Gently flowing harmonies, with many chords broken between the hands.

Comment: A pleasant and undemanding song, though not nearly as interesting as those written 30 years earlier. The play was written in collaboration with John Fletcher.

(2) **When icicles hang by the wall**. (*Love's Labours Lost*, 1595, Act V, Scene ii.)

                C major/minor, f'-f "(e"b), [f'-c"]; *Eb major/minor*. 2/4, Allegro con spirito e ben marcato, crotchet = 84. 1'45". V/me, P/m.

For: *Sop, Ten*; Mezzo, Bar.

Subject: A description of life in winter.

Voice: Skips, steps, repeated notes; melisma at end of each verse; fairly simple rhythms.

Piano: Rhythmic chords, decorated, leaping at times; much 8ve work.

Comment: Would do well in a musical comedy by Lionel Monckton! Page 4, bar 4: keel = stir and skim, to prevent boiling over. Page 5, bar 5: saw = moral maxim; bar 12: crabs = crab-apples.

PETER WARLOCK
1894-1930

Warlock's songs are set out in order of composition, as given in Copley. The **Tonality** is the original if in print; other published keys are given in italics. If the original key is known but not in print the printed key is used followed by a note as to the original. In Colls 8-11 'transposed' indicates new transpositions specially provided for this edition. Collections are referred to as follows:

Coll 1 = *A Book of Songs*, OUP, 1931.
Coll 2 = *A Second Book of Songs*, OUP, 1967.
Coll 3 = *13 Songs for High Voice*, Galliard, 1970.
Coll 4 = *Songs*, B & H, 1967.
Coll 5 = *A Heritage of English Song*, vol. 2, B & H, 1977.
Coll 6 = *Eight Songs*, Thames, 1972.
Coll 7 = *Sociable Songs*, vol. 1, Thames.
Coll 8 = *Songs of Peter Warlock*, vol. 1, Thames, 1982.
Coll 9 = *Songs of Peter Warlock*, vol. 2, Thames, 1983.
Coll 10 = *Songs of Peter Warlock*, vol. 3, Thames, 1984.
Coll 11 = *Songs of Peter Warlock*, vol. 4, Thames, 1986.

The Peter Warlock Society is preparing more volumes in the series published by Thames. Much out of print material is obtainable from the Society, on application to the secretary, Malcolm Rudland, 17 Gledhow Gardens, London SW5 0AY, telephone 01-373-9292.

PETER WARLOCK

1 **The wind from the west**. Blow high, blow low, O wind from the West. (Ella Young, *Poems*, 1906.) Comp. 1911. Pub. Thames, 1972. [Colls 6, 8]. E*b* major. d'-f ", [g'-e"*b*]. 9/8,12/8,6/8, etc, Fairly fast. 1'45". V/me, P/md

For: Mezzo, Bar.
Subject: Asking the wind for news of a country left long ago.
Voice: Steps, simple skips, repeated notes; some chromatics; simple rhythms.
Piano: Thick moving chords; much 8ve displacement, and some hand crossings in the more decorative middle section.
Comment: Much influenced by Delius and Quilter, these first three songs are the earliest of Warlock's output to survive. Coll 6, page 12, bar 1, beat 9, RH: quaver rest needed. Coll 8, page 9, bar 5, beat 7, LH: low E*b* needs quaver tail.

2 **A lake and a fairy boat**. (Thomas Hood, 'For Music', *The Plea of the Midsummer Fairies and Other Poems*, 1827.) Comp. 1911. Pub. Thames, 1972. [Colls 6, 8].
No key sig. d'-g"*b*, [f'-f "]. 6/8, Fast: very soft and light; the phrases well marked. 1'. V/m, P/m.
For: Bar.
Subject: You should wear jewels and sail in a fairy boat, but 'wishing has lost its pow'r'.
Voice: Steps, skips; 9th and 8ve drops, 6th drop and leap; several augmented and diminished intervals; rhythms straightforward, with two hemiolas.
Piano: Decorated chordal; chromatic; many skips.
Comment: The notation of bars 14 and 15 indicates some very awkward hand crossings, which can be avoided by taking the triads in LH. Coll 6, page 5, bar 4, beat 4, RH: c'# needs dot; page 6, bar 3, beat 1, RH: c" needs dot. Coll 8, page 10, bar 1, beat 6, voice: g' needs a natural.

3 **Music, when soft voices die**. (Percy Bysshe Shelley, *Posthumous Poems*, 1824 [1821].) Comp. 1911. Pub. Thames, 1972. [Colls 6, 8, transposed down a minor third.]

F major. d'-f ", [f'-d"]. Original key Ab major. 3/4. Fairly slowly, with expression. 1'30". V/me, P/me.

For: *Mezzo, Bar*. [Sop, Ten].
Subject: Beauty stays in the memory.
Voice: Steps, small skips; somewhat chromatic; varied but fairly simple rhythms.
Piano: Chordal, with decoration; occasional rhythmic complications.
Comment: Two rather different versions survive in MS; one, dated 21 September 1911, is printed as 3A in Coll 8; the other, printed in both volumes, as given here, was probably written after October 1911, and is paired with 2 as 'Two Songs'. In both cases the key is Ab major. Coll 6, page 8, bar 7, beat 1, RH: b' needs b. Coll 8, page 15, bar 1, beat 1, LH: first note semiquaver, not quaver.

4 **The everlasting voices**. O sweet everlasting voices, be still. (W.B. Yeats, *The Wind Among the Reeds*, 1899.) Comp. Winter 1915. Pub. Thames, 1976. [Coll 8].

Bb minor. e'b-a"b(g"b), [f'-f "]. 3/8, Quietly, not too fast. 1'30". V/m, P/m.

For: Sop, Ten.
Subject: Call us no more, for we are old.
Voice: Mostly steps and thirds; one quick 8ve leap, and some chromatics; several f "s; rhythms simple.
Piano: Sliding chords, very chromatic in places; more difficult to read than to play.
Comment: The MS has the last four bars crossed out, and 'rewrite the end' added. The Peter Warlock Society organised a competition in 1976 for a new ending. Anthony Ingle's winning entry is given as an alternative in both published copies. The single copy of 1976 has a long note by Fred Tomlinson on Warlock's relationship with W.B. Yeats; this has not been included in Coll 8. Warlock re-used the introduction for **32**. Single copy, bar 13, beat 1: a° needs a natural. Tomlinson gives f " as alternative top note, in error.

5 **The cloths of heaven**. Had I the heaven's embroidered cloths. (W.B. Yeats, *The Wind Among the Reeds*, 1899.) Comp. March, 1916, revised May, 1919. Pub. Thames, 1982. [Coll 8].

No key sig. c'-g", [g'-f "]. No time sig. or tempo mark. 1'30". V/m, P/m.

For: Sop; Ten.
Subject: Being poor, I can but offer you my dreams.
Voice: Mostly by step, some skips; two 6th drops; ends with climb from c' to held e"; simple speech rhythms.

Piano: Sliding chords over pedal notes; slightly contrapuntal; some
                long-held wide-spread arpeggiated chords and big stretches.
Comment: This formed part of the original version of *The Curlew* song
                cycle, but was never published owing to copyright
                difficulties over the words. The MS is in BL (Add. 52912).
                The texture of the accompaniment betrays its instrumental
                origin. The music was reworked for 53 (2).

6 **The lover mourns for the loss of love**. Pale brows, still hands and dim
  hair. (W.B. Yeats, *The Wind Among the Reeds*, 1899.) Comp. ?1916,
  revised 1920. Pub. S & B, 1924, as part of *The Curlew*. [Coll 8].
                No key sig. d'-e"b, [f'#-c"#]. 12/8, Very quietly, slow and
                very still. 1'30". V/me, P/me.
For: Bar, C-Ten.
Subject: My new love saw you in my heart, and went away.
Voice: Almost a monotone; what little movement there is is
                chromatic.
Piano: Slowly moving chromatic harmonies; mostly in four parts,
                with some big stretches.
Comment: Beautiful, but despairing. It really needs the instrumental
                accompaniment of *The Curlew*, but with a sensitive pianist
                it can be very moving.

7 **SAUDADES**. Pub. Chester, 1923. [Coll 8]. Three songs published as a
  group under this title, which is taken from an essay on poetry by L.
  Cranmer Byng: '...that haunting sense of sadness and regret for days
  gone by which the Portuguese call *Saudades* – a word which has no
  equivalent in the English Language.' As a group they may be found
  rather too successful in conveying this mood! They are all much
  influenced by Bernard van Dieren. Copley notes many differences in
  the MS copy (BL Add. 52906), compared with the first edition. It is a
  pity that Thames, having decided to print the songs twice, once in order
  of composition and again as they appear in Saudades, should have
  ignored the MS versions and used the first edition in both cases.
For: Mezzo; Bar.

(1) **Along the stream**. The rustling nightfall strews my gown with roses.
    (Trans. from the Chinese of Li-Po by L. Cranmer Byng, *A Feast of
    Lanterns*, 1916.) Comp. December 1917.
                No key sig. e'-f"#, [g'-e"]. No time sig., Andante, quaver =
                about 96. 2'30". V/m, P/m.
Subject: Changing moods, walking by a stream at night.

Voice: Steps, repeated notes, skips; two 6th leaps; chromatic; rhythm governed entirely by the words.

Piano: Chordal and contrapuntal alternating; highly chromatic; free rhythm but not over complex.

Comment: Atmospheric, if rather overcomplicated harmonically. The MS has many variants, including one totally different vocal phrase and an extra word in the poem. First page, line 2, note 2, RH: d′ should have a #.

(2) Take, O take those lips away. (William Shakespeare, *Measure for Measure*, 1604, Act IV, Scene i.) Comp. 1916.

F minor. c′-f ″, [c′-c″]. 3/4, Andante con moto, crotchet = 72. 1′30″. V/me, P/m.

Subject: Go, but give me back my kisses.

Voice: Steps and thirds; slightly chromatic; rhythm mostly simple; the f ″ lasts a bar.

Piano: Chordal, with throbbing repetitions below the melodic line; some bursts of arpeggio decoration.

Comment: The music seems rather congested; Warlock's later setting, 11, is much more successful. Some variants in MS, including crotchet = 100! See WSNL 40.

(3) Heraclitus. They told me, Heraclitus, they told me you were dead. (Trans. from the Greek of Callimachus by William Johnson Cory, *Ionica*, 1858.) Comp. 30 September 1917.

No key sig. c′-f ″, [e′-c″]. No time sig., Slow, tempo very free – the voice murmuring to itself, quaver = about 80. 2′45″. V/m, P/m.

Subject: Mourning the loss of a friend.

Voice: Steps, thirds; two 6th leaps; chromatic; varied speech rhythms.

Piano: Contrapuntal, mostly slow-moving in four parts, but some elaboration at times.

Comment: Composed on hearing of the death of a school friend, Hugh Sidgwick, who knew the poem, this is the best of the three songs. Some variants in MS, and some corrections in Warlock's copy of the printed version, all given in Copley. In the latter the quotation marks around the piano interlude on the second line of the second page are deleted, which suggests the phrase has a purely personal significance. No one has yet offered to identify it. Chester and Coll 8, 1st page, line 2, tenor note 8: the a° needs a natural. Chester: *Heracleitus* for *Heraclitus*; 2nd page, line 3, alto note 1: c′ needs a natural.

8 **The water lily.** The lily floated white and red. (Robert Nichols, *Ardours and Endurances*, 1917 [1913].) Comp. Summer 1917. Pub. Thames, 1972. [Colls 6, 8, transposed down a tone].

No key sig. d'-g", [e'-d"]. Original a tone higher. 3/4, Very slow; veiled, as though in a dream. 2'. V/m, P/m.

For: Sop, Ten; *Mezzo, Bar.*
Subject: 'Beauty is its own reward'.
Voice: Steps, small skips; 6th drop; chromatic; one high phrase; some rhythmic complications.
Piano: Chordal, with decorations; chromatic.
Comment: Awkward vocal range, mostly low with one high phrase. It would perhaps have been better to print the song in the original key, for soprano or tenor, or a third down, for mezzo or baritone. Warlock thought of including this song in *Saudades*, but decided against it. Coll 6, page 15, bar 1, beats 2-3, RH: b° flats should be tied. Coll 8, page 24, bar 1, beats 2-3, RH: c' sharp should be tied to d'b; page 25, bar 4, beat 1, RH: two quavers, not quaver semiquaver; bar 8, beat 1, LH: fingering given in Coll 6 – 2 & 5.

9 **I asked a thief to steal me a peach.** (William Blake, MS notebook, 1793-1811, fair copy 1796, first published 1905.) Comp. 31 December, 1917. Pub. Thames, 1972. [Colls 6, 8].

Eb major. c'-f ", [e'b-e"b]. 6/8, Capriccioso e rubato. 45". V/m, P/m.

For: Bar.
Subject: Angels succeed where men fail.
Voice: Steps, repeated notes; 6th drop, two 8ve drops; slightly chromatic; rhythm straightforward, with many pauses.
Piano: Decorated chordal; some wide skips; ends with prestissimo arpeggio.
Comment: The first Warlock song which can be immediately recognised as such. A second, undated version exists, which is given in Coll 8 as 11A; there is disagreement as to which came first. Tomlinson gives F major as an alternative key. Last bar: the arpeggio has one beam in Coll 8 and three in Coll 6.

10 **To the memory of a great singer.** Bright is the ring of words. (Robert Louis Stevenson, *Songs of Travel*, 1895.) Comp. June 1918, revised 1922. Pub. Augener, 1923. [Coll 3; Coll 8, transposed down a tone].

Ab major. d'b-g", [f'-f "]. *Gb major.* 3/4. Andante. 1'40". V/m, P/m.

For: Sop, Ten; *Mezzo, Bar, C-Ten.*
Subject: Good songs will live after poet and composer are dead.
Voice: Steps, broken chords; a few accidentals; mostly crotchets

and quavers, with some triplets; last phrase climbs from f'
to g"b and back in three bars; fairly long legato phrases.

Piano: Fairly simple chordal with decorations, but a few complex
chromatic passages.

Comment: Has charm, though the chromatics are not always
convincing. The 1918 version was in A major; it is printed in
Coll 9, in Gb major, with the title: 'Bright is the ring of
words'. All versions, bar 9: *are they = they are* in Stevenson's
original poem. Tomlinson suggests that this is a *Little
Peterism*, see **27**.

11 Take, O take those lips away. (William Shakespeare, *Measure for
Measure*, 1604, Act IV, Scene i.) Comp. September 1918. Pub. W.R.,
1919. *High* [Colls 4, 5] and Low [Coll 9].

E minor. b°-f"#, [e'-d"]. *F# minor.* 12/8,6/8,9/8,etc. Lento,
con tristezza. 1'30". V/m, P/m.

For: *Sop, Ten*; Mezzo, Bar.

Subject: Go, but give me back my kisses.

Voice: Mostly by step; some 4ths and 5ths; one phrase starts down
from f"#; rhythms straightforward.

Piano: Chordal, sometimes widespread, needing careful use of
pedal.

Comment: A wonderful song, which might be even better in Warlock's
1927 string quartet version (BL Add. MS 52909), on hire
from Boosey, in E minor. Coll 9 gives 'not spread' three bars
from the end; this does not appear in the F# minor versions,
perhaps because in that key it would be impossible for most
pianists.

12 As ever I saw. She is gentle and also wise. (Anon, Harleian MS 7578;
EEL.) Comp. 1918. Pub. W.R., 1919. High and *Low* [Colls 4, 9].

Db major. d'b-g"b, [f'-d"b]. Eb major. 4/4. Allegro, minim =
92. 1'15". V/me, P/m.

For: Ten; *Bar*.

Subject: I shall have the best and fairest girl I have ever seen.

Voice: Steps, simple skips; few accidentals; strong climax at end
includes only g"b and f" in whole song.

Piano: Mostly in four parts; rhythmic, with hints of counterpoint;
thicker chords and a leap in last verse; much important
contrast of legato and staccato.

Comment: Warlock's first great success, and deservedly so. *EEL* has an
introductory burden omitted here, but included in Warlock's
1919 setting of the same poem for high voice and string
quartet, 'My lady is a pretty one' (BL Add. MS 52909; pub.
OUP, 1956, in facsimile; parts obtainable from the Warlock

Society). There is also a string quartet version of this setting, in 6/8, with various modifications, dated 6.11.1930 (BL Add. 52909), obtainable from the Warlock Society, in C major and E*b* major, entitled 'The Fairest May'. Bar 18: conceit = opinion. Bar 23: wonderly wrought = worked wonders. Bars 24-25: Christ, by his death on the Cross bought forgiveness for the sins of all mankind. Bar 37: may = maiden. Coll 9: page 13, bar 9, beat 2, voice: c″ needs a flat.

13 My gostly fader, I me confesse. (Charles d'Orleans? BL Harleian MS 682; *EEL, EV*, Davies.) Comp. 1918. Pub. W.R., 1919. High [Colls 4, 9] and *Low*.

G major. e′*b*-f ″#, [f′ #-d″]. *E major*. 4/4,2/4,3/2, etc, Moderato – rubato (declaim confidentially). 1′45″. V/me, P/me.

For:	Sop, Ten; Mezzo, Bar; *Cont, C-Ten, Bass.*
Subject:	See below.
Voice:	In the style of plainchant; many repeated notes, with occasional melodic phrases, one of which starts down from the only f ″#. Free speech rhythm.
Piano:	Sustained chords, changing part by part, chromatically.
Comment:	If the fifteenth-century language can be accepted this is a gift for the imaginative singer. The poem may be paraphrased as follows: 'Holy father, I make my confession, first to God and then to you. At a window – you know how – I stole a sweet kiss; it was done without premeditation, still, it is done and cannot be undone. But I will give it back, if I can. That I promise to God, otherwise I ask forgiveness'. John Barrow, in *EV*, reads the last line as – 'And for the rest, I ask pardon'. Lack of premeditation lessens sin, and a promise of restoration is necessary for forgiveness for theft. Though Tomlinson comments that *EEL* 'unaccountably changes some of the the spelling' both Davies and *EV* make similar changes in the interest of easier reading. Warlock also wrote a string quartet version in 1918; when this was revised in 1927 he modified the barring and some details of rhythm in the voice part (BL Add. MS 52909). On hire from Boosey, in G major. The changes are given in Copley.

14 The bayly berith the bell away. The maidens came when I was in my mother's bow'r. (Anon; BL Harleian MS 7578; *EEL*.) Comp. 1918. Pub. W.R., 1919. *High*, and Low [Coll 4; Coll 9, transposed up a tone].

E*b* major. g°-e″*b*, [c′-c″]. *G major, F major*. 3/8, Lento quasi andantino, dotted crotchet = 50. 2′15″. V/m, P/me.

For:	*Sop, Ten*; *Mezzo, Bar*; Cont, C-Ten, Bass.
Subject:	See below.

Voice: Steps, simple skips; bottom note c′ save for one unimportant g°; chromatic, but easier than it looks; rhythm quite simple.

Piano: Chordal, with moving parts; mostly thin texture; chromatic.

Comment: A great song, in spite of Warlock's confession that 'at the time of making the setting he had not the faintest idea of what it was all about. He was first attracted by the sheer "witchery of the sound of the words"' (Copley). Gordon Bottomley wrote to Arnold Dowbiggin (both friends of Warlock's) in 1945: ' "The Bailey is the name of the principal thoroughfare in Durham Cathedral precincts. Fairly recently there has been discovered a MS medieval poem about the beauties of Durham and what a fine city it was; and there embedded in the middle come the famous lines which were thought to be a separate poem, and which Warlock set! [*EEL* says – 'We have only printed a short extract from the poem, which is a long one'. This was in 1907!] Their effect in their place is that the Bailey is, of all the fine places in Durham, the very finest and takes the cake; that is the Bell!"' (Copley).

    This explanation may well seem unconvincing; where do maidens and young love fit in? If considered, as in *EEL*, as a separate item, another view is possible. Suppose the speaker to be a child about to be married. (As late as 1695 the Duke of Bedford, aged 14, was married to Elizabeth Howland, aged 13!) He, or she, has slept in his mother's room, where he was happy, for the last time. The maidservants come early to make preparations. Bayly is the normal sixteenth-century word for a steward, who would be in charge of such arrangements, and the rose and lily, red and silver, may refer to coats of arms. The robes are all laid out for the ceremony. The sun rises to herald the wedding day – how can he love anyone at his age? It must be admitted that 'berith the bell away' can mean 'takes the prize', and 'I lay' can mean 'I bet'! Could the child be expressing pride in the city he must now leave? See WSNL 21 and 22. A version for two voices and piano in E♭ major was published by W.R. in 1928. Coll 4, page 25, bar 9, beat 3, LH: e′ needs a natural.

15 There is a lady sweet and kind. (Anon, From Thomas Ford's *Musicke of Sundrie Kindes*, 1607.) Comp. 1918/19. Pub. W.R., 1920. *High* and Low [Colls 4, 9].

        B♭ major. b°♭-f″, [d′-d″]. *Db major*. 3/4. Quasi allegretto. 1′30″. V/me, P/me.

For: *Ten*; Bar, C-Ten.

Subject: Though I have only seen her passing by I still love her.

Voice: Steps, broken chords; 6th drop; held f " at the ends of three
              phrases; no accidentals; nearly all in quavers.
Piano: Four-part harmony, slightly contrapuntal; a few widely
              arpeggiated chords and big stretches.
Comment: Pleasant if unexciting. The three verses omitted in this
              setting, as in *OB*, are included in the 1928 version, 'Passing
              by', **72**. High key copy, page 3, bar 4, quaver 5, RH: a'*b* not g'.

16 Lullaby. Golden slumbers kiss your eyes. (Thomas Dekker, *The Pleas-
ant Comoedy of Patient Grissill*, 1603, Act IV, Scene ii.) Comp. ?1918.
Pub. W.R., 1919. *High* and Low [Colls 4, 8].
              D minor. a°(b°)-d", [d'-d"]. *F minor*. 4/4, Allegretto, crotchet =
              152. 1'. V/me, P/m.
For: *Mezzo, Bar*; Cont, C-Ten, Bass.
Subject: Go to sleep, and I will sing a lullaby.
Voice: Mostly by step; a few 4ths and repeated notes; simple
              rhythms with many paired quavers; few accidentals.
Piano: Chordal, with much incidental counterpoint, some of it hard
              to control accurately; slightly chromatic.
Comment: Beautifully Elizabethan in effect. Sung by Janicola, father to
              Grissill. Bar 9: wantons = roguish, playful children, or spoilt,
              pampered children (*OED*). A version for SSA and piano in F
              minor was published by W.R., 1928. A cradle song. See also
              22. Alternative bottom note not given in Tomlinson.

17 Whenas the rye reach to the chin. (George Peele, *The Old Wives Tale*,
1595, Act I, Scene i]. Comp. 1918. Pub. W.R., 1920. High [Colls 4, 5] and
Low [Coll 9].
              G major. c'(d')-f ", [e'-e"]. *F major*. 2/4, Quasi presto, crotchet
              = 108-112. 35". V/m, P/md.
For: Ten; *Bar, C-Ten*.
Subject: My true love says she cannot wait another year.
Voice: Steps, 3rd sequences, broken chords; 6th, 7th, and 8ve leaps;
              much sequential modulation; simple rhythms.
Piano: Quick changes of full chords; many 8ves and thick texture;
              much rapid modulation.
Comment: A lively song making a good finisher. However, Warlock
              wrote to Colin Taylor in 1922: ' "don't let that song [this one]
              get too popular, for I have done a much better setting of the
              same delightful poem – this ['Chopcherry', 1922, **35** (1)] is
              altogether fresher and nearer the spirit of the words; the
              other setting begins, as you justly remarked four years ago,
              like Percy Grainger, and becomes mechanical and unspon-
              taneous in its devious modulations" ' (Copley). Bar 5: chop-
              cherry = a game in which one tries to catch a suspended

cherry in one's teeth (*OED*). G major copies, bar 20, beat 1, both hands: f′ and f ″ natural, not f′ and f ″ flat.

18 Dedication. Doubt you to whom my Muse these notes intendeth. (Sir Philip Sidney, *Astrophel and Stella*, 1591. The First Song]. Comp. ?1919. Pub. W.R., 1919. [Coll 9, transposed down a minor third.)

        Bb major. b°b-f ″, [d′-d″]. D*b* major. 2/4, Allegro molto, con fuoco, crotchet = 100. 2′. V/m, P/d.

For:	*Bar*; Ten.
Subject:	You have all the virtues and deserve all praise.
Voice:	Broken chords, steps, skips; slightly chromatic; only one f ″, at end; rhythm straightforward.
Piano:	Continuous arpeggios and broken chords in both hands, mostly in semiquavers, but sometimes faster; some thick quaver chordal passages with many leaps; fairly chromatic.
Comment:	Given a singer with a powerful voice, and a first-class pianist this would be a most exciting song, and a great finisher. The original key lies a little low for many tenors. The earliest copies indicate an alternative for low voice, which was never printed (Tomlinson). Coll 9, page 32, bar 6, beat 2, voice: a′ needs a flat. The poem has nine stanzas, the last repeating the first, the others praising in turn eyes, lips, feet, breast, hand, hair and voice.

19 Love for love. My joy it is from her to hear. (Anon; BL Harleian MS 3362.) Comp. ?1918/19. Pub. W.R., 1920. High and *Low* [Coll 9].

        G major. d′-g″, [e′-e″]. *E major*. 4/4, Allegretto con moto, minim = 100-108. 1′15″. V/m, P/m.

For:	Ten; *Bar, C-Ten*.
Subject:	I love her and she loves me.
Voice:	Short scales, short sequences of 3rds and 4ths; almost continuous crotchets, each verse should be sung in one breath if possible.
Piano:	Contrapuntal, mostly in three parts; some three against two which may cause problems.
Comment:	Effective in the right hands. Dedicated to 'Puma', Minnie Lucy Channing, whom Warlock married in 1916. See WSNL 37 for further information. Bar 5: my mind = my desire. Bar 17: me convert = change my opinion. Bars 29-30: Christ wolt = would God. There are a few minor discrepancies in phrasing between the high and low key versions. W.R., low key copy, page 2, bar 10, and page 3, bar 6, beat 1, LH: minim, not semibreve. Coll 9, page 38, bar 1, beat 1, RH: a′ and b″ minims not dotted minims.

20 **My little sweet darling**, my comfort and joy. (Anon; BL Add. MS 17786-91; set by William Byrd in *Elizabethan Songs with String Quartet*, edited by Warlock, OUP, 1922, 'from a Christ Church MS'.). Comp. ?1918/19. Pub. W.R., 1920. High [Coll 5] and *Low* [Coll 9, transposed down a tone].G major. b°-g″, [d′-d″]. *F major, E major.* 6/8, Andantino – poco lento e rubato. 2′. V/m, P/m.

For: Sop; *Mezzo.*
Subject: Cradle song.
Voice: Steps, 3rds, broken chords; one unimportant b°; some modulation; simple rhythms, becoming continuous semiquavers.
Piano: Contrapuntal, mostly in four parts; chromatic; some big stretches.
Comment: Charming, if a little repetitive. Warlock arranged it for string quartet in 1927, in G major (obtainable from the Warlock Society), adding a two-bar introduction in place of a single note for the singer. Coll 9 prints this. *MB* XXII gives the original Consort song; it does not mention a Christ Church MS, but does list a version for voice and lute in Trinity College Dublin MS D. 3.30. *MB* considers the attribution to Byrd unjustified.

21 **Mourn no moe**. Weep no more, nor sigh, nor groan. (John Fletcher, *The Queen of Corinth*, 1617, Act III, Scene ii.) Comp. Spring 1919. Pub. W.R., 1920. High and *Low* [Coll 9].
              E♭ major. e′b-a″b, [g′-g″]. *C major. 6/8,* Andantino, ma con moto. 1′45″. V/me, P/me.
For: Sop, Ten; *Mezzo, C-Ten, Bar.*
Subject: Grief will not last.
Voice: Steps, simple skips; 6th leaps; some modulation; simple rhythms.
Piano: Decorated chordal, mostly in four parts; chromatic; a few big stretches.
Comment: Warlock arranged the C major version for string quartet (on hire from Boosey) in 1927, adding a two-bar introduction, and altering some of the vocal line. (BL Add. MS 60749). Both versions of the voice part and the introduction are given in Coll 9. A version for SSA and piano, also in C major, was issued by W.R. in 1928. Coll 9, page 45, bar 1, beat 1, voice: b′ should have a flat.

22 **Sweet content**. Art thou poor, yet hast thou golden slumbers? (Thomas Dekker, The Basket-Maker's Song from *The Pleasant Comoedy of Patient Grissill*, 1603, Act I, Scene ii.) Comp. ?1918-19. Pub. W.R.,

1920. [Colls 4, 5; Coll 9, transposed down a tone].

        G major. d'-g", [e'-e"]. *F major*. 2/4, Quasi presto. 1'35". V/m, P/md.

For: Sop, Ten; *Mezzo, C-Ten, Bar*.

Subject: Happiness lies in peace of mind, not wealth or position.

Voice: Steps, simple skips, 3rds sequences; ends with 6th skip to g", short; slightly chromatic; rhythms very varied but not actually complicated.

Piano: Contrapuntal, mostly in three parts; full of false relations; a tricky coda to each verse with wide leaps needs memorising; careful fingering required throughout.

Comment: A delightful song. W.R. and Colls 4, 5, bar 18, beat 1, RH: c' needs a sharp. Sung by Janicola, father to Grissel; he also sings **16**. St. 2, line 1: crisped = closely curled.

23 Romance. I will make you brooches. (Robert Louis Stevenson, *Songs of Travel*, 1895.) Comp. 1919. Pub. Curwen, 1921. [Coll 9].

        B*b* major. b°*b*-f ", [d'-d"] 4/8, Quietly, not too fast, quaver = 120. 1'15". V/me, P/m.

For: C-Ten, Bar.

Subject: Let us travel the world together, and I will make you happy.

Voice: Steps, 3rds, broken chords; few accidentals; regular dotted rhythms with a few Scotch snaps and a couple of triplets.

Piano: Alternating quaver chords over pedal notes; easy save for first bar of coda which has some thick stretchy chords awkward to manage in tempo.

Comment: A 'walking song', totally unlike the Vaughan Williams setting.

24 Balulalow. O my deir hert, young Jesus sweit. (Translation of St. 13/14 of Luther's 'Vom Himel hoch da kom ich her', *Geistliche Lieder*, 1535, by the brothers Wedderburn, *Ane Compendious Buik of Godly and Spirituall Sangis*, 1567.) Comp. 1919. Pub. OUP, 1923. [Coll 9].

        E*b* major. e'*b*-f ", [f'-e"*b*]. 3/4, Slow and very quiet throughout. 1'45". V/e, P/e.

For: Mezzo, C-Ten, Bar; *Cont, Bass*, see Comment.

Subject: Cradle song for the infant Jesus.

Voice: Almost entirely by step; slightly chromatic; very simple rhythm.

Piano: Gently moving chords over pedal notes.

Comment: A charming Christmas carol. The old Scots dialect is easy to follow (spreit = spirit; richt = right and proper; Balulalow = Lullaby). String quartet arrangement on hire from OUP. In 1923 Warlock arranged it for choir and orchestra, and a reduction of this version is given in *OCB*. In 1925 OUP issued C major versions for both piano and string quartet (Tomlinson). See long article in WSNL 37. Now printed in *Sing Solo Christmas*, ed. John Carol Case, OUP 1987. High voice in E♭ major, Low voice in C major.

25 **Play-acting**. There's a jolly lot of laughter. (Anon.) Comp. 1920. Pub. Thames, 1972. [Colls 6, 10, transposed up a tone].

E minor. b°-g″, [e′-e″]. Original a tone lower, no key signature. 4/4, With a brutal emphasis – rather slow. 1′10″. V/m, P/m.

For:	Bar.
Subject:	The play concerns failure in love, and is too much for me.
Voice:	Steps, 3rds, broken chords; some chromatics; speech rhythms.
Piano:	Heavy chords with many big stretches; very chromatic.
Comment:	An excellent small drama if the north country accent can be managed. The comment on range in Coll 10 makes no sense; the original key would suit most baritones better, and the given key is uncomfortably low for tenor. Coll 6 gives some instructions missing in Coll 10: bar 9 – Faster; bar 10 – (desperately); Bar 12 – Much slower; bar 13 – (almost spoken).

26 **TWO TRUE TOPER'S TUNES**, to Troll with Trulls and Trollops in a Tavern: No 1: Rum; No 2: Beer. Never actually issued under this title (in MS only).

(1) **Captain Stratton's Fancy**. Oh, some are fond of red wine. (John Masefield, *Ballads and Poems*, 1910.) Comp. 1921. Pub. Augener, 1922. *High*, Medium [Colls 3, 10], *Low*.

F major. c′-f ″, [f′-e″b]. *G major, D major*, 4/4. With great heartiness. 1′45″. V/me, P/md.

For:	*Ten*; Bar; *C-Ten, Bass*.
Subject:	Rum is better than all other drinks, and drinking is the finest occupation.
Voice:	Steps, repeated notes, 3rds; 8ve leap; five stanzas to same tune, with minor adjustments for words; dotted rhythms throughout.
Piano:	Thick chords with wide stretches; many 8ves; dotted march rhythms; if every note is played this must be considered P/md, but a little judicious pruning can eliminate the worst problems and bring it down to P/m.
Comment:	One of the best drinking songs ever. At one time hackneyed,

it has now gone out of fashion and should be restored. St. 5 and 7 are here omitted (Copley gives 4 and 7, in error); Ivor Gurney had set St. 1, 3 and 7, adding a chorus, in a version published in 1920 (see Gurney, **17**). A fine finisher. The transposed editions have many differences of layout for the accompaniment. Coll 10, page 12, bar 8, beat 3, voice: e″ needs a flat.

(2) **Mr Belloc's Fancy**. At Martinmas, when I was born. (Sir John Squire, *Tricks of the Trade*, 1917.) Comp. 1921. Pub. Augener, 1922. G major. [Coll 10, transposed down a major third]. Revised version, Pub. Augener, 1930, High [Coll 3] and *Low* [Coll 10].

G major. d'-g″(a″), [d'-e″]. *Eb major*. 2/2, Very brisk, minim = 92 or thereabouts. 1'30″. V/m, P/m [Original, P/d].

For: Ten; *C-Ten, Bar*.
Subject: I drink beer wherever I go, but the best comes from Sussex.
Voice: Steps, 3rds, 8ve leaps; regular crotchet rhythms; (a″) at end.
Piano: Fast staccato chords, periodic legato melodic lines; wide stretches and leaping chords; texture considerably thinner in revised version, and some of the harmonies altered.
Comment: A most entertaining song, and another good finisher. Some singers have changed the words in verse two, *the Jews* becoming *others*. Since the poem is a deliberate parody of Hilaire Belloc, whose anti-semitic views were notorious, this is not really necessary. Original version, Coll 10, page 13, bar 9, beat 4, RH: a° needs a natural; page 14, bar 9, beat 3, LH: bass needs crotchet rest; page 15, bar 7, beat 2, LH: c° needs a flat; staccato dots missing as follows: page 13, bar 2, RH: notes 1, 2, 3, of treble; bar 5, RH: notes 3, 5, 6; page 14, bar 4, RH: notes 4, 5, of treble. The low key copies of the revised version (Augener and Coll 10) have a number of differences which would appear to be errors: bars 1, 20, 39, 59, beat 2, LH: add a°; bar 16, beat 1, RH: add g°; bar 17, beat 1, LH, add C; bar 18, beat 1, LH: add B; bar 43, beat 3, LH: add a° (this is given in Coll 10). The two other changes make sense: bars 23, beat 1, to 30, beat 3, LH: all 8ve lower in high key; bar 40, beat 3, RH: add e″ – this puts the c' in the LH, giving a 10th which is playable in C but not in Eb. Coll 10, page 19, bar 12: add 'staccato sempre'; page 21, bar 8, beat 1, LH: minims not dotted; bar 12, beat 1, LH: d° needs a flat. Tomlinson gives a″ as top note, with no alternative.

27 LITTLE PETERISMS. Four songs composed at the beginning of 1922 while Warlock was at Cefn Bryntalch. On 7 February Warlock wrote to

Colin Taylor: '…as soon as my last batch of "little Peterisms" is ready. I have sketched half a dozen of these and tomorrow Philip Wilson is coming down for a few days so that between us we may be able to make them fit for the Enoch Ballad Concerts – Enoch have actually asked me to send them something "in a simple style!" These at least are simple to the point of sheer imbecility' (Coll 10). Though never published under this title it is clear that the next four songs are the ones referred to. Tomlinson suggests that **10, 29** and **30** also belong to this group.

(1) **Good ale**. Bring us in no brown bread, for that is made of bran. (Anon; Bodleian MS Eng. Poet e.1; *EEL* and Davies.) Pub. Augener, 1922. High and *Low* [Colls 7, 10].

> A♭ major. e'♭-a"♭, [f'-f "]. *F major*. 3/4, Fast. 1'45". V/me, P/me.

For: Ten; *C-Ten, Bar.*
Subject: Bring plenty of ale; we want nothing else.
Voice: Steps and 3rds; a few accidentals; straightforward rhythms.
Piano: Chordal, in varying rhythms; a few big stretches.
Comment: One of the best drinking songs, it makes a fine finisher. Warlock wrote on his F major copy: A♭ 'is the original key, and is much better than the low key as here. But for roaring unaccompanied it doesn't matter.' For this latter purpose he also indicates that the verse belongs 'In the Saloon Bar', and for the chorus 'Public and Private Bars join equally' (Coll 10). The poem has four more stanzas, and Warlock has changed the order. At the end of verse 3 *boars* is spelt *bores* in *EEL* and Davies; both meanings apply! Low key copies, bar 44, beat 3, LH: the original high key has g° and a° natural to be played with thumb (note the whole chord is printed too far right); since the equivalent e° and f °# cannot be played in the same way the e° is omitted; since the f °# is doubled in the RH it might be better, and easier, to omit f °# and play e° instead. See **49** for another setting of a very similar poem.

(2) **83 Hey, troly loly lo**, maid, whither go you? (Anon; BL. Add. MS 31922; *EEL*, Stevens.) Pub. Augener, 1922. [Colls 3, 10].

> No key sig. c'-f ", [f'-e"♭]. 12/8,9/8,15/8, No tempo mark. 1'30". V/m, P/md.

For: Mezzo, C-Ten, Bar.
Subject: Dialogue: Give me a kiss – no, mother might see!
Voice: Steps; many 5ths, 8ves, broken chords; many accidentals but not difficult; fairly straightforward triplet rhythms.
Piano: Alternation of thick chords and wide-ranging arpeggios; many accidentals which come and go.

Comment: An original and effective song, needing a lively tempo. 'The poem appears in the MS in many not very intelligible repetitions; we have re-arranged it so as to eliminate these' (*EEL*). Warlock has changed it even further, losing seven lines in the process. Bar 6: *rare* = *fair* in *EEL* and Stevens; bar 9: wis = know; bars 12-13: make us sport = take our pleasure; bar 14: sith = since, because; bar 18: mell = associate with, make love (*OED*), meddle (*EEL*). All editions: bar 16, beat 1, RH: a' needs a natural, as in bar 6; beat 3, RH: perhaps d" not c", as in bars 6 and 26; bar 24, beat 3, LH: g° needs a natural. Coll 10, page 30, bar 2, beat 1, LH: A not B; page 31, bar 10, beat 1, LH: treble clef missing. See Stevens for further information.

(3) **The bachelor**. In all this world nis a meriar life. (Anon; Bodleian MS Eng. Poet e.1; *EEL*.) Pub. Augener, 1922. [Coll 3; Coll 10, transposed down a tone].

F# minor. c'#-f"#, [e'-e"]. *E minor*, 2/4. Briskly. 45". V/m, P/m.

For: Ten; *Bar*.
Subject: Life is more fun for a bachelor.
Voice: Steps, 3rds, repeated notes; ends on held f"#; a patter-song.
Piano: Chordal, with much decoration.
Comment: A lively modal song, somewhat reminiscent of Capriol Suite. A good finisher, or encore. The third verse of the poem is omitted, also the burden, which runs: 'A, a, a, a, / Yet I love wherever I go.' Coll 10, page 33, bar 1, beat 2, LH: quavers not crotchets; bar 3, beat 1, RH: g' should be dotted crotchet; bar 18, beat 2, LH: treble clef missing.

(4) **Piggesnie**. She is so proper and so pure. (Anon, early sixteenth century; *EEL*.) Pub. Augener, 1922. High [Coll 3] and *Low* [Coll 10, transposed down a tone].

G major. d'-g", [e'-f"#]. *F major, E major*, 2/4. Moderately fast: very lightly and in strict time throughout. 45". V/m, P/m.

For: Ten; *Bar, C-Ten*.
Subject: There is none sweeter than my beloved.
Voice: Thirds and broken chords, steps; continuous quavers, save for final minim g".
Piano: Chordal, in quavers, not too thick.
Comment: A delightful song, provided the singer can manage a whole verse to a breath. The burden, omitted by Warlock, runs: 'Ah, my sweeting, / My little pretty sweeting, / My sweeting will I love wherever I go.' It is included in Harold Samuel's

charming setting in *Heritage 1*. Bar 18: minion = dainty,
elegant; bar 20: meet = fit and proper; bar 38, and title:
piggesnie (lit. pig's eye) = a term of endearment; cf. Chaucer,
The Miller's Tale, where a girl is described thus: 'She was a
primerole, a piggesnie' – translated by Neville Coghill as
'She was a daisy, O a lollypop!'

28 Little trotty wagtail he went in the rain. (John Clare, [9 August
1849] First published 1934.) Comp. 1922. Pub. OUP, 1923. [Coll 10].

D minor. c'-f ", [d'-d"]. 4/4, Allegretto. 1'15". V/e, P/me.

For: Mezzo, C-Ten, Bar. [Unison].

Subject: Describes a wagtail's behaviour.

Voice: Short scales and 3rds, broken chord; few accidentals; fairly
simple rhythm.

Piano: Light bouncing chords, with patches of counterpoint.

Comment: Originally published as a unison song, and quite suited to
children's voices. Bars 20 and 28: water-pudge = puddle.

29 Late summer. The fields are full of summer still. (Edward Shanks,
The Queen of China and Other Poems, 1919.) Comp. 1921-22. Pub.
Augener, 1925. [Colls 3, 10].

E major. b°-f "#, [e'-d"#]. 3/4, Lento – molto tranquillo. 2'10".
V/me, P/md.

For: Mezzo, C-Ten, Bar.

Subject: The sweetness of late summer is like an old loving couple.

Voice: Steps, 3rds, broken chords; 8ve leap, 6th drop; simple speech
rhythms, mostly quavers.

Piano: Thick and luxuriant, with many accidentals, including
double sharps in profusion; some hand crossings and
stretches.

Comment: A rich and beautiful song, though some may find Armstrong
Gibbs's setting more immediately attractive. Tomlinson
suggests this is a *Little Peterism*, see **27**. Coll 10, page 41,
bars 10-11, RH: grace-note e' should be tied across the
barline; bar 14, beat 2, LH: B should have a natural.

30 The singer. In the dim light of the golden lamp. (Edward Shanks, *The
Queen of China and Other Poems*, 1919.) Comp. 1919-22. Pub.
Augener, 1925. [Coll 10, transposed down a tone].

G major. d'-g", [g'-e"]. *F major*, 2/4(6/8), Allegretto. 1'20".
V/me, P/me.

For: Sop, Ten; *Mezzo, C-Ten, Bar*.

Subject: The pleasure of listening to music.

Voice: Steps and 3rds, broken chords; 6th drop; some accidentals;
simple rhythms though many triplets.

Piano: Three-part counterpoint; much parallel movement, texture
              becoming thicker in the middle of the song.
Comment: Very atmospheric, though much simpler than Gurney's set-
              ting. The note in Coll 10 about Augener's file copy is not quite
              correct; 'Good Ale' is another Augener publication and is also
              missing from the Galliard album. Tomlinson suggests this is
              a *Little Peterism*, see **27**. Coll 10, page 43, bar 1, RH: slur from
              b″-a″ missing; bar 3, beat 2, RH: f′ needs a sharp, last quaver
              add d″; bar 6, beat 1, RH: top note marked LH in Augener; bar
              11, voice: c′ not d′; bar 18: add ritenuto; bar 19: add dimi-
              nuendo hairpin, both these above the vocal part.

31 Adam lay ybounden, bounden in a bond. (Anon; BL Sloane MS 2593;
   EEL, EV and Davies.) Comp. 1922. Pub. OUP, 1923. [Coll 10].
              C minor. c′-f″, [f′-e″*b*]. 2/4, Allegretto. 1′. V/e, P/e.
For: Mezzo, C-Ten, Bar. [Unison].
Subject: But for Adam's sin Mary would not have become Queen of
              Heaven.
Voice: Steps, 3rds, 4ths; a few accidentals; simple rhythms.
Piano: Crotchet chords, mostly in four parts, with some decoration;
              fuller chords to finish.
Comment: A good modal style carol for solo or unison singing, it is
              included in *OCB*. The first two lines refer to the belief that
              Adam was rescued from Hell by Christ between Good Friday
              and Easter, thought to be 4000 years after Creation. Bars
              20-21: Ne had = had not; bar 34: moun = may; bars 35-36: Deo
              gratias = Thanks be to God. Coll 10, page 44, bar 4, beat 1,
              RH: OUP and *OCB* omit c″. See comments in *EV* and Davies.

32 Rest, sweet nymphs, let golden sleep. (Anon; in Francis Pilkington's
   First Booke of Songs or Ayres, 1605.) Comp. 1922. Pub. OUP, 1923.
   [Colls 1, 10].
              F major. f′-f″, [f′-e″*b*]. 6/8, Allegretto tranquillo. 2′15″. V/me,
              P/me.
For: Mezzo, C-Ten, Bar.
Subject: Lullaby for young ladies, wishing them sweet dreams and joy.
Voice: Steps, skips; 8ve leap; regular crotchet quaver rhythm.
Piano: Gently moving chords, sometimes broken.
Comment: A charmer. The middle stanza of the poem is omitted. Coll 10,
              page 46, bar 5: pedal release should come before last quaver,
              not after it.

33 Sleep. Come, sleep, and with thy sweet deceiving. (John Fletcher, *The
   Woman Hater*, 1607, Act III, Scene i.) Comp. 1922. Pub. OUP, 1923.
   [Colls 1, 10].

G minor. d'-e''*b*, [g'-d'']. 3/4,5/8, etc, Rather slow. 2'30''. V/m, P/m.

For: Mezzo, C-Ten, Bar.

Subject: Let me sleep, if only for a little while.

Voice: Mostly by step; some 4ths and 5ths; long legato lines in free speech rhythms.

Piano: Chromatic contrapuntal writing, nearly all in four parts.

Comment: A great song, by any standards. When Warlock made a fair copy of his string quartet version in 1927 (BL Add. MS 52909; on hire from OUP) he made two alterations in the vocal line: bar 7, beat 1: quaver rest, quaver d'', instead of crotchet d''; bar 16, beat 1: quaver b'*b* instead of quaver a'. Coll 1 incorporated these two variants after 1967; Coll 10 gives both versions. Coll 10, page 49, bars 4-5, LH: G should be tied across the barline; page 51, bar 2: 3rd note of arpeggio, e', should have a flat. All editions, bar 21, RH: last note of treble should be quaver. St. 1, line 5: *There may steal = I may feel*, all editions of the poem. *The Woman Hater* is now thought to be the work of Francis Beaumont, not John Fletcher. The lyric is sung by Oriana, attempting to show Gondarino, the woman-hater, that he need not hate women.

34 **Tyrley tyrlow**. About the field they pipèd right. (Anon; Balliol MS 354; *EEL*.) Comp. 1922. Pub. OUP, 1923. [Coll 10].

A minor. e'-f '', [g'-e'']. 6/8, Fast and gay. 2'. V/me, P/m.

For: Mezzo, C-Ten, Bar. Unison.

Subject: The shepherds go to Bethlehem.

Voice: Repeated notes, steps, broken chords; few accidentals; simple rhythms on the whole.

Piano: Decorated chordal, with some hand crossings.

Comment: Lively and effective Christmas carol. *OCB* gives a reduction of the 1923 version for chorus and orchestra. *EEL* has a burden: 'Terly, terlow, terly, terlow, / So merily the shepardes began to blow.' The first stanza reads: 'About the feld they piped full right, / Even about the middes of the night; / A down from heven they saw cum a light, / Terly, terlow.' St. 3 in *EEL* is omitted by Warlock, and St. 5 and 6 in Warlock do not appear in *EEL*, which notes that they were added in 1591, as 'The Shepherd's Song', to the MS of the Two Coventry Corpus Christi Plays. Coll 10, page 52, bars 10-11: *OCB* has *they saw a light*; *OCB* and *EEL* both give: page 52, bar 6: *piped full right*; page 54, bar 2: *Bethlem*; bar 4: *sunnès beam*; bar 7: *stream*. Both leme and stream = ray of light.

35 PETERISMS (FIRST SET). Three songs, Pub. Chester, 1923, as a set, for high voice and piano. A nicely varied group, which would make a good end to a programme for tenor, though the first song is a little low; Coll 11 transposes the last song to make the set available for baritone. Copley explains the name as follows: 'A well known firm of brewers had created an errand-boy character – named Peter, who, from time to time, gave tongue to amusingly perky sayings (in their advertisements) which were headed *Peterisms*. These appealed to Warlock's sense of fun, and he adopted the title as a suitable collective noun to cover some of his more frivolous items.'

(1) Chopcherry. Whenas the rye reach to the chin. (George Peele, *The Old Wives Tale*, 1595, Act I, Scene i.) Comp. 4 June 1922. [Coll 11].
A major. e′-e″, [f′#-c″#]. 6/8, Very fast and light. 1′. V/me, P/m.

For:	Ten; C-Ten; Bar.
Subject:	My true love says she cannot wait another year.
Voice:	Steps, skips, broken chords; rhythms fairly simple, with some occasional syncopation.
Piano:	Four-part chordal, with dotted rhythm top line; some very wide skips at times.
Comment:	See comment to **17**. There is a version for string quartet obtainable from the Warlock Society in A major (BL Add. MS 52909). Chopcherry was a game in which one tried to catch a suspended cherry in one's teeth. In the following half-bars the string quartet version has for the voice the rhythm – dotted quaver, semiquaver quaver, the latter slurred together: bar 12: 2nd half; bar 17: 2nd half; bar 21: both halves. These are given as alternatives in Coll 11, as is a change of notes in bar 29, beat 2: e′, f′#, g′, for b′, a′, g′. Coll 11 also adds half-bar phrase marks to the piano as follows: bar 12: both halves, alto and bass; bar 19: both halves, treble; bar 20: 1st half, treble; bar 25: 2nd half, bass; bar 27: 1st half, bass; bar 28: 1st half, tenor. Missing staccato marks have been restored to make the two hands consistent.

(2) A sad song. Lay a garland on my hearse. (John Fletcher, *The Maid's Tragedy*, 1619, Act II, Scene i.) Comp. 9 June 1922. [Coll 11].
B minor. e′#-f″#, [f′#-f″#]. 6/8, With a gentle lilt. 1′45″. V/m, P/me.

For:	Sop, Ten; Mezzo, Bar.
Subject:	Let earth lie light on my grave, for I died of love.
Voice:	Steps, 3rds; 8ve leap, 7th drop; many phrases lie high; basically simple rhythms, but some irregularities, and some dissonance with the piano.

Piano: Mostly four parts, somewhat contrapuntal; very chromatic; gentle dotted rhythms.

Comment: Warlock quoted the following from the play in his MS: '*Evadne*: That's one of your songs, Madam. *Aspatia*: Believe me, 'tis a very pretty one. *Evadne*: Fie on it, Madam! The words are so strange, they are able to make one dream of hobgoblins.' The same comment might be made of the music in this very individual song. *The Maid's Tragedy* is now considered to be by Beaumont and Fletcher, not Fletcher alone, though the lyric may well be his. It was performed in 1610 or 1611. Bar 18: *lie* = *lay*, in some editions. Warlock made a version for soprano and small orchestra in C minor (1927-28; BL Add. MS 52910, as 'Two Songs for Soprano and Small Orchestra', with 'Pretty Ringtime', **52**), and for string quartet, also in C minor, which Coll 11 considers to have been the original key. Both these versions available from the Warlock Society. See WSNL 35.

(3) **Rutterkin** is come unto our town. (?John Skelton. BL Add. MS 5465; *EEL*, Stevens.) Comp. 1922/3. [Coll 11, transposed down a minor 3rd]. Ab, modal. e'b-a", [g'-e"b]. F modal. 7/8, Boisterously. 1'. V/md, P/d.

For: Sop; Ten; *Mezzo; Bar*.
Subject: Cheerful nonsense; but see comment.
Voice: Short scales, many 4ths; 6th leaps, 8ve drops; very varied rhythms, ending prestissimo.
Piano: Complex chords in varying rhythms; decorative passages, some in two parts, over held bass; many skips.
Comment: Not easy, but good fun and a good finisher. Last verse of poem omitted, as in *EEL*. The poem is given, with music, in Sir John Hawkins's *General History of Music*, 1776, iii, 9-16, where he says it 'is supposed to be a satire on those drunken Flemings who came to England with the Princess Anne of Cleves, upon her marriage with Henry VIII'. Since this was in 1541, and Fayrfax, owner of the MS, died in 1521, this seems unlikely! *EEL* gives it to William Cornish. He may have written the tune and Skelton the words: 'Courtly Abusion', in Skelton's *Magnyfycence* has the line 'Rutty bully, joly rutterkin, heyda'. See the note in Vaughan Williams's *Five Tudor Portraits*, OUP, 1935. Rutterkin = a swaggering gallant or bully. Bar 25 = a tankard of ale at one go (stoup, for a drinking vessel, is Dutch in origin). The omitted verse runs as follows, according to Hawkins: 'When Rutterkin from borde will ryse / He will drink a gallon pot full at twice / And the overplus under the table of the new

guise [in the modern fashion] / Like a Rutterkin, hoyda.'
However, *drink* should be read *piss* (Stevens, who dates the
MS c. 1500, and sees no reason to involve Skelton). One bar
from the end: voice has pause on 1st crotchet, omitted in Coll
11.

36 PETERISMS (SECOND SET). Pub. OUP, 1924, as a set. [Coll 2; but
not grouped together]. For the title see note to **35**. As a group the range
is awkward; the first song is low for a tenor, and the others rather high
for baritone, though the a″ in the last can be avoided. Coll 11 transposes
the last two to make the set available for baritone.

(1) Roister Doister. I mun be married a Sunday. (Nicholas Udall, *Ralph
Roister Doister*, Act III, Scene iii; performed c. 1552, printed c. 1566.)
Comp. 4 January 1923. [Colls 2, 11].

F major. c′-f ″, [f′-d″]. 6/8, Rumbustiously. 1′15″. V/e, P/md.

For:	Bar.
Subject:	We will have a great time at my wedding, for 'I must be married on Sunday'.
Voice:	Steps, 3rds, broken chords; 8ve drop and leap; very simple rhythms; no accidentals.
Piano:	Thick chords with many skips; some decoration; chromatic; some big stretches.
Comment:	A fine finisher. Warlock's MS has further instructions: the first verse is marked 'Squiffeylike', and for the last there should be 'Stamping of feet, clapping of hands, pounding with pint pots, and expectoration ad libitum, but in strict time on the first beat of the bar'. Coll 11 gives the original tempo mark as 'Roisterdoisterously'! A roister, or roister-doister, was a roisterer, a noisy and rude reveller; Udall's play seems to have been the word's first appearance in print; a roister changed to a roisterer in the early nineteenth century. See WSNL 36 for a reproduction of Warlock's MS which, as WSNL admits, contains some 20 variants from the OUP printed version, these being actual notes, not merely dynamic and other markings. It should certainly be studied by anyone performing the song. Though Tomlinson tells us Warlock checked the proofs himself, the MS version sounds more characteristic in almost every case.

(2) Spring the sweet spring is the year's pleasant king. (Thomas Nashe,
Summer's Last Will and Testament, 1600.) Comp. 1922/3? [Coll 2; Coll
11, transposed down a semitone].

A♭ major. c′-g″b, [e′b-f ″]. G major. 3/8, Very fast and light. 1′.
V/m, P/md.

For: Sop, Ten; *Mezzo, high Bar.*

Subject: Spring is the best time of the year.

Voice: Steps and 3rds; 6th leaps; many high lying phrases, but only one note below e'*b*, an upbeat semiquaver *c'*, for which g'*b* could possibly be substituted; rhythms a little tricky in places; slightly chromatic.

Piano: Chordal, with Scotch snap decorations; many leaps; big stretches; chromatic.

Comment: Effective, if the pianist can keep the thickly written accompaniment light enough; however, it does not really compare with Gurney's great setting. Bar 25: palm = willow; bar 26: may = hawthorn; bar 54: *there = these*, all editions of the poem. Coll 11; tempo mark: 'Very fast and gay'; bars 48, 52: cresc. mark missing; bar 50: dim. mark missing; page 18, beat 1, RH: f' needs a natural; bar 21, beat 1: both hands need staccato marks.

(3) **Lusty Juventus**. In a harbour grene aslepe whereas I lay. (Robert Wever, *Lusty Juventus*, 1555.) Comp. 1922/3? [Coll 2; Coll 11, transposed down a minor third].

               C major. d'-a''(g''), [g'-g'']. *A major.* 3/4. Fast and gay. 1'15". V/m, P/md.

For: Ten; *Bar.*

Subject: The joy of youthful love.

Voice: Steps and 3rds; one repeated angular phrase of 5ths and 8ves; no accidentals; fairly varied rhythm; the alternative to final held a'' is not given in the original edition.

Piano: Thick quickly changing chords, with much decoration; many wide stretches; some big skips; chromatic.

Comment: A good finisher; a fairly powerful voice is needed to balance the heavy accompaniment; given this, a fine song. St. 1, line 2: middes = midst; line 3: fast = firmly, with concentration; St. 3, line 1: pyght = fixed, pledged. 'The archaic spellings from one of his favourite anthologies, *Corn from Olde Fieldes*' (Coll 11), however they are also identical with the version in *OB*; Ault agrees except for some spelling, but *OB 16* and *NOB* agree in the following variants: St. 1, line 1: *whereas = where*; line 2: *middes = mids*; St. 2, line 2: *I could = could*. The dates given for the poem also vary, with some odd results! *OB 16* has both c. 1560 and 'temp. Edward VI', while *NOB* has c. 1550 over poem and c. 1560 in the notes; *OB* has c. 1550, and Ault states: 'This is from the earliest edition, which is undated, but contains a prayer for Ed. VI, who died 1553.' See also **39** and **73** (3). Coll 11, bar 10: pedal mark lasting a crotchet missing; staccato marks added: bar

10, bass, 3rd quaver; bar 25, bass, last quaver; bar 28, treble, last quaver.

37 LILLYGAY. Five songs, the poems from *Lillygay: an anthology of anonymous poems*, published by the Vine Press, Steyning, Sussex, 1920. Comp. July-August 1922. Pub. Chester, 1923, as a set. Coll 11 transposes just three of the songs, a procedure not to be recommended with a work clearly intended to be sung as a whole. All the poems except the last are traditional, and the tunes are in folk-song style, though none of them are actual folk-songs. However, 'I have been unable to find the first three items of the Lillygay cycle in any of the most comprehensive ballad collections. Perhaps these should also be ascribed to Neuburg the poet' (Tomlinson). They make an excellent group for soprano. There are many valuable comments by Brian Collins in WSNL 39, which should be read by all performers of the set.

(1) **The distracted maid**. One morning very early, one morning in the spring. (Old English.) [Coll 11].

	Bb minor. d'b-f ", [f'-f "]. 4/4, Moderato. 2'45". V/me, P/md.
For:	Sop, Ten; Mezzo, Bar.
Subject:	A girl gone mad from the loss of her lover, whom she cannot forget.
Voice:	Scales, a few 3rds; all quavers; pause on f " at the end of each of the six verses.
Piano:	Quaver ostinati, becoming more and more complex as the song progresses; chromatic; littered with double flats; many leaping chords.
Comment:	Effective narrative song, with scope for dramatic interpretation. Coll 11, page 29, bar 10, beat 1, LH: g° needs a natural.

(2) **Johnnie wi' the tye**. Johnnie cam' to our toun. (Old Scots.) [Coll 11, transposed down a tone].

	No key sig. d'-g", [a'-f "#]. *Tone lower*, 4/4. Moderato. 1'. V/me, P/me.
For:	Sop; *Mezzo*.
Subject:	When Johnnie came I forgot to cry.
Voice:	Repeated notes, 3rds; dotted rhythms with many Scotch snaps; high lying.
Piano:	Sliding harmonies, mostly in four parts; very chromatic.
Comment:	The tune sounds like a typical Scots folk-song, with fascinating chromatics below it. Bar 6: tye = pigtail; bar 7: kittl'd = tickled, stirred with excitement, cuddled.

(3) **The Shoemaker**. Shoemaker, shoemaker, are ye within? (Old Scots.) [Coll 11].

B*b* minor. f'-f". 6/8, Gaily, dotted crotchet = 120. 45". V/m, P/md.

For: Sop, Ten; Mezzo, Bar.

Subject: Have you shoes for me? Yes, and a kiss too!

Voice: 4ths, 3rds, steps; mostly in quavers; several pauses and tempo variations.

Piano: Chordal, in crotchet-quaver rhythms; some arpeggios and wide skips.

Comment: A cheerful little story, suggesting all sorts of things! The original poem has seven more verses, given in WSNL 38. Bar 10, beat 2, LH: semiquaver rest missing in Coll 11; bar 11, beat 1: Ped in Chester missing in Coll 11; bar 13: may = maiden; bar 14, beat 6, LH: a° has natural in Chester, missing in Coll 11; bar 18; Chester's *do* should read *to*, as in Coll 11; bar 27, LH, end: bass clef missing in Coll 11; bar 30: pedal relase under pause mark in Coll 11, not in Chester.

(4) **Burd Ellen and young Tamlane**. Burd Ellen sits in her bower windowe. (Maidment's *North Country Garland*, 1824.) [Coll 11, transposed down a tone].

A minor. e'-g"#, [g'-e"]. *G minor*. 4/4, Moderato (rather slow). 2'30". V/m, P/m.

For: Sop, Ten; *Mezzo, Bar.*

Subject: A dramatic tale of a deserted mother.

Voice: Folk-song style with steps and 3rds till last verse, then a 7th leap to g"# and 6th leap to a pause on f"; rhythms quite simple.

Piano: Basically chordal, sometimes broken; thick and dramatic at end.

Comment: A small-scale but concentrated version of a dramatic Border ballad. Burd = lady. Bar 11: whiles = sometimes; twisted = twisted yarn for weaving; bar 12: twan = divided or cut off the yarn. Coll 11, bar 9, LH: g° tied to next bar in Chester; page 39, bar 1, end, LH: treble clef missing; bar 3, beat 3, LH: bass clef missing; bar 12, RH: f#s should have double dots; penultimate bar: pause mark added to piano chords, missing in Chester.

(5) **Rantum Tantum**. Who'll play at Rantum Tantum. (Victor Neuburg.) [Coll 11, transposed down a semitone].

D*b* major. d'*b*-f"#, [f'-f"]. *C major*. 9/8, At a rollicking pace. 1'05". V/me, P/md.

For: Sop, Ten; *Mezzo, Bar.*

Subject: May is the time for love.
Voice: Skips, steps; 8ve leap and drop; fairly chromatic; simple rhythms.
Piano: Double note ostinati in RH, chords in LH, sometimes crossing RH. Chromatic.
Comment: Fairly conventional Warlock, but a lively end to the set. Neuberg's poem has two more verses, given in WSNL 39.

38 **Autumn twilight**. The long September evening dies. (Arthur Symons, *London Nights*, 1895, [12 September 1891].) Comp. 1922. Pub. OUP, 1923. [Coll 11].
               C minor. c'-e"b. [d'-d"]. 3/4, Very quietly. 2'. V/m, P/m.
For: Mezzo, C-Ten, Bar.
Subject: As evening falls lovers can be seen wandering along the lanes.
Voice: Skips, steps; 8ve leap and drop, 6th leap; slightly chromatic; varied rhythms; long legato phrases need good breath control.
Piano: Broken chords with interweaving melodic lines; some hand crossings; chromatic.
Comment: A beautiful and atmospheric song, with a much more naturally pianistic accompaniment than is usual with Warlock. Coll 11, page 50, bars 9/10: g's in RH need flats.

39 **In an arbour green**, asleep whereas I lay. (Robert Wever, *Lusty Juventus*, c. 1560.) Comp. 1922. Pub. Paterson & Sons, 1925. [Coll 11, transposed down a tone].
               G major. d'-g", [e'-f "]. *F major*. 3/4, Fast and gay. 1'15". V/m, P/m.
For: Ten; *Bar*.
Subject: The joy of youthful love.
Voice: Steps and 3rds; slightly chromatic; the mixture of single sustained notes and quick patter needs careful control.
Piano: Rapidly changing and skipping chords, but not too thick a texture.
Comment: Good finisher. Perhaps more obvious and straightforward than **36** (3), but none the worse for that. Don't start too fast! See **36** (3) for notes on poem, and **73** (3) for another setting. Coll 11 prints this in F major, without mentioning the original key, though listed as G major in Tomlinson.

40 **Milkmaids**. Walkeing betimes close by a green wood side. (Dr James Smith's *Wit Restored*, 1658; included in *Larkspur: a lyric garland*, published by the Vine Press, Steyning, 1922.) Comp. 3 January 1923. Pub. Enoch, 1924, High and *Low* [Coll 11, transposed down a tone].

G major. d'-g″, [e'-e″]. *F major, E major.* 4/4, Allegretto, crotchet = 114. 1'45″. V/me, P/me.

For:	Sop, Ten; *Mezzo, C-Ten, Bar.*
Subject:	I met some pretty milkmaids; they are more friendly than the ladies.
Voice:	Steps and 3rds; only one g″, in last verse; simple rhythms.
Piano:	Mostly crotchet chords; simple harmonies in variable texture; occasional big stretches.
Comment:	A 'walking song', sounding like a folksong arrangement; simple and charming. The words may seem pseudo-folk, with artificially wrong spelling; however, Tomlinson found the poem in *Wit Restored*, 'a collection of poems by a Dr James Smith', though whether it is the poems or the collection that is by the good doctor is unclear. Anthony Wood included Dr Smith among his biographies of Oxford writers (*Athenae Oxoniensis*, 1691) giving his dates as 1623-1667 (Tomlinson gives 1605-1667). Wood says of *Wit Restored* that it 'is mostly of our author Smith's composition'. But certainly not all of the poems are his. Warlock omitted St. 5-8: 'Silk points, with silver tags, / About their wrists were shown; / And jet-Rings, with poesies / Yours more than his own. // And to requite their lover's points and rings / They gave their lovers bracelets / And many pretty things. // And there they did get gowns / All on the grass so green, / But the taylor was not skilful / For the stitches they were seen. // Thus having spent the long summers day / They took their nutbrown milk pails / And so they came away.' Bar 23: sillibubs – a drink or dish made of milk or cream, often straight from the cow, curdled by adding wine or cider, and often sweetened; bar 37: aporns – presumably a misprint for aprons; the form aporns does not occur in *OED*. The accompaniment of the 1924 low key version was much modified from the original in G major, many of the chords being thinned out; Coll 11 has transposed this modified version up into F major, rather than transposing the original down. Both transposed versions give crotchet = 144 as the metronome mark, much too fast for an allegretto. Coll 11, page 45, bar 2, voice: last note should be a crotchet; page 46, bar 5, piano: marked mp in original key. The MS is in Cambridge University Library.

41 Consider. Now green comes springing o'er the heath. (Ford Madox Ford, *Collected Poems of Ford Madox Hueffer*, 1916.) Comp. 1923. Pub. OUP, 1924.

F major. c'-g″, [d'-d″]. 3/4, Allegro con fuoco. 1'45″. V/m, P/md.

For:	Sop, Ten; Mezzo, high Bar.

Subject: It is good to be alive.
Voice: Steps, simple skips; no accidentals; only one g", but that is a minim, not many f "s, and generally low-lying; the rhythm appears more complicated than it is, switching from 3/4 to 9/8 during the first two pages, but the notation of triplets in 3/4 in the rest of the song could well have been used throughout.
Piano: Elaborate semiquaver triplet arpeggios and broken chords throughout, with much hand crossing; moderately chromatic; lying reasonably well under the hands.
Comment: An exciting song. The accompaniment is very unlike Warlock's usual style; it is possible that the dedication to C.W. Orr, a songwriter who frequently used this texture, is significant. The poet changed his name from Hueffer to Ford in 1919.

42 CANDLELIGHT. A Cycle of Nursery Jingles. (The versions used have been selected from a collection of nursery rhymes published by The Poetry Bookshop as *Nurse Lovechild's Legacy*, 1916.) Comp. July 1923 for Warlock's son. A collection of twelve short contrasting songs, which could easily be rearranged to make other shorter groups if desired; though the whole only lasts just over six minutes. Pub. Augener, 1924.

For: Mezzo, Bar.
Voice: Few problems; the last song lies high, but has only 8 bars, all ff, three phrases using d"b-g"b, only the fourth using the whole range.
Piano: Considerable variety from song to song, but even the last is not as hard as it appears.

(1) **How many miles to Babylon.**
 F minor, modal. f'-f ". 12/8, Slow. 25". V/e, P/e.
(2) **I won't be my father's Jack.**
 E*b* major. d'-c". 6/8, Quick. 25". V/me, P/me.
(3)   **Robin and Richard** were two pretty men.
 A major, modal. d' #-e". 2/4, Allegretto. 25". V/me, P/me.
(4) **O my kitten**, a kitten, and O my kitten, my dearie.
 D major. d'-f "#. 9/8, Allegretto. 45". V/me, P/me.
(5) **Little Tommy Tucker** sings for his supper.
 G major. d'-e". 3/4, Presto. 20". V/me, P/m.
(6) **There was an old man** in a velvet coat.
 B*b* minor. f'-f ". 6/8, Allegretto. 30". V/e, P/me.
(7) **I had a little pony**, his name was Dapple Grey.
 C minor. c'-e". 2/4, Presto. 20". V/me, P/m.
(8) **Little Jack Jingle.** Now what do you think of little Jack Jingle?
 F major. c'-f ". 6/8, Fairly quick. 25". V/me, P/me.

(9) **There was a man of Thessaly** and he was wondrous wise.
F# minor. b°-d″. 2/4, Fast. 35″. V/e, P/m.

(10) **Suky, you shall be my wife** and I'll tell you why.
E*b* major. e′*b*-f ″. 6/8, Allegretto con moto. 45″. V/me, P/me.

(11) **There was an old woman** went up in a basket.
F minor. c′-f ″. 6/8, Fast. 30″. V/me, P/me.

(12) **Arthur O'Bower** has broken his band.
A*b* major. c″*b*(yes, c″*b*)-a″*b*. 4/4, Tumultuosissamamente. 30″.
V/m, P/m.

43 **Jenny Gray**. I had a little nobby mare. (Anon.) Comp. 1923? Pub.
Thames, 1972. [Coll 6].
E minor. d′-e″, [e′-d″]. 6/8, No tempo mark. 30″. V/e, P/me.

For: Mezzo, C-Ten, Bar.
Subject: I had a pony made of straw.
Voice: Steps and 3rds.
Piano: Mostly four parts, with some gracenote decorations.
Comment: Presumably a reject from *Candlelight*, **42**, perhaps to make
that a set of 12 songs rather than 13.

44 **TWO SHORT SONGS**. (Robert Herrick, *Hesperides*, 1648.) Comp.
1923. Pub. Boosey, 1924, as a pair. [Coll 4].

(1) **I held love's head** while it did ache. ('Upon Love.')
F minor. c′-f ″, [f′-c″]. 3/4, Andante affettuoso. 1′15″. V/me,
P/m.

For: Mezzo, Bar.
Subject: I comforted Love, only to find I had acquired his pain.
Voice: Steps, skips, broken chords; simple rhythms; some triplets.
Piano: Rhythmic chords with traces of counterpoint; not too thick,
but some leaps.
Comment: An excellent piece of imitation Roger Quilter!

(2) **Thou gav'st me leave to kiss**. ('Chopcherry.')
G major. d′-f ″, [e′-e″]. 6/8, Allegretto scherzando. 45″. V/me,
P/m.

For: Mezzo, Bar.
Subject: You gave me hope of love, but then gave yourself to another.
Voice: Steps, 3rds, broken chords; some chromatics; rhythms simple
in spite of some strategically placed rests.
Piano: Light leaping chords in usual dotted rhythms; some big
stretches.
Comment: Typical Warlock scherzo; a useful encore.

45 Sweet and twenty. O mistress mine, where are you roaming? (William
Shakespeare, *Twelfth Night*, 1601, Act II, Scene i.) Comp. 31 March
1924. Pub. OUP, 1924. [Coll 2].

Ab major. e'b-f ", [e'b-e"b]. 3/8, Allegretto con moto. 1'. V/me,
P/m.

For: Bar.
Subject: Don't run away – stay and kiss me, for we will not always be
            young.
Voice: Steps and 3rds; 8ve leap; crotchets and quavers with many
            hemiolas.
Piano: Swiftly but smoothly changing chords, mostly in four parts;
            some chromatics; a few leaps.
Comment: Captivating in its flexible rhythm and natural flow. An
            alternative F major version is listed in Tomlinson. MS held by
            OUP.

46 I have a garden of my own. (Thomas Moore, *Ballads, Songs, and
Miscellaneous Poems*, 1841.) Comp. 1924. Pub. OUP, 1925.

D minor. d'-e", [d'-d"]. 2/4, Andantino, crotchet = c. 63. 1'45".
V/me, P/m.

For: Mezzo, C-Ten, Bar.
Subject: My garden is lovely, but will be better still when you are there
            too.
Voice: Steps, skips; 8ve and 7th leaps; simple rhythms, though
            many triplets.
Piano: Chordal and decorative passages alternate; some hand
            crossings; slightly chromatic.
Comment: A pleasant little song, which may be a revival of a setting
            from 1913, which itself may have been a revision of a 'Child's
            Song' of 1910.

47 SOCIABLE SONGS. Two songs for baritone and optional unison
chorus, published separately.

(1) The Toper's song. The landlord he looks very big. (Anon, from an
eighteenth-century ballad sheet.) Arr. 1924. Pub. W.R., 1926. [Coll 10].

E minor. b°-e", [e'-e"]. 4/4, Fairly fast. 1'30". V/me, P/m.

For: Bar. [Optional unison chorus.]
Subject: Ale may cause me some trouble, but still gives me great joy.
Voice: Steps, repeated notes, simple skips; simple rhythms with
            many paired quavers.
Piano: Chordal, with many rests; some chromatics; a few leaps and
            stretches.
Comment: A strong tune with effectively varied accompaniment. The
            chorus is not really necessary.

(2) **One more river**. The animals came in two by two. (Words and tune from *The Weekend Book*, 1924.) Comp. 1925. Pub. W.R., 1927.

F major. c'-d", [f'-c"]. 4/4(12/8), In march time. 2'. V/e, P/me.

For: Mezzo, C-Ten, Bar. [Unison chorus.]
Subject: The odd animals in the ark.
Voice: Steps and 3rds, easy rhythm.
Piano: Rhythmic LH with chords above, some sections chromatic chords alone; some big stretches.
Comment: The well known tune, meant for solo with unison chorus. A version for two tenors, baritone, bass and piano was published by W.R., and an MS version for piano, timpani and strings exists, both in C major.

48 **Twelve oxen**. I have twelve oxen that be fair and brown. (Anon; Balliol MS 354; *EEL*]. Comp. 1924. Pub. OUP, 1924. [Colls 1, 7].

E major. b°-e", [e'-e"]. 6/8, Fast. 1'45". V/me, P/e.

For: Mezzo, C-Ten, Bar. [Two-part male chorus.]
Subject: I have four lots of twelve oxen grazing in different places; have you seen them?
Voice: Steps, skips; 7th leap; few accidentals; simple rhythms.
Piano: Decorated chordal, covering the full range of the keyboard at times; thick texture, but few big stretches.
Comment: Straightforward, with a good swing; it needs the optional two-part male chorus, and does not really challenge Ireland's version published five years earlier. MS held by OUP.

49 **Peter Warlock's Fancy**. Bring us in no beef, sir, for that is full of bones. (Anon; BL Harleian MS 541; in Ritson's *Ancient Songs and Ballads*.) Comp. 1924. Pub. Paterson, 1925 and Chappell, 1927. Medium and *Low* [Coll 7].

Eb major. b°b-e"b, [e'b-e"b]. F major. 2/4, With decided vigour and emphasis. 1'45". V/e, P/m.

For: Bar, *Bass*. [Optional unison chorus.]
Subject: Bring plenty of ale; we want nothing else.
Voice: Descending scales in quavers; some 5th, 8ve, and 6th leaps.
Piano: Crotchet chords, often leaping, sometimes parallel; tenor melodies need agile LH.
Comment: Four-square, but enjoyable to play and to sing. Having the unison chorus would add to the fun. See **27 (1)** for a setting of an earlier version of these words.

50 **Yarmouth Fair**. As I rode down to Yarmouth Fair. (Hal Collins.) Comp. 1924. Pub. OUP, 1925. High, *Medium, Low*.

G major. d'-g", [g'-g"]. *E major, D major*. 2/2, Fast, minim = 108. 2'. V/me, P/m.

For: Ten; *C-Ten, Bar*; *Bass.*
Subject: On the way to Yarmouth I met a girl, and took her with me to the Fair.
Voice: Steps, 3rds; 6th leaps, 7th drop; almost all in crotchets.
Piano: Chordal; some decoration, and becoming gradually thicker in texture.
Comment: The tune was composed by Mr John Drinkwater, of Cley, Norfolk, taken down by E.J. Moeran. The words turned out to be in copyright; when Warlock made this arrangement his Maori friend Hal Collins provided a new text and title. The lower key versions have accompaniments much altered by the composer. Note the metronome mark, this song is often taken too fast. An excellent song, it makes a fine finisher. G major copy, 6 bars from the end, RH last note: c′ needs a natural.

51 **Chanson du jour de noël**. Une pastourelle gentille. (Clément Marot, 'Chanson 25 du Jour de Noël', *38 Chansons Musicales*, 1530.) Comp. 1925. Pub. W.R., 1926.
            C major. g′-a″, [g′-g″]. 6/8,9/8, Allegretto con moto. 1′30″. V/me, P/m.
For: Sop, Ten.
Subject: Christmas Carol, of the shepherds and Mary.
Voice: Repeated notes, steps, 3rds, broken chords; 6th leap; some high-lying phrases; quite simple rhythms.
Piano: Chordal, changing quite quickly; mostly in four parts; some big stretches; a few bars of fast wide skips.
Comment: No singing translation is given for this attractive song; a prose version would run as follows: 'An agreeable shepherdess and a shepherd, in an orchard, played marbles together, to be brief. Happy shepherd, careless shepherdess, it is all very well to play ball. We sing Noel. Do you no longer remember the prophet who told us about such high deeds, that of a perfect virgin would be born a child quite perfect? The deed is done. The beautiful virgin has dedicated a son to heaven. Sing Noel.' It was published by B & H in New York in 1961 as 'Noel', with a translation by D'Alton McLaughlin (Tomlinson).

52 **Pretty ring time**. It was a lover and his lass. (William Shakespeare, *As You Like It*, 1599, Act V, Scene iii.) Comp. 1925. Pub. OUP, 1926. [Coll 1].
            Eb major. d′-g″(f ″), [f′-e″b]. 4/4,5/4, Allegretto con moto. 1′20″. V/m, P/md.
For: Sop, Ten; Mezzo, Bar.

Subject: Spring is the time for lovers.
Voice: Steps, repeated notes, sequences of 4ths and 3rds; strongly
               rhythmic, almost a patter song.
Piano: Quick chord changes throughout, some of them very thick
               and needing a big stretch; in places it may be advisable to
               omit notes rather than spread the chords, for example, five
               and six bars from the end.
Comment: A lively and effective setting; good finisher. The voice must
               keep legato above the staccato accompaniment. Not too fast,
               it is not marked allegro; a slight allargando before verse
               four, itself taken a little more steadily, is allowable. Bar 12,
               beat 4, RH: d" not e"b, both editions. The second word of the
               refrain, throughout, does not appear in Shakespeare: 'In *the*
               springtime'. Bar 9: ring-time = wedding season; bar 26: carol
               = a song for dancing, with no necessary religious
               connotation; bar 42: prime = the first part of the day, of the
               year (spring), or of human life (about 21 to 28, *OED*).
               Warlock made an effective arrangement of this song for
               soprano and small orchestra in E major (BL Add. MS
               52910), see 35 (2).

53 TWO SONGS. The words by Arthur Symons. Comp. 1925. Pub. OUP,
1928, as a pair. [Coll 2]. Intended to be sung together – at the end of
the first song the word 'attacca' is printed; however, they can stand
separately, and indeed they do not really both suit the same voice.

(1) A prayer to Saint Anthony of Padua. Saint Anthony of Padua,
   whom I bear. (*London Nights*, 1895 [7 September 1894].)
               Eb major. e'b-e"b. 3/4, Very quietly, rather slow. 1'10". V/me,
               P/me.
For: Sop, Ten; Mezzo, C-Ten, Bar.
Subject: Kind saint, bring back my love's heart, for I have lost it.
Voice: Repeated notes, steps, simple skips; 8ve drop; simple speech
               rhythms.
Piano: Gently contrapuntal and fairly chromatic.
Comment: A charming little song. In bar 13 *her* could be changed to
               him, if desired. The poem is the eleventh and last of a cycle
               of poems, *Céleste*.

(2) The sick heart. O sick heart, be at rest. (*The Loom of Dreams*, 1901
   [18 April 1900].)
               No key sig. c'-g", [e'b-f "]. 12/8, Slowly. 1'25". V/m, P/m.
For: Sop, Ten; Mezzo, high Bar.
Subject: Only age will cure the suffering in my heart.

Voice: Steps and 3rds; 8ve leap, 7th leap and drop, 6th drops; only
                one g″, but sustained pp e″ at end.
Piano: Chords, with contrapuntal decoration; mostly in four or five
                parts, sometimes thicker; some big stretches.
Comment: Perhaps a little congested harmonically, but a magical
                ending. See comment to 5.

54 The countryman. Oh! the sweet contentment the countryman doth
   find. (John Chalkhill, 'Corydon's Song', in *The Compleat Angler*, 1653.)
   Comp. 20 January 1926. Pub. W.R., 1926. Ab major, as a unison song,
   pub. Hawkes, 1926. High and *Low* [Coll 4].
                F major. c′-f ″, [c′-c″]. Ab major. 2/4, At a brisk walking pace.
                1′30″. V/e, P/me.
For: *Mezzo, Bar*; Sop, Ten.
Subject: Countryfolk have a hard life, but are happier than city-
                dwellers.
Voice: Steps, 3rds, broken chords; 8ve leaps; no accidentals; simple
                rhythms with Scotch snaps.
Piano: Decorated chordal, not thick except in last verse; often
                staccato chords with sustained melody above; few acci-
                dentals; some big stretches.
Comment: Very enjoyable 'walking song'. Originally published as a
                unison song, with the three a″bs [f ″s] given as optional
                alternatives to f ″s [d″s]; a″b is clearly better, but could be
                reserved for the last verse only, if necessary. To make the
                transposed (F major) edition match the original: bar 27, beat
                2, RH: add b° natural; bar 28, beat 1, RH: add c′. According to
                Izaac Walton, John Chalkhill was 'an acquaint and friend of
                Edmund Spenser' (1552-1599). He has now been identified as
                the brother of the stepmother of Walton's second wife, Ann
                Ken. He went up to Trinity College Cambridge in 1610 and
                died in 1642. Warlock omits stanzas 4 and 6-8: (4) 'Our
                clothing is good sheepskins / Gray russet for our wives; / 'Tis
                warmth and not gay clothing / That doth prolong our lives.'
                (6-8) 'To recompense our tillage / The heavens afford us
                showers, / And for our sweet refreshments / The earth affords
                us bowers. // The cuckoo and the nightingale / Full merrily do
                sing, / And with their pleasant roundelays / Bid welcome to
                the spring. // This is not half the happiness / The countryman
                enjoys; / Though others think they have as much / Yet he who
                says so lies: / Then come away, turn countryman with me'
                (note altered refrain).

55 Maltworms. I cannot eat but little meat. (?Bishop Still, *Gammer
   Gurton's Needle*, Act II. See Comment.) Comp. February 1926. Pub.
   OUP, 1926. [Coll 2].

F major. c′-f ″, [d′-d″]. 2/2, Briskly. 2′. V/e, P/me.

For:	Bar. [Unison chorus.]
Subject:	The pleasure of drinking ale.
Voice:	3rds, short scales; 8ve drop; almost all in crotchets.
Piano:	Chords, many in parallel; many rests; a few leaps and stretches.
Comment:	A drinking song, originally for baritone solo, unison male chorus, and brass band; it was later scored for full orchestra (available from the Warlock Society) (BL Add. MS 52911) with some harmonic elaboration – see Copley, p. 248. All but the first two lines of the melody were provided by E.J. Moeran, (*Musical Times*, March 1955). Warlock uses the version of the poem given in *OB*, taken from *Gammer Gurton's Needle*. The date and authorship of the play are in dispute; it was published in 1575, as being by 'Mr S. Mr. of Art', now thought to be William Stevenson of Cambridge, where it was 'Played on Stage, not longe ago'; the old attribution to Bishop Still appears to be out of favour. Warlock's favourite source, *EEL*, gives a longer version of the poem, as found in MS Dyce 45 (Victoria and Albert Museum), as does *OB 16*. This may be older than the play, the earliest date suggested for its first performance being 1553, and Dyce 45 being dated late fifteenth to early sixteenth century in *EEL*. Maltworm = one who loves malt-liquor, that is, ale. This is the word's first appearance in print, and it remained in use till the nineteenth century. St. 1, line 4: one wears a hood – 'some see this as a reference to a monk, but since many of the laity wore hoods, I take the phrase to mean "I'll have a drink with anybody" ' (Tydeman); line 6: *am nothing* = *nothing am*, in *OB*, though in no other source; line 3 of refrain: *thee* = *the* (Tydeman). St. 2, line 1: toast = toasted bread; line 2: crab = crab-apple; line 3: do me stead = suffice me; line 6: *I* = *it*, in old version of poem, which makes better sense; line 7: thoroughly lapped = well enfolded. St. 3, line 5: troll = pass around. St. 4, line 5: scoured = emptied by drinking.

56 Away to Twiver. And did you not hear of a mirth that befell. (*The Famous History of Friar Bacon*, printed before 1600.) Comp. 1926. Pub. OUP, 1927. [Coll 2].

B minor. d′-f ″#, [e′-d″]. 6/8,2/4, Fast. 1′30″. V/m, P/m.

For:	Mezzo, Bar.
Subject:	A description of some wedding celebrations.
Voice:	Steps, skips, repeated notes; few accidentals; rhythms straightforward, with some mixture of 6/8 and 2/4.
Piano:	Basically chordal, with much variety of layout and texture; some chromatic passages; a few big stretches.

Comment: Most enjoyable, and a good finisher. Bar 15: quintain = target
for tilting lances; bar 20: jade = worn-out horse: bar 26:
fiddle-dee-dees = string players; bar 27: a-cock-horse = up on
a perch: bar 37: forehorse = leader of a team of horses; bar 47:
fuddling = drinking; bar 59: posset = drink of warm milk
curdled with wine or ale; bar 64: laid on the lip = kissed.

57 The birds. When Jesus Christ was four years old. (Hilaire Belloc,
Verses and Sonnets, 1896.) Comp. 1926. Pub. Joseph Williams, 1927.
[Coll 3].

E*b* major. d'-e″*b*, [e′*b*-c″]. 4/4, Allegretto simplice. 1′15″. V/me,
P/me.

For: Mezzo, C-Ten, Bar. [Unison.]
Subject: When Jesus was a child he made clay birds come alive.
Voice: Steps, simple skips; some modulation; very simple rhythm.
Piano: Simple chordal, with many accidentals.
Comment: Charming, if rather sentimental; suitable for Christmas. It
was composed as a unison song for the boys' preparatory
school of Port Regis, Broadstairs, Kent, and published as
such in G*b* major.

58 Fair and true. Lovely kind, and kindly loving. (Nicholas Breton,
Melancholic Humours, 1600.) Comp. 1926. Pub. OUP, 1927. [Coll 1].

E*b* major. e′*b*-e″*b*, [e′*b*-c″]. 4/4, Rather slow, with simplicity
and tenderness. 2′30″. V/me, P/m.

For: Mezzo, C-Ten, Bar.
Subject: You have all virtues – bless you.
Voice: Steps, simple skips; mostly crotchets; ends with held e″*b*.
Piano: Chordal, with much contrapuntal decoration; one bar of
awkward wide skips in final stanza.
Comment: Warlock gave a copy of this song to the accompanist John
Longmire, inscribed: 'To John Longmire, fellow admirer of
the Reverend J[ohn] B[acchus] D[ykes], from whom this song
obviously derives.' This is true. It can and should be sung as
intended, 'with simplicity and tenderness', but some may find
it hopelessly sentimental.

59 Jillian of Berry. For Jillian of Berry she dwells on a hill. (Beaumont
and Fletcher, *The Knight of the Burning Pestle*, 1607, Act IV; but it is
probably older than the play.) Comp. 1926. Pub. OUP, 1927. [Coll 1].

B*b* major. d'-f ″, [f′-d″]. 6/8, Fast and gay. 35″. V/me, P/m.

For: Bar.
Subject: Let's visit Jillian, who gives good fellows beer.

Voice: Steps, sequence in 3rds, broken chords; 6th and 8th leap; simple rhythms, mostly quavers.
Piano: Chordal, wide ranging, with many cross-rhythms.
Comment: Fairly big voice needed to surmount the noisy piano part in this lively drinking song. Good finisher or encore. Sung by 'Old Merrythought', who sings popular songs throughout the play. The play is now thought to be by Beaumont alone.

60 Robin Goodfellow. And can the physician make sick men well? (*Robin Goodfellow: commonly called Hob-goblin, with his mad pranks and merry jests.* The Second Part, printed 1628, reprinted by The Percy Society, vol. 9, 1837.) Comp. 1926. Pub. OUP, 1927. [Coll 1].
              A major. e'-f"#, [e'-e"]. 9/8,6/8, Fairly fast, but wayward and capricious in time. 1'30". V/m, P/md.
For: Sop, Ten; Mezzo, Bar.
Subject: Doctors and magicians need their special plants.
Voice: Steps, skips, broken chords; 8ve drop; slightly chromatic; fairly simple rhythms; little help from piano.
Piano: Bouncing chords leaping all over the piano at times, otherwise sliding; many rests; highly chromatic.
Comment: A nonsense poem, its liveliness makes it a good finisher. Bar 7: divine = discover, guess; bar 9: germander = speedwell; bar 10: sops-in-wine = clove-pink, or gilly-flower; bar 14: strawberry wire = strawberry plant runners. Robin Goodfellow is a series of prose tales, with occasional verses, about Robin, who is the same character from English folklore as Puck, of *A Midsummer Night's Dream* and Kipling's *Puck of Pook's Hill*. The preface to the Percy Society edition suggests there is 'little or no doubt that it was first printed before 1588'.

61 THREE BELLOC SONGS. Settings of poems by Hilaire Belloc. Composed in January 1927, published separately by OUP the same year. [Coll 2]. An extremely satisfying group for medium voice.

(1) Ha'nacker mill. Sally is gone that was so kindly. (*Sonnets and Verse,* 1923.)
              D minor. c'-f", [d'-d"]. 12/8, Fairly slow. 2'. V/m, P/m.
For: Mezzo, Bar.
Subject: The end of the old familiar English countryside.
Voice: Steps, 3rds, 5ths, 6ths; 8ve and 7th drops; quite chromatic and often somewhat angular; rhythms simple.
Piano: Chordal; much in four parts; some widely spread passages, needing a good stretch; very chromatic.

Comment: A haunting atmospheric song. Bar 7, beat 3, RH: c′ needs a
               natural; bar 17: *thistle* = *Thistle*, with capital, in poem.

(2) **The night**. Most holy night, that still dost keep. (*Verses and Sonnets*,
    1896.)
               E minor. d′-e″, [e′-e″]. 2/4, Soft and chantlike, very slowly.
               1′45″. V/m, P/m.
For: Mezzo, C-Ten, Bar.
Subject: May I have rest and peace this coming night.
Voice: First stanza consists entirely of quaver e′s till the last note, a
               minim e″; thereafter steps and 3rds, most notes repeated, and
               held e″ to end; one chromatic phrase.
Piano: Simple chords till third page, where they become thick and
               widely spread.
Comment: Not easy to bring off, but can produce a wonderful atmo-
               sphere. Bar 34, beat 2, LH: add crotchet B, see Copley.

(3) **My own country**. I shall go without companions. (*The Four Men*,
    A Farrago, 1912.) *High* and Low.
               F major. c′-e″, [d′-d″]. *Ab major*. No time sig., Very quietly.
               2′15″. V/me, P/me.
For: *Sop, Ten*; Mezzo, C-Ten, Bar.
Subject: I shall return to the land where I belong.
Voice: Steps, 3rds, broken chords; some modulation; free but simple
               rhythms.
Piano: Gently changing harmonies, in quavers; nearly all in four
               parts.
Comment: Deservedly one of Warlock's best known songs, it breathes
               contentment; the modulations are simple but extraordinarily
               effective, and the whole is one of the most soul-satisfying
               songs ever written. Belloc's country was Sussex: the woods
               are deciduous, and therefore have new leaves in spring; there
               are also the notable groups of a few trees round ancient
               hill-forts such as Chanctonbury and Cissbury Rings. Copley
               gives a number of dynamic and phrasing variants, none of
               which seem of great importance.

62 **The lover's maze**. O be still, be still, unquiet thoughts. (?Thomas
   Campion, from *Giles Earle, His Booke*, 1615.) Comp. July 1927. Pub.
   OUP, 1928. [Coll 1].
               F minor. e′b-f ″, [f′-e″b]. 4/4, Briskly. 1′30″. V/m, P/md.
For: Mezzo, Bar.
Subject: 'Love is like an endless maze, more hard to get out than to
               enter.'
Voice: Nearly all by step; slightly chromatic; simple rhythms with

	many paired quavers; diction vital.
Piano:	Quickly changing staccato crotchet chords with much quaver decoration; chromatic.
Comment:	One of Warlock's most successful pseudo-Elizabethan songs, full of false relations. Not easy, but well worth the effort involved. Do not let the dry piano affect the legato vocal line. Bar 6: adventer = chance, good luck; bar 24: affected = endeavoured to have, aimed at; bar 47: cull = hug and fondle; bar 48: clip = hold tightly in the arms. Mezzos may like to sing *him* for *her* in bar 28. Though attributed to Campion by Warlock, on grounds of style, the poem is not accepted as his by Vivian or Davis.

63 Sigh no more, ladies, sigh no more. (William Shakespeare, *Much Ado About Nothing*, 1599, Act II, Scene iii.) Comp. 9 August 1927. Pub. OUP, 1928. [Coll 1].

	E♭ major. e'♭-f ", [e'♭-e"♭]. 6/8,5/8, Fast and in strict time (Allegretto con moto). 1'15". V/m, P/m.
For:	Sop, Ten; Mezzo, Bar.
Subject:	Do not sigh, ladies; men cannot be trusted, so let them go, and be happy.
Voice:	Steps, many skips, sequences; much chromaticism; free rhythm mostly in quavers.
Piano:	Rapidly sliding chords; very chromatic; some wide stretches.
Comment:	Lively, with interesting rhythms; a rather thick texture needs careful handling. Good finisher. Bar 23: dumps = sad songs, usually about love. Bars 20 and 38, the 'non rit' is followed by '!' in MS.

64 Cradle song. Be still, my sweet sweeting. (John Philip, The Nurse's Song in *Patient and Meek Grissill*, 1566.) Comp. August 1927. Pub. OUP, 1928. [Coll 1].

	D minor modal. d'-f ", [f'-e"]. 6/8, With a gentle lilt. 2'45". V/m, P/m.
For:	Mezzo.
Subject:	A lullaby, wishing the infant good fortune.
Voice:	Steps and skips; sequences; 7th and 6th leaps; some accidentals; dotted 6/8 rhythm throughout.
Piano:	Gently moving chords, chromatic and decorated; some big stretches.
Comment:	A charming song, with much more of the character of a lullaby than Britten's highly original setting in *A Charm of Lullabies*. Watch out for the change of rhythm in the final vocal phrase.

65 Mockery. When daisies pied and violets blue. (William Shakespeare, *Love's Labour's Lost*, 1595, Act V, Scene ii.) Comp. 9 August 1927. Pub. OUP, 1928. [Coll 2].

No key sig. e'-g", [g'-g"]. 2/4, Fast and in strict time. 1'. V/m, P/m.

For: Sop, Ten.
Subject: In spring the cuckoo mocks married men. (His call sounds like 'cuckold'.)
Voice: 3rds and 4ths; 8ve leap; chromatic; mostly quavers, with some cross-rhythms.
Piano: Staccato quaver chords; frequent skips; highly chromatic.
Comment: A sardonic setting, more appropriate to the point of the words than most versions. Bar 5: ladysmocks = cuckoo-flowers; bar 7: cuckoo-buds = buttercups; bar 24: oaten straws = pipes made from oat stems; bar 26: ploughman's clocks – ploughmen rise with the lark; bar 27: turtles tread = turtle-doves mate.

66 Walking the woods. I would I were Actaeon whom Diana did disguise. (Anon, from *A Gorgeous Gallery of Gallant Inventions*, 1578.) Comp. September 1927. Pub. Hawkes, 1927. [Coll 4].

F major. c'-f ", [f'-d"]. 3/4, Allegretto (poco rubato, colla voce). 1'30". V/me, P/me.

For: Bar.
Subject: I would undergo much to see and speak with my lady.
Voice: Steps and 3rds; 6th leap and drop; continuous quavers.
Piano: Continually changing chords, in three or four parts; occasionally more elaborate.
Comment: A 'walking song' with flexible rhythms and attractive modal inflexions. 'A shorter version of the poem which appears in *The Paradyse of Daynty Devises*, 1576, is ascribed to M.B., probably the otherwise unknown Mr Bewe, who appears elsewhere in that collection' (*OB 16*). Bars 4 & 5: Actaeon saw Diana (Goddess of Hunting) bathing, and she in anger changed him into a stag; bar 17: fain = glad; bar 21: quite = quit, repay; bar 26: shaling = falling from the husk as ripe; mast = the fruit of the beech, oak, chestnut, etc, as fed to pigs; bar 32: *alone = all day* with no following comma, according to *OB 16*; perhaps *alone* was taken from the previous line in error.

67 The first mercy. Ox and ass at Bethlehem. (Bruce Blunt.) Comp. 1927. Pub. Hawkes, 1927. [Coll 4].

F major, modal. f'-f ", [g'-d"]. 6/8, Allegretto con moto. 2'45". V/me, P/me.

For:	Mezzo, Bar.
Subject:	When an infant at Bethlehem Jesus called even the smallest creatures to his company.
Voice:	Steps, 3rds, 5ths; a few accidentals; simple rhythms, though the last two verses need careful choice of breathing places to make the sense clear.
Piano:	Decorated chordal, mostly in four parts; some big stretches.
Comment:	A charming carol, originally issued as a unison song, and later arranged for SSA. A French translation by Lilian Fearn was added for the series *Mélodies Anglaises* in 1946.

68 The jolly shepherd. The life of a shepherd is void of all care-a. (Anon, from *Wit and Drollery*, 1661.) Comp. 1927. Pub. Hawkes, 1930. *High* [Coll 4] and Low.

> *A major.* d'-f "#(a"), [e'-e"]. G major. 3/4, Allegretto con moto. 2'30". V/me, P/m.

For:	*Sop, Ten*; Mezzo, C-Ten, Bar.
Subject:	A shepherd's life is a happy one.
Voice:	Broken chords, steps, 3rds; 6th leaps and drops; optional g" at end; continuous crotchets throughout.
Piano:	Chordal, with much variety of layout, many 10ths.
Comment:	In spite of the effectively varied accompaniment the sameness of rhythm can easily become monotonous. To make transposed (A major) version match the original: bar 83, beat 1, LH: add c'#; RH: add f "#, delete f'#; bar 96, beat 1, RH: delete d'; bar 127, beat 2, RH: add d'; beat 3, RH: add e'. Bar 13: ruffles = bears himself proudly; bar 49: cantle = slice; bar 79: cabin = hut, rather than cottage.

69 What cheer? good cheer! Lift up your hearts and be ye glad. (Anon, medieval, Balliol MS 354; Davies.) Comp. 1927. Pub. W.R., 1928.

> E*b* major. b°*b*-e"*b*, [e'*b*-e"*b*]. 6/4, With a good swing, but not fast. 1'30". V/me, P/me.

For:	Mezzo, C-Ten, Bar. [Unison].
Subject:	A New Year carol; be happy, since Christ is born.
Voice:	Broken chords, steps, repeated notes; sequence of 5ths; simple rhythms.
Piano:	Or organ. Chordal, with a few big stretches.
Comment:	Very straightforward; three verses all to the same music; better suited to unison than solo singing. Variants in Davies: St. 2, line 1: *The King = Now the King*; line 2: *Now joy = Joy*; line 3: *His dear sake = His sake*. St. 3, line 2: *be all to me = be to me*. A fourth stanza runs: 'The gudman of this place, in fere, [together in company] / You to be merry he prayth you here, / And with gud hert he doth to you say, / "What cher" etc.'

70 Where riches is everlasting. Into this world this day did come. (Anon, medieval.) Comp. 1927. Pub. OUP, 1928.

D minor. d'-f ″, [d'-d″]. 6/4, Fast, with a good swing. 2'40″. V/e, P/me.

For: Mezzo, Bar. [Unison, with optional 4-part chorus].

Subject: Almighty God became a poor child for our sakes.

Voice: Steps, simple skips; simple rhythms.

Piano: Or organ. Good straightforward carol which can be performed solo, in unison, and with or without chorus. Verse 2, bar 4: right poor weed = truly poor clothing. Verse 3, bar 2: cratch = crib or manger; bar 7: lapped = wrapped.

71 Queen Anne. I am Queen Anne. (Anon.) Comp. 12 January 1928. Pub. Nelson, 1929 in *The Roundabout Song Book* (Part I, for Juniors); reissued OUP, 1970.

C major. e'-e″, [f'#-d″]. 3/4, Tempo di Minuetto. 1'. V/e, P/me.

For: Mezzo.

Subject: I, Queen Anne, am chiefly famed for being dead!

Voice: Steps, repeated notes, broken chords; some paired quavers; simple rhythms.

Piano: Chordal, with some decoration; some big stretches, which can be omitted.

Comment: A delightful children's song.

72 Passing by. There is a lady sweet and kind. (Anon, from Thomas Ford's *Musick of Sundrie Kinds*, 1607.) Comp. July 1928. Pub. OUP, 1929. [Coll 1].

G major. d'-g″, [d'-e″]. 4/8, Moderato – poco lento – semplice. 2'30″. V/me, P/m.

For: Ten, high Bar.

Subject: Though I have only seen her passing by I shall always love her.

Voice: Steps, skips; 6th leap; only one g″, sustained near end; simple rhythms, mostly quavers.

Piano: Chordal with decorations; some chromatics.

Comment: One of the few settings of the complete poem; straightforward and effective, with opportunities for a singer with story-telling ability.

73 SEVEN SONGS OF SUMMER. Composed in August 1928. Warlock could find no publisher willing to take them all, so they were published separately. MS in BL (Add. 52907).

(1) **The passionate shepherd**. Come live with me and be my love. (Christopher Marlowe, c. 1589.) Pub. Elkin, 1929. High and *Low*.

G major. d′-g″, [g′-f″#]. *F major*. 6/4, Fast. 1′50″. V/m, P/md.

For: Ten; *Bar*.

Subject: If you will live with me I will give you all the pleasures a shepherd can.

Voice: Steps, 6ths, broken chords; some chromatics; rhythms simple but varied, with many paired crotchets.

Piano: Decorated chordal; chromatic; many leaps; many big stretches.

Comment: If the pianist can keep the luxurious accompaniment light this can be effective. The words are as given in *OB*, which is a conflation from the two sources, *The Passionate Pilgrim*, 1599, and *England's Helicon*, 1600. St. 1, lines 3-4 read, in 1599: 'That hills and valleys, dales and fields, / And all the craggy mountains yield.' 1600 gives: 'That valleys, groves, hills and fields, / Woods, or steepy mountain yields.' *OB 16* and *NOB* follow 1599, Ault follows 1600, except that *mountain* becomes *mountains*. However, neither *OB 16* or *NOB* follows 1599 consistantly, though Ault has only one further emendment to 1600 (see bar 47 below). Bar 26: kirtle = gown or outer coat; bar 47: *England's Helicon* gives *shepherds*, *OB 16* and *NOB* give *shepherds'*, with apostrophe; since swains are always male Ault and *OB* must surely be correct in giving *shepherd*. Bar 54, voice, note 2: Warlock changed the g″ to a c″ in his own copy.

(2) **The contented lover**. Now sleep and take thy rest. (James Mabbe, *The Spanish Bawd*, 1631.) Pub. Augener, 1929. [Coll 3].

A♭ major. e′♭-a″♭, [f′-f″]. 3/4, Lento affettuoso. 1′40″. V/m, P/m.

For: Ten.

Subject: Rest now, for she loves you.

Voice: Steps; 7th and 6th leaps and drops; long slow legato phrases.

Piano: Broken chords in both hands, often with descant; many accidentals.

Comment: Some strange harmonies in this very individual and rather beautiful love-song. Bar 12: wight = fellow. *The Spanish Bawd* is based on Fernando de Rojas' *Celestina*, of 1499.

(3) **Youth**. In an arbour green. (Robert Wever, *Lusty Juventus*, c. 1560.) Comp. July 1928. Pub. Elkin, 1929.

F major. c′-f″, [e′-e″]. 2/2, Fast and in strict time. 1′15″. V/m, P/md.

For: Bar.

Subject: The joy of youthful love.
Voice: Broken chords, steps, skips; 6th drops and leaps, 7th leap; fast melisma at end of each verse.
Piano: Chordal, with many 10ths, and much 8ve skipping in third verse; chromatic.
Comment: See also **36 (3)** for comments on the words, and **39**. In spite of an attractive start this is perhaps the least successful of Warlock's three settings of these words; but if the pianist can keep the accompaniment light and the singer bring off the melismas in tempo it could be effective.

(4) **The sweet o' the year.** When daffodils begin to peer. (Shakespeare, *A Winter's Tale*, 1611, Act III, Scene iv.) Comp. August 1928. Pub. Elkin, 1929.

    F major. c'-f ", [f'-d"]. 6/8, Allegro vivace. 1'. V/me, P/m.

For: Bar.
Subject: Spring is the time for me, with girls and beer to be had.
Voice: Steps, simple skips; two verses end with a climb to f "; rhythms simple but very varied.
Piano: Bouncing chords; fairly chromatic.
Comment: More appropriate to the character of Autolycus than most settings – Warlock clearly understood the words! Bar 4: peer = appear; bar 5: doxy = female beggar or prostitute; bars 9-11: replaces winter's pallor, or, reigns in Winter's domain; bar 17: pugging = ?pilfering? but see note to Ireland 24 (2); bar 28: aunts = prostitutes; bars 31-33: tumbling = making love. Tomlinson lists an alternative Eb major version.

(5) **Tom Tyler.** I am a poor tiler, in simple array. (Anon, *Tom Tyler and his Wife*, ' "An excellent old Play, as it was Printed and Acted about a hundred years ago.", 1661. (Song registered 1558-9),' Ault.) Pub. Augener, 1929. [Coll 3].

    G major. d'-f "#(g"), [g'-e"]. 6/8, Allegretto e con umore. 2'40". V/m, P/md.

For: Ten, high Bar.
Subject: The misfortunes of unhappy marriage.
Voice: Steps and 3rds; optional g" at end of each of five strophic verses; bouncing dotted triplet rhythm.
Piano: Decorated chordal; staccato; many LH 10ths can cause problems.
Comment: Rather a routine example of Warlock's humorous songs. Warlock wrote to a friend: 'The tune of my Tom Tyler is based almost entirely on an improvisation of his'; referring to Hal Collins, his Maori servant and friend. See also 'Yarmouth Fair', **50**. Tom Tyler became a term for a

henpecked husband. Bar 12: wot = know; bar 25: shrows = shrews; bar 27: glike = trick, flout.

(6) **Eloré lo**. In a garden so green in a May morning. (Anon, from John Forbes's *Cantus, Songs and Fancies*, 1662]. Pub. Augener, 1929. [Coll 3].

F major. c'-f ", [c'-e"b]. 6/8,3/4, Allegretto con moto. 1'30". V/m, P/m.

For:	Bar.
Subject:	I heard my lady sing of love, and we were happy together.
Voice:	Steps, 3rds, broken chords; continuous quavers, 'to be sung in strict time "trippingly on the tongue", without any regard for barline accentuation'. (Warlock's note).
Piano:	Parallel quaver chords, legato, with a few bars of staccato leaps; fairly thin texture; some chromatics.
Comment:	Very satisfying free rhythm. Many Scottish dialect words are used. Bars 5 and 6: pleen of paramours = complain about lovers; bar 9: Heght = promised; bar 17: kythe = make known; bar 21: Jo = sweetheart; bar 31: law-tie = loyalty; bars 23-24 = so that your consent, genuine and unchanging; bar 26: ruth = compassion. The poem was included in the anthology *Lilligay*, see **37**.

(7) **The droll lover**. I love thee for thy fickleness. (Anon, seventeenth century; BL Add. MS 53723.) Pub. Augener, 1929. [Coll 3].

F major, modal. b°-e"b, [c'-c"]. 2/4, Fast. 1'. V/m, P/md.

For:	C-Ten, Bar.
Subject:	I love you for your faults, for without them you would never have loved me.
Voice:	Steps, 3rds, broken chords; some accidentals; a patter-song.
Piano:	Decorated chordal, quick-changing, with very varied rhythms; many accidentals; occasional fast arpeggios with crossing hands.
Comment:	One of Warlock's best humorous songs; a good finisher.

74 And wilt thou leave me thus? (Sir Thomas Wyatt, before 1533; BL Add. MS 17492.) Comp. August 1928. Pub. OUP, 1929. [Coll 1].

Bb minor. c'#-f ", [e'-e"b]. 3/4,4/4,3/8, etc, Poco agitato e rubato. 1'50". V/m, P/m.

For:	Mezzo, Bar.
Subject:	Surely you cannot really be going to leave me.
Voice:	Steps, simple skips; slightly chromatic; many descending phrases starting on f ", and ends on sustained f "; fairly continuous quavers in speech rhythms.
Piano:	Gently moving chromatic harmony, some counterpoint.

Comment: Fairly complex but very beautiful, getting to the heart of
            this anguished poem.

75 The cricketers of Hambledon. I'll make a song of Hambledon. (Bruce
    Blunt.) Comp. 1928. Pub. Augener, 1929. [Coll 3].
            E♭ major. b°b-f″, [e′b-e″]. 4/4, At a moderate pace. 2′15″.
            V/m, P/md.

For: Bar.
Subject: Cricket.
Voice: Steps, simple skips, repeated notes; dotted rhythms
            throughout.
Piano: Thick chordal with some decorations; many big stretches,
            but could be simplified.
Comment: Composed for the Hampshire Eskimos' New Year's Day
            cricket match at Hambledon, 1929. For baritone solo, unison
            male voice chorus, and brass. When issued with piano
            accompaniment the long instrumental coda was omitted.
            See WSNL 10.

76 Fill the cup, Philip, and let us drink a dram. (Anon; in BL Cottonian
    Vesp. A. xxv; *EEL*]. Comp. 1928. Pub. Thames, 1972. [Coll 6].
            E♭ major. b°b-e″b, [c′-c″]. 4/4, (Briskly). 45″. V/e, P/me.

For: [Mezzo], C-Ten, Bar; [Cont], Bass. [Unison chorus.]
Subject: I will drink to you if you will drink to me.
Voice: Steps and 3rds; nearly all quavers.
Piano: Chordal; some wide intervals for LH.
Comment: A nice lively piece for low voice, it would make a good encore.
            Originally written for Hambledon brass band, and chorus.
            Bar 5: *your* = *you*, in *EEL*, but there is a note to the effect
            that one earlier editor reads it as *your*, as given in the song.
            Using *you* changes the meaning considerably, and might
            well make the song suitable for women.

77 The frostbound wood. Mary that was the Child's mother. (Bruce
    Blunt.) Comp. 1929. Pub. OUP, 1931.
            No key sig. d′-e″, [e′-a′]. 4/4, Very slow and quiet
            throughout. 2′30″. V/me, P/me.

For: Mezzo, C-Ten, Bar.
Subject: Mary, alone, passed me without a word.
Voice: A single phrase – e′ d′ e′ g′ a′ e′ – repeated some sixteen
            times, with repeated notes and rhythms continuously varied
            to suit the words; a single e″ held at end.
piano: Slowly moving chromatic harmonies, often dissonant
            against the voice.
Comment: A very strange song indeed, but unforgettable, and almost

hypnotic in its affect. The poem equally is both beautiful and mysterious – am 'I' the planter of the tree which became the Cross? There is no hint of Resurrection in this tragic verse; it is not by any means suited to Christmas. Bar 5: The rit molto applies only to this bar, perhaps only to its first half; last bar, 4th quaver LH: d°, tied to following minim, not B and slur.

78 The five lesser joys of Mary. When Mary lay fretting that night in the cold. (D.L. Kelleher, *Augustan Books*, 1927.) Comp. December 1929. Pub. Novello, 1930.

Db major. d'b-e''b, [e'b-d''b]. 3/4, At a moderate pace. 2'30". V/e, P/me.

For: Mezzo, C-Ten, Bar. [Unison.]
Subject: Five events in Mary's life.
Voice: Steps, and a few 3rds; crotchets with some paired quavers; no accidentals.
Piano: Or organ. Four-part harmony in crotchets; last verse chromatic, with some big stretches.
Comment: A useful Christmas song. It was republished by Novello in 1961 in a version for SATB by Basil Ramsay, which can easily be restored to the original unison version by using the accompaniment to verse 1 for the first four verses, and then singing the top line only with the accompaniment to verse 5. Last bar but one, the treble should be three crotchets. See Notes on Sources: *Augustan Books*.

79 Carillon, carilla. On a winter's night long time ago. (Hilaire Belloc, 'Noël', *Verses and Sonnets*, 1896.) Comp. 1930. Pub. Novello, 1930.

G major. c'-e'', [e'-d'']. 6/8, Allegretto con moto. 3'. V/m, P/m.

For: Mezzo, C-Ten, Bar. [Unison.]
Subject: The Holy Family's reception at Bethlehem.
Voice: Steps and small skips; chromatic; simple rhythms.
Piano: Organ, but can be played without much adjustment on the piano. Four-part harmony throughout; chromatic; the long pedal note at the end needs repetition on the piano.
Comment: Some may find the rather anti-semitic line at the start of verse 5 a problem. The music may be thought attractively original, or awkwardly over-chromatic. Warlock's own opinion, on a copy given to E.J. Moeran, runs as follows: 'Poor folk that may this carol hear / (The bells ring single and the bells ring clear) / Deserve a free quart mug of beer. // Balls like this cannot be borne / The tune is trite and the style's outworn / And the harmony's a mixture of Bax and Vaughan.' This was printed by Gerald Cockshott in the

Musical Times for March 1955. He comments: 'A joke of course, but the feeling that his music was no good often attacked him, and in the end prevailed.'

80 After two years. She is all so slight. (Richard Aldington, *Images*, 1919.) Comp. 1930. Pub. OUP, 1931.
   D♭ major. d'b-f ″, [e'b-d″b]. 6/8, Allegretto con moto. 1′50″. V/m, P/m.

For:	Bar.
Subject:	Love unreturned, but living still in hope.
Voice:	Steps, 3rds, broken chords; 6th and 7th leaps and drops; some unexpected rhythms at times; few accidentals.
Piano:	Decorated chordal, in dotted 6/8 rhythms; many accidentals; a few wide stretches; mostly thin texture.
Comment:	An unusual love song, with some strangely dissonant harmony; well worth singing.

81 The fox. At 'The Fox Inn' The tatter'd ears. (Bruce Blunt.) Comp. July 1930. Pub. OUP, 1931.
   D minor. d'-f ″#, [d'-d″]. 3/4, Very slow. 2′40″. V/m, P/m.

For:	Mezzo, Bar.
Subject:	You and I will have been long dead when the fangs fall from the fox's mask.
Voice:	Repeated notes, 3rds, steps; highly chromatic; speech rhythms.
Piano:	Chordal, with hints of counterpoint; dissonant; mostly in four parts.
Comment:	A truly terrifying song, which can stand comparison with anything in German lieder. The story of its creation shows the pressure of inspiration under which it was composed: 'He [Warlock] was staying with me at Bramdean in the summer of 1930, and we had spent a long evening in "The Fox" which is the local pub. When we got home, Philip went almost straight to bed, but I stayed up and opened a bottle of Chablis (what an inadvisable addition to a lot of beer) and wrote the words of The Fox. As I did not go upstairs till about 3.0, I thought Philip would probably be down before me, so I left the poem on the table with a note to the effect that I thought it was unsuitable for setting on account of the shortness of the lines. When I got down at about noon next day, I found Philip sitting at the table with MS paper in front of him, and he was working at the song. He said, "On the contrary, my dear sir, I think this admirably suited for setting to music." We were going to Salisbury that afternoon, and, when we got there, Philip hired a room with

a piano at some music shop, played and whistled the thing over, and finished the song on the spot. So The Fox, words and music, was conceived and completed within about 18 hours, which may, or may not, be a record.' (Bruce Blunt, Letter to Gerald Cockshott, 20 May 1943. See Copley.) The accompaniment was arranged for flute and string quartet by Bernard van Dieren, obtainable from the Warlock Society.

82 Bethlehem down. 'When He is King we will give Him the Kings' gifts.' (Bruce Blunt.) Comp. 1 December 1930. Pub. W.R., 1931.

	D minor. *c'#-e″b*, [d'-d″]. 6/4, Very slow. 3'15″. V/me, P/md.
For:	Mezzo, C-Ten, Bar.
Subject:	Mary's dreams for her child's future, and its reality.
Voice:	Mostly by step, some 3rds; 6th leap; some modulation; simple rhythms with many paired quavers.
Piano:	Intended for organ, with piano as an ad lib alternative. Chordal, with much counterpoint and parallel writing; chromatic; often thick texture. Whether organ or piano is used some modifications will be required; it is not playable as it stands on either instrument.
Comment:	A lovely melody with a strangely dissonant accompaniment. It may be thought suitable for Christmas. There is an earlier version (September 1927) for SATB (W.R., 1928) which with its simpler harmony is much more successful as a carol.

Notes on Sources

This provides additional information on MSS and other early sources.

Augustan Books of English Poetry, second series, no 18, edited by D.L. Kelleher, 1927. All the poems are given as Anon, but Warlock **78** gives Kelleher as author. Tomlinson says none of the carols appears in Sandys, Wright, Ritson, etc, however Warlock **70** comes from Balliol 354.

Balliol 354. 'Commonplace book of Richard Hill, who describes himself as "servant with Mr Wyngar, alderman of London". John Wyngar, grocer, was alderman in 1493, mayor 1504, and died 1505. Richard Hill married in 1518 Margaret, daughter of Harry Wyngar, haberdasher, "dwellyng in bowe parishe in London", and the births of his seven children are recorded in the MS from 1518 to 1526. The MS is a miscellany of the widest character, English, French and Latin, poems, ...romances, fabliaux, legal notes, London customs, etc. Some pieces, signed by Hill, must be in his own hand; so probably is most of the MS. The latest date in it is 1535, but part must have been written before 1504' (*EEL*). See also *Oxford Book of Carols* no 36.

Bassus. ' "In this boke ar conteynyd XX songes. IX of IIII partes and XI of thre partes. Anno domini M.CCCCC.XXX." Printed by Wynken de Worde. BL Shelf mark of only known copy K.1.e.1' (*EEL*). Davies suggests Cornish 'probably wrote words as well as music'.

Bodleian Eng. Poet e.1. 'Seventy-six songs, religious and other, including some Christmas carols and drinking songs' (Madan). Dated 1460-80 by Madan and 'about 1485-90' by Nicholson (*EEL*).

BL Add. MS 5465. This belonged to Robert Fairfax, Gentleman of the Chapel Royal and organist of St Albans (1464-?1521) and may be in his hand. It contains words and music throughout; the composers include R. Fairfax, G. Banistre, W. Cornish, R. Davy, Sheringham, and Browne; these range from Henry VI to Henry VIII. See *EEL*.

BL Add. MS 31922. 'Music throughout, with and without words of lyrics. ...At least one of the poems is by Sir Thomas Wyatt; this may be dated 1518-1528. Another poem can be exactly dated 1 January – 22 February 1511. The MS is said to have belonged to Henry VIII; it is certainly well decorated' (*EEL*).

BL Add. MS 53723. A large autograph manuscript containing over 300 songs and dialogues composed by Henry Lawes between 1630 and 1650. Six songs from this collection, edited by Gwilym Beechey, were published by Peters in 1979.

BL Cottonian Vesp. A xxv. 'Poems and ballads, mainly religious, but with secular and jovial poems as well...One poem is dated 1578...and certain poems are in the early Tudor manner' (*EEL*).

BL Harleian 7578. 'Note...in Kitson's writing "An oblong paper book...containing the treble part of a collection of old songs & set to musick, used within and about the bishop[ric] of Durham, in the time of Queen Elizabeth" ' (*EEL*).

BL Sloane 2593. 'Songs and carols, seventy-four in number, of which three are in Latin, and the rest in English. Mainly religious or moral, but some trivial and satirical...According to Bradley-Stratmann, the MS was written in Warwickshire at the beginning of the fifteenth century' (*EEL*).

D'Orleans, Charles. BL Harleian 682 contains more than 200 English poems which may well have been written by Charles when prisoner in England from 1415-1440. About two-thirds have equivalents in a French series of love poems which are certainly by Charles, and the French collection does include some English poems. However, there is no French version of 'My Ghostly Fader', Warlock 13. See *EV*.

Fletcher, John. There is considerable debate as to the authorship of plays under the names of Beaumont and Fletcher, and even when the author of the play is agreed that is not considered evidence as to the authorship of any lyrics therein. Such evidence as there is is given under each song.

Hawkins, Sir John, *A General History of the Science and Practice of Music*, 5 vols, 1776; reissued by Dover Books in 2 vols in 1963, a facsimile of the 1853 edition, with an introduction by Charles Cudworth.

Kelleher. See *Augustan Books*, above.

Lilligay: an anthology of anonymous poems, published by Victor Neuburg at his own press at Vine Cottage, Steyning, Sussex, 1920. Apart from the poems in the cycle of the same name the anthology included 'Eloré Lo', Warlock 73 (6). For further information see *The Magical Dilemma of Victor Neuburg* by Jean Overton Fuller, W.H. Allen, 1965. 'This book relates the strange fact that Neuburg, after many years in which he had been unable to read poetry, was inspired to write several poems in the Scottish dialect, which later turned out to be well-known border ballads' (Tomlinson).

Nursery rhymes. 'Candlelight', Warlock 42, 'selected from *Nurse Lovechild's Legacy*, an anthology of nursery rhymes printed by the Poetry Bookshop, 1916, compiled from chapbooks of the eighteenth and early nineteenth century' (Tomlinson). Though 'Jenny Grey', Warlock 43, appears to be similar Tomlinson does not allocate it to the same source.

The Paradyse of Daynty Devises 'An anthology of works by poets of the early part of the sixteenth century. It was collected by Richard Edwards (1523-66), a playwright of the time, and published in 1576 after Edwards's death. The poets in the volume are not major figures, the most considerable one being Thomas Vaux' (*Cambridge Guide to English Literature*).

Select Bibliography

Composers

Gurney

Hurd, Michael, *The Ordeal of Ivor Gurney*, OUP 1978.
Moore, C.W., *Maker and Lover of Beauty*, Triad Press 1976.
Thornton, R.K.R., ed., *Ivor Gurney, War Letters*, Carcanet New Press 1983.

Ireland

Chapman, Ernest, *Catalogue of Works*, Boosey & Hawkes 1968.
Longmire, John, *John Ireland, Portrait of a Friend*, John Baker 1969.
Scott-Sutherland, C., *John Ireland*, Triad Press 1980.
Searle, Muriel V, *John Ireland, The Man and his Music*, Midas Books 1979.

Quilter

Hold, Trevor, *The Walled-in Garden*, Triad Press 1978.

Warlock

Copley, Ian, *The Music of Peter Warlock*, Dobson 1979.
Gray, Cecil, *Peter Warlock: A Memoir of Philip Heseltine*, Cape 1934.
Tomlinson, Fred, *A Peter Warlock Handbook*, vol. 1, Triad Press 1974.
Warlock Society Newsletters (obtainable from Malcolm Rudland, 17 Gledhow Gardens, London SW5 0AY.)

General reference

Banfield, Stephen, *Sensibility and English Song*, 2 vols, CUP 1985.
Early Bodleian Music, with an Introduction by E.W.B. Nicholson, edited by Sir John Stainer, 2 vols, 1901.
Madan, Falconer, *Summary Catalogue of the Western Manuscripts in the Bodleian Library*, 1895-?

Mulgan, John; revised Dorothy Eagle, *The Concise Oxford Dictionary of English Literature*, OUP 1979.

Musica Britannica, series published by S & B for the Royal Musical Association, 1954-.

New Grove Dictionary of Music and Musicians, ed. Stanley Sadie, Macmillan 1980.

New Larousse Encyclopedia of Mythology, Hamlyn 1968.

Northcote, Sidney, *Byrd to Britten: A Survey of English Song*, John Baker 1966.

Oxford English Dictionary.

Stapleton, Michael, *The Cambridge Guide to English Literature*, CUP 1983.

Stevens, Denis, ed., *A History of Song*, Hutchinson 1960.

Stevens, John, *Music and Poetry in the Early Tudor Court*, Methuen 1961.

Anthologies

Ault, Norman, ed., *Elizabethan Lyrics, from the original texts*, Longmans, Green & Co. 1925, revised and corrected 1949, republished Faber 1986.

Burrow, John, ed., *English Verse 1300-1500*, Longman 1977.

Chambers, E.K., ed., *The Oxford Book of Sixteenth Century Verse*, Clarendon Press 1932.

Chambers, E.K. and Sidgwick, F., eds, *Early English Lyrics, Amorous, Divine, Moral & Trivial*, Sidgwick and Jackson 1907 (1947).

Clayton, Thomas, *Cavalier Poets*, [Herrick, Carew, Suckling, Lovelace], OUP 1978.

Davies, R.T., ed., *Medieval English Lyrics: A Critical Anthology*, Faber 1963.

Earle, Giles, *His Booke*, 1615, ed. Peter Warlock, Houghton Publishing Co. 1932.

England's Helicon (1) ed. Hyder E. Rollins, 2 vols. Harvard University Press 1935; (2) ed. Hugh Macdonald, Routledge and Kegan Paul 1949.

Fellowes, E.H., *English Madrigal Verse*, 3rd edition revised F.W. Sternfeld and David Greer, Clarendon Press 1967.

Gardner, Helen, ed., *The New Oxford Book of English Verse*, OUP 1972.

Grierson, H.J.C., ed., *Metaphysical Lyrics and Poems of the Seventeenth Century*, Clarendon Press 1921.

Kelleher, D.L., ed., *Augustan Books of English Poetry*, second series, no. 18, London 1927. See Notes on Sources.

Love, Harold, ed., *The Penguin Book of Restoration Verse*, Penguin Books 1968.

Marsh, Edward., ed., *Georgian Poetry 1911-1912*, The Poetry Bookshop 1912.

—— *Georgian Poetry 1913-1915*, The Poetry Bookshop 1915.

—— *Georgian Poetry 1916-1917*, The Poetry Bookshop 1917.

—— *Georgian Poetry 1918-1919*, The Poetry Bookshop 1919.

Neuberg, Victor, ed., *Lilligay: An Anthology of Anonymous Poems*, Vine Press 1920.

—— *Larkspur: A Lyric Garland*, Vine Press 1922. See Notes on Sources.

Poems of To-day, First Series, 1915; Second Series, 1922, Sidgwick and Jackson 1924.

Quiller-Couch, Arthur, ed., *The Oxford Book of English Verse, 1250-1900*, Clarendon Press 1912.

Ritson., ed., *Ancient Songs and Ballads, from the reign of King Henry the Second to the Revolution*. 2 vols, 1829, revised W. Carew Hazlitt, Reeves and Turner 1877.

Tydeman, William, *Four Tudor Comedies* [*Jake Jugeler, Roister Doister, Gammer Gurton's Needle, Mother Bombie*], Penguin Books 1984.

Poets

Aldington, Richard, *Collected Poems, 1915-1923*, George Allen and Unwin 1933.

Beaumont and Fletcher, *The Works*, Cambridge English Classics, ed. A.R. Walker, CUP 1905-1912.

Beddoes, Thomas Lovell, *The Poems*, ed. Ramsay Colles, Routledge 1907.

Belloc, Hilaire, *Complete Works*, Duckworth 1970.

Blake, William, *The Complete Writings*, ed. Geoffrey Keynes, OUP 1972.

Bodenstadt, Frederick von, *Die Lieder des Mirza-Schaffy*, Berlin 1851.

Breton, *The Works in Verse and Prose*, ed. A.B. Grosart, 1879, reprinted Hildersheim 1969.

Bridges, Robert, *Poetical Works*, OUP 1971.

Brooke, Rupert, *The Complete Poems*, Sidgwick and Jackson 1932.

Brontë, Emily Jane, *The Complete Poems*, ed. C.W. Hatfield, Columbia University Press 1967.

Byron, George Gordon, Lord, *The Complete Poetical Works*, ed. Jerome J. McGann, 5 vols Clarendon Press 1980-86.

Campion, Thomas, *The Works*, ed. Walter R. Davis, Doubleday 1967.

—— *Campion's Works*, ed. Percival Vivian, Clarendon Press 1909.

Carman, Bliss, *Sappho: One Hundred Lyrics*, Chatto and Windus 1921.

Chaucer, Geoffrey, *The Canterbury Tales*, translated into modern English by Neville Coghill, Penguin Books 1951.

Clare, John, *Poems Chiefly from Manuscript*, ed. Edmund Blunden and Alan Porter, Cobden Sanderson 1934.

—— [The Oxford Authors], ed. Eric Robinson and David Powell, OUP 1984.

Coleridge, Mary, *Collected Poems*, ed. Theresa Whistler, Rupert Hart-Davies 1954.

Cory, William Johnson, *Ionica*, George Allen 1905.

Daniel, Samuel, *The Complete Works*, ed. A.B. Grosart, 5 vols, privately printed 1885-96, reprinted New York 1963.

Davidson, John, *The Poems*, ed. Andrew Turnbull, Scottish Academic Press 1973.

De La Mare, Walter, *Peacock Pie*, Constable 1913.

—— *Complete Poems*, Faber 1969.

Dekker, Thomas, *Dramatic Works*, ed. F. Bowers, Clarendon Press 1955-61.

Dowson, Ernest Christopher, *The Poetical Works*, ed. Desmond Flower, Cassell, 1934.

—— *The Poems*, ed. Mark Longaker, University of Pennsylvania Press 1962.

Ford, Ford Madox, *Collected Poems [of Ford Madox Hueffer]*, Martin Secker, 1916.

Freeman, John, *Memories of Childhood and Other Poems*, Selwyn and Blount 1919.

Gibson, Wilfrid, *Collected Poems*, Macmillan 1926.

Graves, Robert, *Over the Brazier*, Poetry Bookshop 1916.

—— *Country Sentiment*, Martin Secker 1920.

Gurney, Ivor, *The Collected Poems*, ed. P.J. Kavanagh, OUP 1982.

Hardy, Thomas, *The Complete Poetical Works*, ed. Samuel Hynes, Clarendon Press 1982-85.

—— *The Poetry of Thomas Hardy: A Handbook and Commentary*, by J.O. Bailey, University of North Carolina Press 1970.

Harvey, F.W., *A Gloucester Lad at Home and Abroad*, Sidgwick and Jackson 1915.

Henley, W.E., *Poems*, David Nutt 1898.

Herrick, Robert, *The Poetical Works*, ed. L.C. Martin, Clarendon Press 1963.

—— See also *Cavalier Poets*, ed. Clayton, listed under Anthologies.

Heywood, Thomas, [The Best Plays of the Old Dramatists], ed. A. Wilson Verity, Fisher Unwin 1923.

Hood, Thomas, *Complete Poetical Works*, ed. Walter Jarrold, Henry Froude 1906.

—— *Selected Poems*, ed. John Clubbe, Harvard University Press 1970.

Housman, A.E., *The Collected Poems*, Cape 1939.

Jonson, Ben, *Works*, ed. C.H. Herford, Percy and Evelyn Simpson, 11 vols, Clarendon Press 1925-1951.

—— *The Complete Poems*, ed. George Parfitt, Harmondsworth 1975.

Joyce, James, *Collected Poems*, The Viking Press 1937.

—— *Musical Allusions in the Works of James Joyce*, by Zack Bowen, Gill and Macmillan 1975.

Keats, John, *Poetical Works*, ed. H.W. Garrod, Clarendon Press, 1958.

Ledwidge, Francis, *Complete Poems*, Herbert Jenkins 1919.

Lovelace, Richard, *Poems*, ed. C.H. Wilkinson, Clarendon Press 1930.

—— See also *Cavalier Poets*, ed. Clayton, listed under Anthologies.

Maquarie, Arthur, *The Wheel of Life*, Bickers and Son 1909.

Marlowe, Christopher, *The Poems*, ed. Millar Maclure, Methuen 1968.

Masefield, John, *The Collected Poems*, Heinemann 1931.

Meynell, Alice, *The Poems*, OUP 1940.

Moore, Thomas, *The Poetical Works*, 10 vols, Longmans, Orme 1840-41.

Munro Harold, *The Collected Poems*, ed. Alida Munro, Duckworth 1970.

Nashe, Thomas, *The Works*, ed. Ronald B. McKerrow, 1904-10, revised F.P. Wilson, Basil Blackwell 1966.

Newbolt, Henry, *Poems New and Old*, John Murray 1912.

Nichols, Robert, *Ardours and Endurances*, Chatto and Windus 1917.

O'Sullivan, Seamus, *Collected Poems*, The Orwell Press 1941.

Ralegh, Sir Walter, *The Poems*, ed. Agnes Latham, Constable 1929.

Rochester, John Wilmot, Earl of, *Complete Poems*, ed. D. Vieth, New Haven 1968.

Rossetti, Christina Georgina, *Poetical Works*, ed. William M. Rossetti, Macmillan 1904.

Rossetti, Dante Gabriel, *Collected Works*, ed. William M. Rossetti, Ellis and Elvey 1890.

Shakespeare, William, *The Complete Pelican Shakespeare*, ed. Alfred Harbage, Penguin Books 1969.

—— *A Shakespeare Lexicon and Quotation Dictionary*, Alexander Schmidt, Berlin 1902. [Dover 1971].

Shanks, Edward, *Poems, 1912-1932*, Macmillan 1933.

Shelley, P.B., *The Complete Poetical Works*, ed. Thomas Hutchinson, OUP 1934.

Sidney, Sir Philip, *The Poems*, ed. William A. Ringler, Jr, Clarendon Press 1962.

Squire, J.C., *Tricks of the Trade*, Martin Secker 1917.

—— *Poems, First Series*, Martin Secker 1918.

—— *Poems, Second Series*, Hodder and Stoughton 1922.

Stephens, James, *Songs from the Clay*, Macmillan 1915.

—— *Reincarnations*, Macmillan 1918.

—— *Collected Poems*, Macmillan 1926.

Stevenson, Robert Louis, *New Poems*, Chatto and Windus 1918.

—— *The Collected Poems*, ed. Janet Adam Smith, Rupert Hart-Davis 1950.

Suckling, Sir John, *The Works...Non Dramatic*, ed. T. Clayton, OUP 1971.

—— See also *Cavalier Poets*, ed. Clayton, listed under Anthologies.

Symons, Arthur, *Collected Works*, Martin Secker 1924.

Tennyson, Alfred Lord, *Poems and Plays*, ed. T. Herbert Warren, revised Frederick Page, OUP 1986.

Thomas, Edward, *The Collected Poems*, ed. R. George Thomas, Clarendon Press 1978.

Waller, Edmund, *Poems*, 1645, facsimile edition, Scolar Press 1971.

Walton, Izaac, *The Compleat Angler*, ed. John Buxton, OUP 1982.

Warner, Sylvia Townsend, *Collected Poems*, ed. Claire Harman, Carcanet Press 1982.

Watson, Sir William, *The Poems, 1878-1935*, George Harrap 1936.

Wyatt, Sir Thomas, *Collected Poems*, ed. Joost Daalder, OUP 1975.

Yeats, W.B., *Collected Works*, vol 1, Shakespeare Head Press 1911.

—— *Collected Poems*, Macmillan 1950.

—— *A Commentary on the Collected Poems of W.B. Yeats*, by A. Norman Jeffares, Macmillan 1974.

Index of titles and first lines

Titles and first lines are given separately for each composer. Titles are in roman, first lines in italic. If the title uses the beginning of a first line it is given thus: Orpheus *with his lute made trees*. Titles in **bold** refer to sets or cycles.

Ivor Gurney

John Ireland

Roger Quilter

Peter Warlock

Index of poets

This index includes all the poets and anonymous sources found in this volume. The composer's name appears before the numbers of the songs set by him. **Bold** numbers refer to sets or cycles.

Aldington, Richard [1892-1962] (Warlock) 80
Anonymous Lyrics: (Ireland) 39 (2); (Warlock) 25, 71
  Augustan Books, see Notes on Sources (Warlock) 69, 70, 78
  Ballad Sheet, 18th century (Warlock) 47 (1)
  Balliol 354, see Notes on Sources (Ireland) 33; (Warlock) 34, 48, 69
  BL Add. MS 5465, *see* Notes on Sources (Warlock) 35 (3)
  BL Add. MS 31922, *see* Notes on Sources (Warlock) 27 (2)
  BL Add. MS 53723, *see* Notes on Sources (Warlock) 73 (7)
  BL Add. MS 17786-91 (Warlock) 20
  BL Cottonian Vesp. A. xxv, *see* Notes on Sources (Warlock) 76
  BL Harleian 541 (Warlock) 49
  BL Harleian 3362 (Warlock) 19
  BL Harleian 7578, *see* Notes on Sources (Ireland) 22 (3); (Warlock) 12, 14
  BL Sloane 2593, *see* Notes on Sources (Quilter) 18 (3); (Warlock) 31
  Bodleian Eng. Poet e.1., *see* Notes on Sources (Warlock) 27 (1, 3)
  Border Ballads (Gurney) 5 (9), 18
  Byrd, William, *Psalms, Songs and Sonnets*, 1611 (Quilter) 10 (2)
  Dowland, John, *Third and Last Book of Songs*, 1603 (Gurney) 8 (2); (Quilter) 8 (1)
  England's Helicon, 1600 (Quilter) 8 (4)
  Famous History of Friar Bacon, The, before 1600 (Warlock) 56
  Forbes, John, *Cantus, Songs and Fancies*, Aberdeen, 1662 (Warlock) 73 (6)
  Ford, Thomas, *Musicke of Sundrie Kindes*, 1607 (Warlock) 15, 72
  Gorgeous Gallery of Gallant Inventions, A, 1578 (Warlock) 66
  Hawkins, Sir John, 1776, *see* Notes on Sources (Warlock) 27 (4), 35 (3)
  Hume, Tobias, *First Part of Ayres*, 1605 (Quilter) 8 (7)
  Lilligay, see Notes on Sources (Warlock) 37 (1, 2, 3)
  Maidment, *North Country Garland*, 1824 (Warlock) 37 (4)
  Manx Ballad (Quilter) 18 (2)
  Nursery Rhymes, *see* Notes on Sources (Warlock) 42, 43
  Pilkington, Francis, *First Booke of Songs or Ayres*, 1605 (Warlock) 32
  Ritson, Joseph, *Ancient Songs and Ballads*, 1829 (Warlock) 49
  Robin Goodfellow, 1628, (Percy Society, vol. 9, 1837) (Warlock) 60
  Scots Ballad (Gurney) 14
  Traditional (Ireland) 36
  Tom Tyler and His Wife, 1661, *see* Notes on Sources (Warlock) 73 (5)

Index of special categories

This index gives lists of cycles, sets, Christmas songs, drinking songs, songs for ending groups ('finishers'), songs with alternative accompaniments, and songs classed as easy or moderately easy for both voice and piano. The composer's name precedes the numbers of his songs. Bold numbers indicate sets or cycles.

Pairs: (Gurney) 1 (6)/3 (10), 3 (4)/4 (3)]; (Ireland) 7 (1, 2), 15 (1, 2), 27 (1,2), 34 (1, 2); (Quilter) 13 (1,2), 19 (1, 2), 23 (1, 2); (Warlock) 26 (1,2), 44 (1, 2), 47 (1, 2), 53 (1, 2)

Sets of three: (Ireland) **13, 20, 25, 39**; (Quilter) **3, 5, 10, 11, 14, 15**; (Warlock) **7, 35, 36, 61**

Sets: (Gurney) **8**; (Ireland) **4, 17, 22, 24**; (Quilter) **1, 2, 4, 7, 8, 9, 16, 17, 18, 20, 22**; (Warlock) **27, 37, 42, 73**

Cycles: (Gurney) **6, 7, 9**; (Ireland) **1, 19, 23**; (Quilter) **6**

Christmas: (Gurney) 10; (Ireland) 4 (1), 42; (Quilter) 18 (3); (Warlock) 24, 31, 34, 51, 57, 67, 69, 70, 78, 79, 82.

Drinking songs: (Gurney) 16, 17; (Ireland) 21; (Warlock) **26**, 27 (1), 49, 55, 59, 76

Finishers: (Gurney) 2 (6), 11, 16, 17; (Ireland) 4 (6), 7 (2), 21, 24 (5), 29, 30, 33, 35; (Quilter) 2 (4), 3 (1), 8 (7), 9 (4), 10 (1, 2), 11 (1), 14 (3), 16 (2, 5), 17 (2), 20 (2); (Warlock) 17, 18, 26 (1, 2), 27 (1, 3), 35 (3), 36 (1, 3), 39, 50, 52, 56, 59, 60, 63, 73 (7), 76.

Alternative accompaniments. String quartet: (Ireland) 16, 42; (Warlock) 11, 12, 13, 20, 21, 24, 33, 35 (1, 2); string trio and piano: (Quilter) 15; string quartet and piano: Gurney **6, 7**; small orchestra: (Warlock) 35 (2), 52.

Easy/moderately easy [voice and piano]: (Gurney) 1 (4, 6, 9), 2 (2, 5, 8), 3 (2, 9), 4 (5, 7, 8), 5 (3, 4, 7, 10), 6 (6), 7 (3), 8 (1, 2, 3), 10, 12, 16, 17; (Ireland) 1 (1), 3, 4 (1, 2, 4, 5), 6, 8, 12, 16, **17**, 20 (2, 3), 22 (2), 24 (1, 5), 27 (1), 28, 29, 30, 31, 32, 34 (1), 36, 40, 42; (Quilter) 1, 2 (3, 4), 3 (2, 3), 4 (2, 3), 5 (2), 6 (3, 5), 7 (2, 4), 8 (1, 5), 9 (1), 13 (1), 14 (1), 15 (1), 16 (1, 4), 17 (1), 18 (2, 3, 5, 6), 20 (3), 22 (1, 2, 3), 23 (1); (Warlock) 3, 6, 13, 15, 21, 24, 27 (1), 28, 30, 31, 32, 37 (2), 40, **42**, 43, 47 (2), 48, 53 (1), 54, 55, 57, 61 (3), 66, 67, 69, 70, 71, 76, 77, 78.

Index of voices

Voices are given separately for each composer. **Bold** numbers refer to sets or cycles.

Ivor Gurney

All for Medium voice except the following:
Sop: 3 (4, 5, 7), 5 (6), **8**
Tenor: 2 (7), 3 (5, 7), 4 (2), 5 (6), **6, 8**

John Ireland

(1) Voices appropriate to songs in their original keys. Numbers in *italics* refer to keys *not* printed in *Complete Works*. Numbers in curly brackets {} refer to songs whose original keys are not known; the key is as found in *Complete Works*. Square brackets [] imply that some such singers might find the text of the song unsuitable.

Soprano: 1 (1, [2, 4, 5, 6]), {2}, 3, 4 (1, 3, 4), {5}, 6, 7 (1, *2*), {8}, 18
Mezzo: **4**, **13**, *14*, **15**, **16**, **17**, 20 (1, *2*, *3*), 22 (1, 2, [3, 4], 5), 24 (1, [3, 4, 5]), [25 (3)], 26, {28}, 32, {33}, 34 (1), {36}, {37}, 38, **39**, {40}, [41]
Contralto: *9*, {11}, 24 (1, [3, 4]), [25 (3)], {28}, {31}
C-Tenor: 4 (5), *9*, {10}, {11}, 13 (2), **16**, **17** (3, 4, 5, 7), *20 (3)*, **22**, **24**, 25 (3), {28}, *29*, {31}, 32, 34 (1), 38
Tenor: 1, {2}, 3, 4 (1, 3, 4), {5}, 6, 7 (1), {8}, *21*, {30}
Baritone: **4**, *12*, **13**, *14*, **15**, **16**, **17** (3, 4, 5, 7, 8), **19**, 20 (1, 3, *21*, **22**, **23**, **24**, **25**, 26, {**27**}, {28}, *29*, {31}, 32, {33}, **34**, {35}, {36}, {37}, 38, **39**, {40}, 41
Bass: *9*, {10}, {11}, 24 (1, 3, 4), 25 (3), {28}, {31}

(2) Voices for which transposed versions were published. *Italic* shows those given in *Complete Works* in error since they were not the original keys.

Soprano: *9*, 11, 13 (1), 14, 20 (2, 3), 28, 31, 33, 36, 37, 40, 42
Mezzo: 1 (1, [2, 4, 5, 6]), 2, 3, 5, 6, 7 (1, *2*), 8, 9, 11, 31, 42 Contralto: 4 (4), 8, 13 (1), *14*, 20 (1, *2, 3*)
C-Tenor: 1 (1, 3, 5), 4 (4), 6, 7 (1), 8, 12, 13 (1), *14*, 20 (1), *21*, *27 (1)*, 30, 35, 37, 40
Tenor: 9, 10, 11, 12, 13 (1), 14, 20 (3), 27 (1), 28, *29*, 31, 33, 35, 36, 37, 40, 42
Baritone: 1, 2, 3, 5, 6, 7 (1), 8, 9, 10, 11, *21*, 30, 31, 42
Bass: 4 (4), 8, 12, 13 (1), *14, 20 (3)*, 27 (1)

Roger Quilter

All the songs were published in more than one key. The list below refers to original keys only. *Italic* signifies that the original key is not known. Square brackets [] indicate that some such singers might find the text of the song unsuitable.

Soprano: 3 (1), **4**, **8** ([1, 2], 4, 6, 7), 10 ([1], 2, 3), 17 (2), 18 (1), [21], *22 ([1], 3, 4)*

Mezzo: **1**, **2**, 3 (2, 3), [5 (1, 3)], **7**, **9**, 12, **13**, **14**, **15**, 16 (1, [2], 3, 4, [5]), 17 (5), **18**, **19**, [20 (2, 3)], *22 ([1], 3, 4)*, **23**

Contralto: 1 (1, 3), **14**, 16 ([2], 4), 18 (3), *22 (3, 4)*

C-Tenor: **1**, 2 (1, 2, 3), 3 (2, 3), **5**, 12, **13**, **14**, **16**, 17 (4), 18 (3, 6), **19**, 20 (2, 3), **22**, 23 (1)

Tenor: 3 (1), **4**, **6**, **8**, **10**, 17 (1, 2, 3), 18 (1), 21, *22*

Baritone: **1**, **2**, 3 (2, 3), **5**, **7**, **9**, **11**, 12, **13**, **14**, **15**, **16**, 17 (4, 5), 18 (1, 2, 3, 5, 6), **19**, **20**, *22*, **23**

Bass: 1 (1, 3), **14**, 16 (2, 4), 18 (3), *22 (3, 4)*

Peter Warlock

Numbers in *italics* refer to transposed versions. Square brackets [] imply that some such singers might find the text of the song unsuitable.

Soprano: [3], 4, 5, 8, 10, *11*, 13, *14*, 20, 21, 22, 30, 35 (2, 3), 36 (2), **37**, 40, 41, 51, 52, **53**, 54, 60, *61 (3)*, 63, 65, *68*

Mezzo: 1, *3*, 7, *8*, *10*, 11, 13, *14*, *16*, *20*, *21*, *22*, 24, 27 (2), 28, 29, *30*, 31, 32, 33, 34, 35 (2, *3*), 36 (2), 37 (1, *2*, 3, *4*, *5*), 38, *40*, 41, **42**, 43, **44**, 46, 47 (2), 48, 52, **53**, *54*, 56, 57, 58, 60, **61**, 62, 63, 64, 67, 68, 69, 70, 71, 74, [76], 77, 78, 79, 81, 82

Contralto: *13*, 14, 16, *24*, [76]

C-Tenor: 6, *10*, *13*, 14, 15, 16, 17, *19*, *21*, *22*, 23, 24, *26*, 27 (*1*, 2, *4*), 28, 29, *30*, 31, 32, 33, 34, 35 (1), 38, *40*, 43, 46, 47 (2), 48, *50*, 53 (1), 57, 58, 61 (2, 3), 68, 69, 73 (7), 76, 77, 78, 79, 82

Tenor: [3], 4, 5, 8, 10, *11*, 12, 13, *14*, *15*, *17*, 18, 19, 21, 22, 26 (*1*, 2), 27 (1, 3, 4), 30, **35**, 36 (2, 3), 37 (1, 3, 4, 5), 39, 40, 41, 50, 51, 52, **53**, 54, 60, *61 (3)*, 63, 65, *68*, 72, 73 (1, 2, 5)

High Bar: 36 (2), 41, 53 (2), 72, 73 (5)

Baritone: 1, 2, *3*, 6, 7, *8*, 9, *10*, 11, *12*, 13, *14*, 15, *16*, 17, *18*, *19*, *21*, *22*, 23, 24, 25, 26 (*1*, *2*), 27 (*1*, *2*, *3*, *4*), 28, 29, *30*, 31, 32, 33, 34, 35 (1, 2, *3*), 36 (1, *3*), 37 (1, 3, *4*, *5*), 38, *40*, **42**, 43, 44, 45, 46, **47**, 48, 49, *50*, 52, 53 (1), *54*, 55, 56, 57, 58, 59, 60, **61**, 62, 63, 66, 67, 68, 69, 70, 73 (*1*, 3, 4, 6, 7), 74, 75, 76, 77, 78, 79, 80, 81, 82

Bass: *13*, 14, 16, *24*, *26 (1)*, *49*, *50*, 76